Venez...

Leonard V. Dalton

Alpha Editions

This edition published in 2024

ISBN : 9789362922069

Design and Setting By
Alpha Editions
www.alphaedis.com
Email - info@alphaedis.com

Contents

INTRODUCTORY NOTE

The author is desirous of expressing his appreciation of the continued courtesy and kindness rendered during his stay in Venezuela by the British Chargé d'Affaires, Mr. W. E. O'Reilly, by Mr. E. A. Wallis, and other British residents, as well as the warm reception accorded by the Venezuelan officials throughout the parts of the country he visited.

Mr. F. A. Holiday, A.R.C.S., F.G.S., has made himself responsible for much of the information on the Llanos, and has assisted largely in the preparation of the tables in Appendix B. Mr. J. D. Berrington, of El Callao, also furnished details relating to the Guayana goldfields and their surroundings.

The author is greatly indebted to Mr. N. G. Burch, F.R.G.S., for reading the manuscript and for many valuable suggestions and criticisms. He would also thank Mr. G. T. Wayman, of Carácas, for many useful documents and items of interest regarding recent developments.

CHAPTER I
PHYSICAL DESCRIPTION OF THE UNITED STATES OF VENEZUELA

Situation—Area—Population—Main physical divisions—The Guayana Highlands—Mountains, rivers, and forests—The Llanos—*Selvas*—*Mesas*—Rivers and *cienagas*—The Delta—*Caños*—The Caribbean Hills—Serrania Costanera—Serrania Interior—Rivers—Segovia Highlands—Drainage—Vegetation—The Andes—Portuguese chain—Cordillera of Mérida—The Sierra Nevada—Mountain torrents—Vegetation—*Páramos*—The Coastal Plain—Lake of Maracaibo—Coro and Paraguana Lowlands—Climate—"White-water" and "black-water" rivers—Seasons—*Tierra caliente, templada, and fria*—Temperature and seasons—"St. John's little summer"—Health.

If we take a map of South America on which the political boundaries are clearly shown, Venezuela will be observed as a wedge of territory immediately to the east of the most northerly point of the continent, separating Colombia from our colony of British Guiana.

The United States of Venezuela, as this republic is officially called, lie wholly within the tropical zone, between latitude 0° 45′ N. and 12° 26′ N. and longitude 59° 35′ W. and 73° 20′ W. (from Greenwich). The area within these limits is some 1,020,400 square kilometres, or 394,000 square miles, according to the Statistical Year Book for 1908, published in Carácas in 1910. The total population, according to the same authority, is 2,664,241, these being the figures of the last census, that of 1891.

Turning to our map once more, it will be seen that the wedge is not a regular one, but suggests rather the lower half of a human head, with the Lower Orinoco as the line of the jaw. The features are easily observed to separate the territory of the republic into four main divisions: (1) the Guayana Highlands, including all the region corresponding to the part of the head below the jaw-line, *i.e.*, south and east of the Orinoco; (2) the great central area of plains or *Llanos*, bounded on the north and west by (3) the north-eastern branch of the great Andine chain, and in the north-west of the country (4) a smaller low-lying region round the Lake of Maracaibo. Each of these divisions includes somewhat varying types of land surface, but has its main features of uniform character.

As already defined, the Guayana Highlands include the whole of that vast, more or less unexplored, tract of Venezuela lying on the right bank of the Orinoco and round the head-waters of that river. The area is primarily one huge elevated plateau about 1,000 feet or more above the sea, and from this rise a few principal mountain ranges, with some peaks over 8,000 feet high, while smaller hills and chains link up the larger systems. The highest ground is found on the Brazilian frontier, beginning at Mount Roraima (8,500 feet), where the three boundaries of Venezuela, British Guiana, and Brazil meet, and extends thence in the Sierras Pacaraima and Parima westward and southward to the head-waters of the Orinoco. From Roraima the Orinoco-Cuyuni watershed extends northward within Venezuela, along the Sierras Rincote and Usupamo and the Highlands of Puedpa, to the Sierra Piacoa, and thence south-east along the Sierra Imataca to the British limits again. The Sierra Maigualida forms the watershed between the Caura and the Ventuari.

The whole area, which amounts to some 204,600 square miles, is well watered by the upper Orinoco and the Ventuari, with the other great tributaries, the Cuchivero, Caura, Aro, Caroni, and their affluents. Large as these rivers are, they are so broken by rapids that travel along them is only possible for much of their length in small portable craft, and even then the passage is fraught with danger. Save for the districts in the immediate neighbourhood of the Orinoco, and scattered areas elsewhere, the whole region is thickly covered with forests of valuable timber, containing rubber, tonka-beans, brazil-nuts, copaiba, and all the varied natural produce of the South American tropics.

The great plains or Llanos of the Orinoco extend from the banks of the Meta in a broad arc parallel to the course of the Orinoco along its left bank. Westward they are bounded by the Cordillera of Mérida, and northward by the Cordillera of Carácas and the hills of Sucre, but between these ranges, at Barcelona, they virtually reach the sea for a short distance. To the east they merge into the low-lying tract of the Orinoco Delta. The total area of the Llanos proper is in the neighbourhood of 108,300 square miles, so that we have in these two thinly populated tracts about 80 per cent. of the territory of the republic.

Vast areas of the Llanos remain, for all practical purposes, still unexplored, and their general character can only be inferred from that of the regions bordering on the "roads." The typical areas are wide grass plains, often stretching to the horizon on all sides without a break, but generally interrupted by little groups of palms and small trees, especially near the banks of the rivers. At some four or five points near the northern edge there are great forests or *selvas*, relics possibly of an earlier, more extensive woodland.

The elevation of the Llanos ranges up to 650 feet, and more than this in the *mesas* of the central region, these being gravel-capped plateaux, of varying extent, beginning in the west with the Mesa de Santa Clara, northward of Caicara, and extending thence in a continuous series eastward and northward to form the watershed between the Orinoco and the Unare-Aragua basin, which drains into the Caribbean Sea west of Barcelona. The lowest part of the Llanos is situated westward of this chain of tablelands, in the valley of the Portuguesa, the lower part of which has large tracts less than 300 feet above sea-level. East of the Mesa de Guanipa the ground falls comparatively rapidly to the Delta.

PENINSULA OF PARIA FROM TRINIDAD.

IN THE DELTA.

While severe drought is experienced over much of the Llano region in summer, the heavy rains, particularly in the western districts, produce floods over the low-lying plains, the mesas being dry at all times. The whole area is traversed by numerous streams and rivers, which rise either on the southern slopes of the Cordillera or in the mesas. North of the Meta, in addition to the large number of smaller streams which here and there broaden out into marshy lakes or *cienagas*, we have the navigable rivers Arauca (the main waterway to eastern Colombia) and Apure, flowing from the Andes to the Orinoco in an easterly direction. The Apure receives many tributaries on its left bank from the Venezuelan Andes, most important of which are the Portuguesa, rising in the plains of the same name south of Barquisimeto and joining the Apure at San Fernando, and the Guárico, whose mouth is east of the same town, flowing from south of Carácas through the State to which it gives its name, and receiving from the east the waters of the Orituco, whose source is less than thirty miles from the coast in longitude 66°. Of the Orinoco tributaries from the north beyond the Apure the most important is the Manapire, all the streams east of this rising in the mesas and having but short courses. The greater part of the eastern Llanos drains northward by the Unare and Aragua into the Caribbean Sea. A few large rivers rise on the east of the mesas, but flow for short distances only through the plains, emptying, not into the Orinoco itself but the *caños* of the Delta. This last-mentioned region of inundated forest, savannah and mangrove swamp, occupies about 11,500 square miles, bringing the total area of the central plains up to 119,800 square miles.

The third great tract, the north-eastern spur of the Andes, divides itself naturally into three parts—the Caribbean Hills, along the shores of the sea of the same name; the Segovia Highlands, linking the former to the higher mountains of western Venezuela; and the Cordillera of Mérida, or the Venezuelan Andes. The total area occupied by these mountain and hill tracts is about 41,800 square miles.

The Caribbean Hills give to the Venezuelan coast its splendid and almost unique aspect, for, save for the interruption near Barcelona, the range extends without much decrease in average height from west of longitude 68° to the east end of the peninsula of Paria, less than 62° west of Greenwich. Two main lines of elevation are plainly discernible in the Carácas region, known as the Serrania Costanera and the Serrania Interior; they continue throughout the range, but are less distinct in the Cumaná Hills. The greatest elevation of the outer line is reached near Carácas itself, a considerable area west of the city rising to over 6,500 feet, while to the east are the famous peaks of La Silla (de Carácas) and Naiguatá (8,620 feet and 9,100 feet respectively). In the inner range the greatest elevation is round Mount Turimquiri, south of Cumaná; the eastern portion of the coast range, in the peninsulas of Araya and Paria, does not rise above 3,200 feet. On the northern side the complex is drained only by mountain torrents falling rapidly throughout their short courses to the sea, while on the south are the head-waters of the Orinoco tributaries. Between the two ranges, however, we have longitudinal valleys with rivers of more or less importance—the Aragua, flowing westwards from Carácas into the lake of Valencia or

Tacarigua, which overflows into the Paito, a tributary of the Portuguesa; and the Tuy, with its affluent the Guaire, flowing eastwards to the sea south of Cape Codera. In the Cumaná Hills we have the Manzanares and other smaller streams emptying their waters into the Gulf of Cariaco, and on the east the Lake of Putucual, though small, is similar in situation to that of Valencia, and its overflow forms the River San Juan, which empties into the Gulf of Paria, forming virtually part of the Orinoco drainage. The lower slopes of all these ranges, and the valleys, are clothed with rich forests, excepting the dry, barren coasts near Carácas, while the heights are bare, save for grass and a few small temperate trees.

Between the western extremity of the Caribbean Hills and the northern spurs of the Venezuelan Andes there is an elevated region, which, though subject to variations of level, possesses the main features of a tableland, and this type of surface extends in a broad belt northward through the States of Lara and Falcón. Their main extent is in the State of Lara, whose capital, Barquisimeto, had as its original name, before any territorial limits were defined round it, Nueva Segovia; it seems appropriate, therefore, to distinguish this area as the Segovia Highlands.

The level of most of the area so designated ranges from 1,500 to 3,500 feet, but the plateau type is best developed in the Barquisimeto region, the dry, barren plains of which, with their cactus vegetation, suggest by their general features the dry bed of an ancient lake, in whose waters the small scattered hills formed islands, while the Andine spurs to the south and the Sierra de Aroa and similar mountain masses north of Barquisimeto, constituted its limits. Beyond the latter, and north of the Tocuyo River, while the larger part of the area maintains its more or less uniform elevation, three well-defined ranges rise from the plateau, in the Cordilleras of Baragua, Agua Negra, and San Luis; the last named is the largest, and extends for 110 miles parallel to the Coro coast, overlooking the Gulf of Venezuela. Practically the whole of this region is drained by the Tocuyo and its tributaries, the other rivers rising merely on its outer edges and falling direct to the sea; from this generalisation should be excepted a small area round Barquisimeto, in the catchment area of the river of the same name, which contributes its waters to the volume of the Portuguesa, and so enters the Orinoco. The Tocuyo, whose principal affluents are the Carora and the Baragua on its left bank, rises in the Andes and flows for some 330 miles in a northerly direction, changing to easterly in the lower river, before it empties itself into the Caribbean. While the southern part of this area is barren, all the lower slopes of the northern hills are forest clad and fertile, with *llanos* in the Carora Valley and grass-covered summits above.

To the south we have the Venezuelan Andes, stretching for some 300 miles south-westward to the Colombian frontier, and forming the highest land in the whole country.

There are two main divisions of this mountain group, the Portuguesa chain south of Barquisimeto, and the Cordillera of Mérida constituting the more important and higher part. The Portuguesa chain reaches its greatest elevation (13,100 feet) in the south near the sources of the Tocuyo, the northern portion rising only to about 5,000 feet. A slight break in the mass is caused by the valley of the Boconó, beyond which the Cordillera of Mérida begins with peaks of nearly 13,000 feet on the north, rising to their maximum in the centre, where the summits of the Sierra Nevada of Mérida have an elevation of about 16,400 feet, and the top of the highest of all, La Columna, is 16,423 feet above sea-level. Southwards the elevations decrease again, until on the borders of Colombia the watershed is less than 5,000 feet above the sea. The streams of this chain, with its steep outer flanks so characteristic of the Andes, naturally belong for the most part to the catchment area of the Orinoco or the Maracaibo Lake, but there is a succession of longitudinal valleys within the chain which may be considered as pertaining more particularly to the Andes. The chief of these rivers are the Motatán, which, rising north of Mérida, flows northwards through Trujillo to the Lake of Maracaibo; the Chama, whose sources are in the same snows that supply the Motatán, though the stream flows southward past Mérida, bending then sharply northward to reach the south shore of the lake opposite the mouth of the Motatán; and the Torbes, flowing south-westward by San Cristobal, and turning there to the east to fall into the Uribante, a tributary of the Apure. Every type of vegetation occurs within this Andine tract, varying according to the geology of the ground and its elevation. At some points there are fertile valleys with tropical flora, others with temperate cereals; sometimes bare mountain slopes and hot gorges supporting only cactus and acacia, and little of these; sometimes grass-clad slopes and summits, with the peculiar heather-like and resinous plants of the "páramos," and, lastly, the eternal snows of the peaks of the Sierra Nevada.

North of the mountain region of Venezuela lies what may be considered as the coastal plain, including the alluvial area of the Lake of Maracaibo, the Coro and Paraguana lowlands, and such few tracts of flat ground as may be found along the coast, with the numerous islands in the Caribbean which belong to Venezuela. The area of this division may be estimated as about 27,800 square miles. The lake has many points of similarity to the Delta, both in hydrography and general character. The southern part has innumerable rivers comparable to the caños, with open lagoons and swamps, bordered by dense forests more or less inundated in the rains. On the east and west shores to the north there are stretches of higher ground between the swamps, and frequent grass plains like the Llanos; the western side is bounded by the Sierra de Perija, forming the frontier of Colombia. Chief of the rivers traversing these plains are the Motatán and Chama, already mentioned as rising in the Andes, the Escalante, and the Catatumbo; the mouths of all are of a deltaic character, and all are navigable to a greater or lesser extent. The largest and most important is the Catatumbo, which, with its great tributary, the Zulia, rises in Colombia.

The Coro and Paraguana lowlands form a stretch of open, sandy, more or less barren and low hills, extending from the neighbourhood of the port of Maracaibo along the coast to Coro, and into the Paraguana peninsula; with them may be grouped the islands, which are similar in character, except Margarita, whose mountains resemble those of the Caribbean chain, though the open, cactus-covered lower ground is a repetition of the western coast (and Curaçao).

The climate of the 394,000 square miles naturally varies greatly according to latitude, elevation, and vegetation. The Guayana region, here also, stands by itself, both from its southern position and comparatively uniform elevation, so that over a wide area the temperature and rainfall are more or less the same. Naturally in those parts of Guayana where mountain ridges rise above the general level of the plateau the temperature is lower than the average, but these must constitute a small part of the whole. There is a marked difference in the meteorological conditions in the various river-valleys of the Orinoco basin, where the "white-water"—*i.e.*, the swiftly flowing but muddy streams, with rocky beds—are always accompanied by a clear sky overhead, and mosquitoes and crocodiles abound; on the "black water"—the deep and slow rivers—the sky is continually clouded, but the air is free from mosquitoes. The Orinoco represents the former type, the Rio Negro the latter. The rainy season in Guayana begins in April and lasts till November; the remaining four months are fairly dry.

The better known region of the north is generally considered as divided, *qua* climate, into three regions, in common with tropical South America generally—that is to say, the hot, temperate, and cold zones. The hot zone or *Tierra caliente* is generally considered as ranging from sea-level to an elevation of 1,915 feet, where the mean annual temperature varies from 74° to 91° Fahr. The intermediate or temperate zone, the *Tierra templada*, lies between 1,915 and 7,030 feet above sea-level, and within those limits the mean annual temperature may fall as low as, or even lower than, 60° Fahr. The *Tierra fria*, or cold zone, including the highest peak of Venezuela, 16,423 feet, has mean annual temperatures ranging from 60° to below zero.

The *Tierra caliente* includes (in addition to the greater part of Guayana) the Llanos, the coastal plains, and the region of the Lake of Maracaibo, the lower slopes and part of the central valleys of the mountains, part of the Segovia Highlands, and the Caribbean islands. The higher ground naturally has a climate varying with elevation, but the typical hot country, the Llanos are the warmest, the islands the coolest. On the Llanos the central, northern, and eastern regions are cooler than the southern and western, the highest mean annual temperature being recorded in San Fernando de Apure. Over this area the rainfall is heavy, and the wet season lasts from April to November. Maracaibo has the highest temperature of the cities of the coastal region, and, while the rains in the greater part of the area last through the same months as in Guayana and the Llanos, the area round the lake is comparatively free from rain until August and September, when the heaviest falls are recorded. The Segovia highlands and the islands alike have a lower mean temperature and rainfall than the remainder of the zone, the position of the one region, behind the coastal range which has precipitated the moisture of the easterly winds, being paralleled by the distance of the islands from these heights in the opposite direction.

The *Tierra templada* includes the greater part of the inhabited region of the hills, in which the climate necessarily varies greatly according to situation, the bottoms of some of the Andine valleys within the zone being more oppressive than parts of the low countries.

In the eastern part of the Caribbean Hills the rains last during the same months as in the Llanos, but in the Andes, particularly to the south, the seasons vary, and it is generally considered that there are two rainy seasons; the first light rains from April to June, separated by "St. John's little summer" (*El Veranito de San Juan*) from the later heavy rains which last from August to November; this arrangement applies rather to the eastern side of the watershed, the western side having an increasing similarity in seasons to the Llanos as one descends towards those plains.

Only the higher peaks and ridges of the Caribbean Hills are included in the *Tierra fría*, but between Tocuyo and the Colombian frontier the greater part of the area is situated above 7,030 feet. The prevalent strong winds and the sparse vegetation of the upper areas render them too unattractive to have become extensively colonised, but the products of the temperate zone grow readily in the lower parts below the timber-limit. Only the peaks of the Sierra Nevada are permanently snow-covered, the line having, it is said, retreated upwards of late years. The snow is apparently more abundant in the hotter months of the year, when the clouds which are dropping rain on the plain hide the peaks for many hours of the day, and then, lifting suddenly, show them white with snow far below the normal point, which is about 14,700 feet above sea-level. A very short period of exposure to the sun's rays restores the mountains to their usual aspect.

PANORAMA OF THE ANDES FROM NORTH OF CARACHE.

From the point of view of health, Venezuela must be looked upon as holding a good record for a country in its latitude, where malaria is to be expected to prevail. The death-rate for the whole republic in 1908 is given in the *Anuario Estadístico* as 25·1 per 1,000, and of the 56,903 deaths in that year, about one-third were infants under four years of age, while malaria (*paludismo*) accounts for 8,239. Tuberculosis and gastric and nervous diseases are the most prevalent causes of death. Yellow fever, once so prevalent, is now rare, thanks to improved sanitary conditions. The Delta region and the lower parts of the Guayana valley are the most unhealthy from a general point of view, while the death-rate of the cities shows that the Llanos are by far the healthiest district, with the Andes next, followed by the Caribbean Hills. In some of the low-lying coast towns, where mangrove swamps abound in the neighbourhood, the death-rate is high, but as a general rule the northern coast, with its dry atmosphere and sea breezes, while hot, appears to be markedly healthy.

CHAPTER II
THE GEOLOGICAL HISTORY OF VENEZUELA

Ancient land of Guayana—Comparison with Scottish Highlands—Gneisses, schists, and granite—Dykes—Roraima Series—Strange peaks—The Caribbean Series—"All that glitters is not gold"—La Galera—Segovia Group—Natural castles—Capacho Limestone—The Golden Hill—Cerro de Oro Series—Formation of mountains—Early outlet of Orinoco—Cumaná Series—Shoals and islands—Llano gravels—Cubagua beds—Igneous rocks—Earthquakes—Hot springs—A natural kettle—Coal—Iron—Gold—Copper—Lead—Petroleum and asphalt—Sulphur—Salt—Urao—Ornamental stones—Wealth in minerals.

A certain interest, often described as spurious but none the less common, generally attaches to the ancient for the sake of its antiquity, and we may, hope, therefore, that the story of the rocks of Venezuela will appeal even to non-geological readers.

The Guayana Highlands appear not only to be formed of the oldest rocks in Venezuela, but from such scanty study as has been made of parts of the region, to represent one of the most ancient land-surfaces in the world. Different as they are in appearance, they offer many analogies with the north-western highlands of Scotland from a geological point of view; and here it is known that the processes of building-up and breaking-down have preserved for us glimpses of a land which stood, as it now stands, long ages ago when living organisms, if there were any, had not reached such a stage in their development as to leave their traces in the deposits of the time.

The great elevated platform from which rise the peaks and mountain chains of Guayana appears everywhere to be composed of similar rocks, gneisses, hornblende schists, and granites, all containing evidence of great antiquity in geological time. This Guayana complex, as it may be called, has been considered by geologists as more or less equivalent in age to the Lewisian gneiss of Scotland, and therefore one of the oldest members of the Archæan system.

What may have been the original condition of the rocks it is impossible now to say, but one of the agencies which has brought them to their present form has left its traces in the form of "dykes" of quartz-porphyries and felsite, which were once forced in a molten condition into crevices and joints of the then less solid deposits.

After the cooling of these intrusions and wearing down of the whole mass by atmospheric influences, the movements of the earth's crust produced a shallow sea or series of lakes over what is now Guayana, and in these waters a series of beds of red and white sandstones, coarse conglomerate, and red shale were laid down to a thickness of about 2,000 feet. Later the area was again elevated into dry land, the sediments were consolidated, and again veins or dykes of basalt, dolerite, and similar dark, heavy rocks in a molten condition forced themselves into the fractures of gneisses and sandstones alike. These sandstones are here named the Roraima Series, from their occurrence in that mountain, and they now remain as isolated peaks or chains of hills all over Guayana, which, since that far-off period when the series was first consolidated, seems to have been always dry land.

The points at which the Roraima beds have been left as upstanding masses of horizontally stratified material, in place of being completely denuded from the ancient foundation of gneiss, appear to have been determined in many cases by the presence of exceptional accumulations of molten igneous rock, which has hardened and remained as a cap to protect the softer sandstones below from the effects of atmospheric weathering. Where this has been the case the strange vertical-sided, flat-topped mountains of Guayana are the result.

While in all probability northern Venezuela has no rocks quite so ancient as those of Guayana, the geological history of this part of the country has been much more eventful, and the number of earthquakes suggest that even yet the form of the earth's crust in this region is undergoing comparatively violent changes.

As is commonly the case, to find the oldest rocks we have to search the hills, and because the masses of gneiss, silvery mica-schist, marble, and so on, which form the highest parts of much of the mountain region, were first studied by Mr. G. P. Wall in the Caribbean Hills in 1860, he named the whole the Caribbean Series. The beds which make up the series may have been deposited at a period corresponding to that of the ancient Silurian rocks of Wales, but it seems very possible that they are older in some parts than in others. They form the central region of the Venezuelan Andes, where there is a core of granite which probably cooled at a date subsequent to the consolidation of the gneiss and schists. The silvery mica-flakes of the latter are very often mistaken by the inhabitants for gold or silver ores, and the author had more than one pretty but valueless specimen offered for sale, with its locality to be revealed as a secret of great worth! The same rocks extend all the way along the coastal range across the Boca del Draco into Trinidad, and northward in Margarita the mountains are formed of similar gneisses and schists. In the Llanos north of El Baúl there is a peculiar elevated plateau known as La Galera, from which rise many hills of gneiss and granitic rock, but these may perhaps be an outlying island of the Guayana complex.

After the deposits of the Caribbean Series had been consolidated and elevated into dry land, but before they had been thrown into high mountains such as they form to-day, perhaps at the same time that the granite of the Sierra Nevada of Mérida was being pushed up under them in a molten condition, the seas around were receiving deposits of quartz sand, mud, and lime, which were later consolidated to form a series of red and yellow sandstones, shales, slates, and black bituminous limestones, which now outcrop along the Sierras, and chiefly in the Segovia Highlands, suggesting for the whole the name Segovia Group. The animals which inhabited the seas of those times left their shells and remains in the rocks, and the forms (Ammonites, *Inoceramus*, &c.) which have been found by various travellers show that these deposits were formed at a period approximately corresponding to that of the lowest parts of our chalk or of the Cretaceous System generally.

Here and there throughout the mountains of northern Venezuela, the traveller is sure to be struck by the sight of great cliffs and castle-like masses of limestone rock, which add greatly to the effect of the scenery where they occur. From their position it is clear that these were originally parts of a more or less continuous accumulation of lime in a deep, still sea, after more turbulent waters had deposited the Segovia Group. The German traveller Dr. Sievers called this limestone the Capacho Limestone, from Capacho in Táchira. The fossils are similar to those of the period of the higher parts of the chalk.

After the deposition of the Capacho Limestone the earth's crust, which had in this region remained tranquil for a considerable period, again underwent some changes, and in the new shallower sea thus formed sand and mud, with some lime, were alternately laid down. The resulting sandstones, shales, and limestones were named by Dr. Sievers the Cerro de Oro Series, from a hill formed of these rocks in Táchira, and called Cerro de Oro, or Golden Hill, because the very abundant iron pyrites in it were mistaken for the precious metal. Many fossils have been found in the group, and from these it seems that in Venezuela, instead of the break between Cretaceous and Tertiary which we have in England, there was a continuous series of deposits, so that at the base we have chalk fossils, and higher up Eocene forms, the general character of the animal life changing gradually from one to the other.

With the consolidation of the Cerro de Oro beds we have a new period of disturbance, in which the mountain chains of northern Venezuela began to be formed as we know them to-day, and the waters of the Orinoco began to flow into the Atlantic more or less by the present mouth of the river. Alongside the newly formed hills, or islands as they would then be, sandstones and shales were deposited to a considerable thickness. They are found outcropping now along the coast and under the Llanos, as well as round the Lake of Maracaibo. The first fossils from them were collected by Mr. G. P. Wall from Cumaná, and it seems fitting to distinguish the whole as the Cumaná Series.

After the deposition of the Cumaná Series, and the crust movements which led to the consolidation and folding of these rocks, the physical features of Venezuela must have been very much what they are to-day, save that many of the smaller islands and parts of the coast were still submerged as shoals, whilst the Llanos seem to have been a great swampy or submerged plain, with deep water in parts, over which the Orinoco sediments gradually accumulated in the form of current-bedded sands and clays surmounted by gravels, which we may term the Llano deposits. At the same time, along the coast and on the shoals shell-beds were being formed, and can now be seen at Cabo Blanco, west of La Guaira, and similar places, while practically the whole surface of the Island of Cubagua is formed of them, suggesting the name Cubagua Beds. About this period some volcanic rocks were thrust up and cooled both in the Peninsula of Paraguana and near San Casimiro, south of Carácas. In the mountains great masses of gravels containing huge boulders and some *Megatherium* and other bones were being piled up by the rivers. Last of all we have the still-accumulating recent alluvium of the modern streams, attaining its widest extent in the Delta and round the Lake of Maracaibo.

No volcanoes, active or recently extinct, are known in Venezuela, but the country has, like most of South America, been continually subject to earthquake shocks of greater or less intensity. Some of these are historic, but of the many others recorded not a few had far-reaching effects on the population. The first important tremor noticed after the discovery and settlement of the shores of the Caribbean was that of 1530, which shook the city of Nueva Cadiz on the Island of Cubagua and destroyed the fortress of Cumaná, thus checking for some time the colonisation of the mainland in this region. Thirteen years later New Cadiz was visited again by earthquake and hurricane, and so disastrous were the results that from that day to the present Cubagua has been, what it was before the arrival of the Spaniards, a desert island. The many shocks experienced in the course of the seventeenth and eighteenth centuries seem to have been generally unaccompanied by much loss of life or property, but this period of comparative quiescence was followed by one of the historical examples of severe earthquake early in the nineteenth century. In March, 1812, a shock destroyed great parts of Carácas, La Guaira, Barquisimeto, Mérida, and other towns, and in the capital alone ten thousand people were killed. The great earthquake which, on August 13, 1868, made itself felt all over South America, so much affected some of the

Venezuelan rivers that their waters over-flowed the banks, and even remained for a short time in new channels. In 1894 Mérida and other towns in the Andes suffered much damage, houses and churches being shaken down; the destruction was in some cases extraordinarily complete. Since that time only slight tremors have been felt.

The internal heat in the north-eastern spur of the Andes, which traverses Venezuela, manifests itself at many points in the form of hot springs. One, containing much sulphur, is found at Las Trincheras, between Valencia and Puerto Cabello. The temperature of this spring varies, but in 1852 it was found by Karsten to be only a few degrees below the boiling point of water; in general, however, it does not exceed 195° F. or 17° below boiling point. Wall found one south of Carúpano actually boiling. All along the flanks of the coastal Cordillera there are mineral springs, generally at fairly high temperatures, and many more are known throughout the Andes. Nearly all these springs have been used in the treatment of various diseases, though none has achieved especial popularity.

While hot springs may be interesting to the visitor, they are hardly valuable assets to a country such as Venezuela, but this part of the world has always, and with much justice, held the reputation of being rich in minerals. There is coal of fairly good quality in more than one of the Cretaceous and Tertiary groups of strata, near Barcelona, Tocuyo, Coro, and Maracaibo, as well as in the Andes, but the often-associated iron is only found in large quantities in the Guayana gneiss south of the Orinoco Delta.

Gold, that great lure for the early European ventures to the west, may be said to occur in almost every State of Venezuela, but it has only been worked with profit in Guayana, even though samples of a quartz-reef near Carúpano are said to have assayed 7 oz. to the ton. When Sir Robert Dudley visited the coast of the Gulf of Paria in 1595, he heard of a goldmine near Orocoa (Uracoa), on the eastern side of the Llanos, which may mean that the gravels are occasionally auriferous, but unfortunately he failed to reach the place. Placer workings are the chief source of the precious metal in the Guasipati goldfields in Guayana, but the reefs from which it is derived have been discovered and worked at odd times. In British Guiana, where the conditions are similar, Mr. Harrison says that the gold is generally found along the later intrusive dykes, the smallest dykes being the richest, while most gold is found where a basalt intrusion crosses one of the older ones.

The ores of copper are fairly common in the northern Cordillera, and the mines of Aroa in Yaracuy have been worked for many years. Here the pyrites veins occur in the Capacho Limestone, not far from where it has been invaded by a mass of granite. In the Andes it seems to occur in the more ancient rocks, as near Seboruco in Táchira, and Bailadores in Mérida. A mine near Pao seems to be in Cretaceous rocks.

Many other metallic ores occur at various points, notably galena in the Andes, but one of the most common minerals of northern Venezuela is petroleum, known in its desiccated form as "Bermudez asphalt" over half the world. Boring for the original mineral oil has only recently been undertaken. Sulphur is one of the less valuable minerals which occur in considerable quantities, but the so-called salt-mines are not strictly mines at all, and are described in Chapter XVI. Humboldt had heard of the strange mineral lake near Lagunillas, which contains a large proportion of *urao* or sesqui-carbonate of soda, a mineral not usually found in nature, and here apparently supplied from springs rising in the Segovia rocks. It is used locally for mixture with tobacco juice to make a chewing mixture called *chimo*, but there have been projects to obtain the salt in large quantities for the manufacture of caustic soda.

In addition to those already mentioned, all the following minerals or ornamental stones have been found in one part or another of Venezuela, viz., marble, kaolin, gypsum, calcium phosphate, opal, onyx, jasper, quartz, felspar, talc, mica, staurolite, asbestos, and ores of antimony, silver, and tin.

The minerals of Venezuela have merely been mentioned casually in this place, an account of the extent to which they have been exploited being deferred to the chapter on the general development of the country. It is evident, however, when one considers their number and the extent of their distribution, that the geological changes which have played their part in the building up of the physical features of the country have left Venezuela in possession of splendid assets in this respect.

CHAPTER III
THE PLANTS AND ANIMALS OF VENEZUELA

The glamour of the South American forests—Hidden treasures—Temples of Nature—"A dim religious light"—*Bejucales*—Forest giants—Brazil nuts—Tonka-beans—Rubber—Quinine—Arctic and tropic forms—The Llanos—*Tierra caliente*—Natural hothouses—Colour and coolness—*Páramo* plants—Monkeys—An old friend—Cannibalism—Vampires and bats—"Tigers" and "lions"—"Handsome is as handsome doesn't"—Wild horses—Dolphins—Prickly mice—The "water-hog"—Sloths—Birds—Many-coloured varieties—Umbrella-bird—"Cock-of-the-rock"—Toucans—Cuckoos—Humming-birds—"Who are you?"—Oil-birds—Parrots and macaws—Eagles and vultures—A national disgrace—Game-birds—Snakes—Lizards—From the Orinoco to a city dinner—A cup-tie crowd—Ferocious fish—When is a mosquito not a mosquito?—Agricultural ants—Gigantic spiders—Ticks—A pugnacious crustacean—A rich field.

Most of us, if possessed of imaginative faculties, have been impressed in our youth by the thought of those vast virgin forests of South America, inhabited, as we often used to think, only by huge boa-constrictors and anacondas which lived to an immense age and continued to grow throughout their lifetime; and even in later years, when experience at first or second hand has taught us that the supposed silent forest of the tropics is generally noisy with the chattering of monkeys and birds or the perpetual hum and chirp of insects, and is often far from a desirable place on account of these last, the glamour of the vastness and fertility of these great untrodden temples of nature remains with us.

More than half of Venezuela is covered by forest, and, indeed, comes within the forest area of South America; what botanical treasures and zoological curiosities may yet be discovered, when some explorer is found to succeed Humboldt and Schomburgk, are not to be guessed at, and it is not our purpose to give a scientific account of what has been done towards classifying and enumerating the many plants and animals already known to live in Venezuela, but to briefly describe what is most interesting and important to the general reader who may be interested in the country as a whole.

Richest in quantity, and probably in variety, of vegetable life is the little-known land of Guayana, with its vast forests, hot climate, and heavy rainfall. Within it the plants range from the alpine shrubs and reindeer moss of some of the higher plateaux and hills to the bamboos and orchids of the river banks. The simile which compares the tropical forest to those darkened lofty cathedrals of Europe has been often used, and is, perhaps, somewhat trite, but its aptness is incontrovertible. The huge timber-trees grow fairly close together, and their spreading tops, fifty, eighty, or a hundred feet from the ground, with the abundant hanging lianes and flowering creepers, keep all but a feeble light from the ground, whence it comes that the under-growth is usually sparse or absent, and progress on foot is comparatively easy. Sometimes, however, there are stretches of *bejucal*, full of tangled ground creepers, and it may take a day to cut a path for one mile through such growth as this.

Of all the forest giants of Guayana, Schomburgk considered the mora the most magnificent; the average diameter of the trunk is about three feet, and it seldom branches at less than forty feet from the ground. The dark-red, fine-grained wood is said to be excellent for shipbuilding purposes. Mahogany or *caoba*, the *palo de arco*, whose wood is very like mahogany in colour, and a big tree called in Venezuela rosewood, which it resembles, are among the timber trees of the region known to us in Europe. The huge *ceibas*, with their buttress-like roots, have a soft, easily worked wood, excellent for the dug-out canoes of the Indians, and the equally large *mucurutu* or cannon-ball tree furnishes a beautiful but hard and fine-grained timber. Unfortunately, the very fertility of the soil becomes a drawback in the exploitation of these timber resources, for all trees grow with equal freedom, and the particular kind for which the lumber-man is searching may only be found at rare intervals; on a large scale, when all the valuable woods are utilised, this difficulty would, to some extent, disappear.

There are two fruit-trees whose products are well known in European markets, and though these grow all over Guayana, they are particularly abundant in certain regions. The Brazil nut was first described by Humboldt, but since his time it has become a common article of merchandise in Europe; the tree which bears it is itself large, and the fruit, with its fifteen or twenty nuts, is tremendously heavy, and generally breaks in falling from the tree when ripe, not infrequently cracking the shells inside, when the birds and monkeys are able to enjoy the oily kernel; otherwise the exterior usually proves too hard. The other fruit we have referred to is the *sarrapia*, or tonka-bean, not so well known to the general public of to-day as formerly, though extensively used in perfumery. The trees grow in greatest abundance and excellence, according to André, in the Caura and Cuchivero valleys. The gums and resins of Guayana include the balatá, copaiba-balsam, and rubber-producing trees, the latter chiefly varieties of Hevea, while *cinchona* or quinine with innumerable creepers and trees possessed of medicinal or toxic properties are found everywhere. The 2,450 species of plants referred to by Schomburgk have since been added to, and it is obvious that in such an assembly there must be many of value, as yet undiscovered and unused.

The vegetation of the higher exposed peaks and plateaux is quite different from that of the forests, and here Schomburgk found such an alpine, or rather Arctic, form as reindeer-moss, associated with semi-tropical rock-orchids and aloes.

The forest plants and trees of Guayana also flourish in the Delta region and in the forests bordering the Llanos of Maturín, but the vegetation of northern Venezuela is generally very different from that of the south.

The great green or brown plain of the Llanos is often beautified by small golden, white, and pink flowers, and sedges and irises make up much of the small vegetation. Here and there the beautiful "royal" palm, with its banded stem and graceful crown, the *moriche*, or one of the other kinds, forms clumps to break the monotony, and along the small streams are patches of *chaparro* bushes, cashew-nuts, locusts, and so forth. The banks of the rivers often support denser groves of ceibas, crotons, guamos, &c.; the last-named bears a pod covered with short, velvety hair, within which, around the beans (about the size of our broad beans), is a cool, juicy, very refreshing pulp, not unlike that of the young cocoa-pod. Along the banks of the streams in front of the trees are masses of reeds and semi-aquatic grasses, which effectually conceal the higher vegetation from a traveller in a canoe at water-level.

IN THE UPPER TEMPERATE ZONE: THE CHAMA VALLEY.

As might be expected, when we enter the region of the Cordilleras, we find very different types of vegetation in the various zones. The *tierra caliente* has generally a heavy rainfall, and then supports thick forest, but along the coast there are barren stretches with only cactus, acacia, croton, and similar plants, picturesque, but hardly beautiful. The mangroves and their associated forms line the shore in a belt of varying width, but behind follow, according to the climate and soil, lowland forests or plains and hills covered with cactus of all shapes and sizes, some being so large that the woody stems are used locally in building.

In the *tierra caliente* we have the plantations of cacao, sugar, bananas, plantains, maize, and cassava, which produce the staple foods of the inhabitants, and the highly profitable coconuts, if not cultivated, are at least encouraged and exploited. In addition, there are the many valuable products of the forests, chief of which are the dye-woods and tanning barks, including logwood, dividive, mangrove, indigo, and many others. A good deal of valuable timber grows in parts of the forest, the chief woods exported being mahogany and "cedar."

As we rise into the cooler regions, we find, naturally, a mixture of the hot-country plants and those of the mountains; particularly is this so in the case of cultivated kinds. One may see in the same valley, within a short distance of one another, bananas, potatoes, sugar-cane, wheat, yuca or cassava, peas, maize, cotton, cocoa, and coffee, all flourishing, and a single orchard may contain guavas and apples, peaches and oranges, papayas and quinces, not to mention many other fruits; the garden adjoining will have a mixture of roses, carnations, violets, and dahlias with bougainvilleas, dragon's blood, magnolias, and other tropical flowers. Strawberries, mint, bulrushes, nasturtiums, and other of our garden plants have been successfully naturalised in these mountain regions within 10° of the equator.

The higher part of the *tierra templada* exhibits the greatest variety of plants peculiar to this zone. As one travels along the mountain roads, in addition to new kinds of palms, one sees screw-pines and beautiful tree-ferns, splendid white rock-orchids and purple parasitic varieties, red and white rhododendrons and heaths, cranberries, blackberries, ivy, passion-flowers, yews, quinine-trees, aloes of all kinds, small bamboos, silver-ferns, and all manner of beautiful flowering shrubs and plants, for it is here and not in the hotter tropical regions that we have the greatest variety of colour and the most beautiful floral scenery.

Nor is the *tierra fria* of the Cordilleras without its beauty and interest to the botanist. The small woods of the temperate zone gradually die out, and towards the snow-line we have the alpine grasses, heaths, and lichens of the *páramos*, amongst which are scattered those peculiar white or yellow, thick-leaved, aloe-shaped plants which, strangely enough, have lumps of resin clinging to their roots, and seem in this respect to supply the place of the pines and firs which are not found in Venezuela.

There is at least one animal found in the forests of Guayana which is familiar even to the untravelled Cockney, namely, the prehensile-tailed capuchin monkey or *sapajou*, of which several species are known in Venezuela, while they are the most common tame kind brought to Europe. Humboldt's woolly monkey, which is nearly allied, is dark grey, the capuchin being generally reddish; its flesh is said to be excellent eating for those who feel no qualms at nearing the verge of cannibalism. Many other kinds are found in the forests, including the black thumbless spider-monkeys, but the variegated spider-monkey, of which the first specimen brought alive to England came from the Upper Caura in 1870, is a gorgeous beast, with black back, white cheeks, a band of bright reddish-yellow across the forehead, and yellow under-surface to body and limbs. The banded douroucouli also occurs in southern Venezuela, and Mr. Bates has described how, on the banks of the Amazon, a person passing by a tree in which a number of them are concealed may be startled by the apparition of a number of little striped faces crowding a hole in the trunk. Their ears are very small. The graceful little squirrel-monkeys, with dark fur shot with gold, the titi, reddish-black, with a white spot on the chest, the white-headed and other sakis, and the abundant and very noisy howlers are all denizens of the Guayana forests. Nor must we omit to mention the pretty little marmosets, which are often kept as pets.

Bats, and their objectionable cousins, the vampires, are abundant in Venezuela, but the true blood-sucking vampire does not seem to be very common.

There are, of course, no tigers or lions, properly so called, in the New World, but the names have been usurped by similar beasts, the jaguar and the puma. The tan-coloured fur of the former, with its large rosette-like spots, is very beautiful, and quite equals that of the tiger in large specimens, while for agility it more than rivals its Asiatic relative, being credited with climbing trees and living there in times of severe flood, to the great danger and annoyance of the usual inhabitants, the monkeys. The tawny puma is also said to chase the monkeys in the tree-tops, even in ordinary times. The other large cats of Venezuela include the ocelot, jaguarondi, and margay, and there is the one fox-like "Azara's" dog.

The peculiar-looking "spectacled bear" is found up in the Andes, and the kinkajou represents the raccoon tribe, while the weasels include the tayra and grison, and their relative, the handsome but most objectionable skunk, occasionally pollutes the atmosphere with his presence. The big Brazilian otter, with chocolate-brown fur, is found in the rivers of the Llanos.

Amongst the hoofed animals, the red Brazilian and Ecuador brockets represent the deer, and there are two species of *vaquira* or peccary, in addition to the now acclimatised European pig. Horses and donkeys live in a semi-wild state on the Llanos, though their nearest relative native to the country is the tapir or *danta*, a very different beast in appearance.

The nailless manati of the Orinoco mouth is fairly common, and higher up the river there is a fresh-water dolphin: the author observed a fish-like beast in the Lake of Maracaibo, which may be the same species, though out in the salt water of the Caribbean the common dolphin is found, as well as the cachalot, and another species of whale is said to have been seen there.

The rodents include a number of species of great scientific interest, but for the ordinary individual one rat or shrew is much like another, and the squirrels, mice, rabbits, hedgehogs, and allied animals are very similar to those of Europe. One of the mice has flattened spines mingled with the fur, and the coypu or *perro de agua* has a very harsh coat, though it is rather like a beaver in appearance and habits, while some near relatives of smaller size have the same peculiar flattened spines on the back. The peculiar Brazilian tree-porcupine is a Guayana species. The gracefully formed aguti or *acure* is common in the Venezuelan forests, and its near relative, the *aguchi*, is found there with the *lappa* or *paca*, the flesh of which is excellent eating. The big "water-hog," *chiguire* or *capybara*, familiar to Zoo visitors, occurs in Guayana and elsewhere.

There are several sloths common in the low-lying parts of the Guayana forests and similar regions of northern Venezuela, and the great-maned ant-eater or "ant-bear," with the lesser ant-eater, is as often seen in Venezuela as in any part of South America, while Guayana is the centre of the small district in which the peculiar two-toed ant-eater is found. The *cachicamos* or armadillos are much esteemed as food in the forest districts.

The marsupials are represented by the *rabipelados* or opossums and the *perrito de agua* or water-opossum.

The birds, being more commonly seen, are perhaps of greater interest than the mammals, and certainly many of the Venezuelan birds are beautiful, though, as frequently happens, what they gain in plumage they lose in song, and few have even a pleasant note.

Beautifully coloured jays, the peculiar cassiques, with their hanging nests, starlings, and the many violet, scarlet, and other tanagers, with some very pretty members of the finch tribe, are all fairly abundant in Venezuela. Greenlets, some of the allied waxwings, and thrushes of various kinds, with the equally familiar wrens, are particularly abundant, nor does the cosmopolitan swallow absent himself from this part of the world. The numerous family of the American flycatchers has fifty representatives in Venezuela, and the allied ant-birds constitute one of the exceptions to the rule, in possessing a pleasant warbling note. The chatterers include some of the most notable birds of Venezuela, and we may specially notice the strange-looking umbrella-bird which extends into the Amazon territory, known from its note as the fife-bird; the variegated bell-bird, which makes a noise like the ringing of a bell; the gay manikins, whose colour include blue, crimson, orange, and yellow, mingled with sober blacks, browns, and greens; the nearly allied cock-of-the-rock is one of the most beautiful birds of Guayana, orange-red being the principal colour in its plumage, while its helmet-like crest adds to its grandeur; the hen is a uniform reddish-brown. The wood-hewers are more of interest from their habits than the beauty of their plumage.

The beautiful green jacamars, the puff-birds, and the bright-coloured woodpeckers are found all over Venezuela in the forests, but their relatives the toucans are among the most peculiar of the feathered tribe. With their enormous beaks and gaudy plumage they are easily recognised when seen, and can make a terrible din if a number of them collected together are disturbed, the individual cry being short and unmelodious. Several cuckoos are found in Venezuela, some having more or less dull plumage and being rare, while others with brighter feathers are gregarious. With the trogons, however, we come to the near relatives of the beautiful quezal, all medium-sized birds, with the characteristic metallic blue or green back and yellow or red breasts. The tiny, though equally beautiful, humming-birds are common sights in the forest, but a sharp eye is needed to detect them in their rapid flight through the dim light; some of the Venezuelan forms are large, however, notably the king humming-bird of Guayana; and the crested coquettes, though smaller, are still large enough to make their golden-green plumage conspicuous. The birds which perhaps most force themselves, not by sight but by sound, upon the notice of travellers are the night-jars; the "who are you?" is as well known in Trinidad as in Venezuela. The great wood night-jar of Guayana has a very peculiar mournful cry, particularly uncanny when heard in the moonlight. The kingfisher-like motmots have one representative in Venezuela, but the other member of the group, which includes all the preceding birds, constitute a family by itself. This is the oil-bird or *guacharo*, famous from Humboldt's description of the cave of Caripe in which they were first found. The young birds are covered with thick masses of yellow fat, for which they are killed in large numbers by the local peasantry. They live in caves wherever they are found and only come out to feed at dusk.

Other birds which are sure to be observed even by the least ornithological traveller are the parrots and macaws which fly in flocks from tree to tree of the forest, uttering their discordant cries. The macaws have blue and red or yellow plumage, but the parrots and parraquets are all wholly or mainly of a green hue. The several owls are naturally seldom seen, and, in the author's experience, rarely heard.

There are no less than thirty-two species of falcons or eagles known from Venezuela, and of these many are particularly handsome, such as the swallow-tailed kite and the harpy eagle of Guayana. Their loathsome carrion-eating cousins, the vultures, have four representatives.

In the rivers and caños of the lowlands there are abundant water-birds, and the identified species include a darter, two pelicans, several herons or *garzas*, the indiscriminate slaughter of which in the breeding season for egret plumes has been one of the disgraces of Venezuela, as well as storks and ibises. Among the most beautiful birds of these districts are the rosy white or scarlet flamingoes, huge flocks of which are sometimes seen rising from the water's edge at the approach of a boat or canoe. There are also seven Venezuelan species of duck.

The various pigeons and doves possess no very notable characteristics, and one or two of the American quails are found in the Andes. Other game-birds include the fine-crested curassows of Guayana, the nearly allied guans, and the pheasant-like hoatzin. There are several rails, and the finfeet are represented. The sun bittern is very common on the Orinoco. There are members of the following groups: the trumpeters (tamed in Brazil to protect poultry), plovers, terns, petrels, grebes, and, lastly, seven species of the flightless tinamous.

Descending lower in the scale, we come to the animals which are, or used to be, most often associated in the mind with the forests of South America. The snakes are very numerous, but only a minority are poisonous. Of the latter the beautiful but deadly coral-snake is not very common, but a rattlesnake and the formidable "bushmaster" are often seen. Of the non-poisonous variety the water-loving boas and *tigres* or anacondas are mainly confined to the Delta and the banks of the Guayana rivers. The *cazadora* (one of the colubers) and the Brazilian wood-snake or *sipo*, with its beautiful coloration, are common; the blind or velvet snake is often found in the enclosures of dwellings.

One of the lizards, the amphisbæna, is known in the country as the double-headed snake, and is popularly supposed to be poisonous, but there are many species of the pretty and more typical forms, especially in the dry regions, while the edible iguana is common in the forests. There are eleven species of crocodiles, of which the *caiman* infests all the larger rivers and caños. The Chelonidæ include only two land tortoises, but there are several turtles in the seas and rivers, and representatives of this family from the Gulf of Paria often figure on the menus of City companies.

There are some six genera of frogs and toads to represent the Amphibians, and the evening croaking of the various species of the former on the Llanos is very characteristic of those regions; one, in particular, emits a sound like a human shout, and a number of them give the impression of a crowd at a football match.

CLOUD-DRIFTS IN THE ANDES.

TORBES VALLEY AND THE COLOMBIAN HILLS.

Fish abound in rivers, lakes, and seas, but, considering their number, remarkably little is known about them. Some are regarded as poisonous, and others are certainly dangerous, such as the small but ferocious *caribe* of the Llano rivers, which is particularly feared by bathers, as an attack from a shoal results in numbers of severe, often fatal, wounds. The *temblador* or electric eel is very abundant in the western Llanos, and is as dangerous in its way as the *caribe*.

The insects are too numerous for more than casual reference, but it may be noted that the *mosquito* of the Spaniards is a small and very annoying sandfly;

the mosquito as we know it is, and always has been, called *zancudo de noche* by the Spanish-speaking inhabitants of Venezuela. The gorgeous butterflies and the emerald lights of the fireflies are in a measure a compensation for the discomforts caused by their relatives, but of the less attractive forms, the most interesting are the hunting ants, which swarm through houses at times devouring all refuse, and the parasol ants, which make with the leaves they carry hot-beds, as it were, for the fungus upon which they feed.

One of the most unpleasant of the lower forms of life in the forests is the *araña mono* or big spider of Guayana, which sometimes measures more than six inches across; it is found in the remote parts of the forest, and its bites cause severe fever. The better-known tarantula, though less dangerous, can inflict severe bites. The extremely poisonous scorpions and the *garrapatas* or ticks must be seen or felt to be appreciated.

We may leave the lower forms of life to more technical works, but the amusing "calling-crab" deserves special mention. With his one enormous paw of pincers the male if disturbed will sit upon the mud or sand and apparently challenge all the world to "come on" in a most amusing fashion.

A host of interesting birds, beasts, and plants have already been found in Venezuela, and it still presents an almost virgin field for the botanist and zoologist, to whom the technical literature given in the bibliography will prove of more use than this necessarily brief sketch.

CHAPTER IV
VENEZUELA UNDER SPANISH RULE AND BEFORE

Pre-Columbian times—No great empire—Primitive Venezuelans—Picture rocks—Invasions—The Guatavitas and the legend of El Dorado—Amalivaca—An Inca prince?—Ancient roads—The discovery of *Tierra Firme*, 1498—Alonso de Ojeda—The name Venezuela—A great geographical fraud—Discovery of the treasures of the west—Arrival of the *conquistadores*—The slave trade—Treacheries of the Cubagua colonists—Gonzalez de Ocampo—Las Casas—First cities of the New World—Settlement of Coro—The Welsers—Alfinger—Ingratitude of Charles V.—New Andalusia—Exploration of the Orinoco—Cruelties of Alfinger—Exploration of the Llanos—First Bishop of Venezuela—Destruction of New Cadiz—Faxardo and the Carácas—Cities of Western Venezuela—The rebellion of Aguirre—Foundation of Carácas—Pimentel moves his capital to the new city—Capture of Carácas by English buccaneers—Inaccuracies of Spanish historians—Explorations of Berrio in Guayana—Raleigh and El Dorado—Attempts to civilise the Indians—Missions—University of Carácas—Guipuzcoana Company—Revolution of Gual and España—Miranda—The last Captain-General—The Junta—Appeals to England—The Declaration of Independence.

The advanced civilisations of early Peru and Mexico have left us, despite the vicious destruction of everything "heathen" by the "Christian" *conquistadores*, in possession of sufficient documents of one kind or another to glean a fairly complete and consecutive story of those countries in pre-Columbian times, as we may term that period before the discovery of the New World by Columbus. It is otherwise in Venezuela; here there seems to have been no advanced civilisation; and the *conquistadores* were as incapable of noticing or recording details of the social organisation and international relations of the savage aborigines as of appreciating the knowledge and skill of Incas or Aztecs; hence we have to depend mainly, if not entirely, on the information gathered with difficulty from buried ruins, tombs, and sepulchre-caves. Dr. G. Marcano has been one of the chief workers in this direction, and his systematic and painstaking work may one day give us a fairly complete picture of Venezuela before the Spaniards.

In the remote past, long (though we do not know how long) before the arrival of the white men from the east, the land appears to have been sparsely peopled by semi-nomadic, primitive tribes of a long-headed race, whose social organisation was limited to a grouping in temporary villages, while in the arts they had advanced as far as the making of rude earthenware, and perhaps the use of curiously shaped stones for personal adornment. They buried their dead in caves, either natural or artificial, placing them in a sitting posture in palm-leaf frails or earthenware urns, accompanied by small pieces of pottery and other household matters. The names of "tribes" in Guayana appear to be far too numerous to be really distinct races, and it is probable that they represent merely the more permanent associations of villages or groups of villages with slight differences of dialect. In Humboldt's time there were traditions of the internecine warfare of these "tribes," and it is possible that in times of strife they were guilty of cannibalism, though in later days authentic occurrences of the eating of human flesh were very rare, if existent at all.

Throughout Guayana there are crude rock inscriptions of comparatively ancient date, apparently representing an early attempt at picture-writing, and it is said that some of the shy and reticent Indian tribes appear to know the meaning of these. As yet no one has obtained any satisfactory clue to the purpose of these *rocas pintadas*.

We have said that these long-headed peoples occupied the land in the remote past, though their descendants were to be found in parts of Venezuela in comparatively recent times, and tribes of mixed race still bear witness to their existence. Many years before the Spanish conquest, however, there was a great influx of the more normal short-headed peoples, divided into more or less civilised communities, and possessed of some proficiency in the arts, with beliefs which were, in some respects, an advance upon the Nature-worship of the earlier inhabitants.

These last were soon compelled to withdraw into the mountain fastnesses, or the equally inaccessible forests of the south, while their conquerors settled in the Caribbean Hills and the lower valleys of the Andes, where at some points excavations have revealed something of their customs. Though greatly inferior to the ruling nations of Peru and Mexico, these races must still be looked upon as intermediate between them and the savages already referred to.

The Guatavitas of the plateau of Bogotá, whose great religious festival probably gave rise to the legend of El Dorado and his golden city of Manoa, may be taken as representing their higher development. The Guatavita chief, according to Acosta, used on the occasion of this annual festival to smear his body with turpentine preparatory to rolling in gold-dust; then, proceeding on a barge to the centre of their sacred lake, he would cast into it gold ornaments, emeralds, and other valuables, finally plunging into the waters himself, an action which was the signal for shouts of applause from the worshippers on the banks.[1]

Whether the Incas ever really held any communication with these lowland peoples it is impossible at present to say, but perhaps the legend of Amalivaca, who, the Indians say, visited them and began to teach them to write, finally sailing away to the east with a promise to return, may be based upon an actual visit of a Peruvian leader, who left on an exploratory voyage to the east, from which he never returned, at least to these shores. It is strange that there was in Humboldt's time on the Llanos between Barinas and the River Apure some twenty miles of well-made road, elevated about fifteen feet above the frequently flooded plains, the remains of a causeway from the mountains made long before Spanish times, and apparently the work of some nation far more advanced in the arts than any living close at hand.

We emerge from these regions of conjecture into the definite historical period rather more than five years after the first discovery of the islands of the New Continent by Columbus, when the great explorer, on his third westward journey, coasted along the south side of the Peninsula of Paria on July 31, 1498. He did not land there, but his son tells us that from the ships they could see men on the shore dressed in vari-coloured turbans and loincloths. When he entered the Gulf of Paria, he had expected to be able to pass out on the west side, believing the peninsula to be an island; realising his error, he turned back and entered the Caribbean through the Boca del Draco, "giving thanks to God who delivered him from so many troubles and dangers, still showing him new countries full of peaceful people, and great wealth." On his way across to Hispaniola (Santo Domingo), he passed by an island which he named Margarita, knowing nothing, as it seems, of the rich pearl fisheries which later rendered the name so appropriate.

Great enthusiasm was naturally kindled in Spain by the news of the discovery of a mainland (*Tierra Firme*) west of the islands, and it was decided to send a special exploratory expedition. Hence we have Alonso de Ojeda setting sail in 1499, and landing several times on what is now the Peninsula of Paria, though he knew it by the native name of Maracapana. The region generally he designated Nueva Andalusia. Encouraged by what he had seen, he sailed on westwards as far as Cabo de la Vela (now in Colombia), and entered the Lake of Maracaibo or Coquibacoa. Here there were at that time, as now, Indian pile-dwellings on the shores of the lake, which so far reminded Ojeda of Venice or Venezia, that he gave to the region the name of Little Venice, or Venezuela.

Thus we have the mainland of the New World or the Indies first sighted by Columbus and partly examined and named by Ojeda, but we may here turn aside from the story of Venezuela for a moment to see how, by a great and successful geographical fraud, the whole of the continent came to be called America.

There was on Ojeda's ship a Florentine merchant by name Amerigo Vespucci, who appeared to have contented himself on this voyage with gazing from the deck at the shores of the new countries. After returning to

Europe, he developed sufficient zeal to make a voyage on his own account to Brazil, and wrote a clever joint account of both voyages, in which he represented himself as a leader in the first expedition which effected a landing on the mainland of the New World. This *suggestio falsi*, if it deserves no harsher term, led Martin Hylacomylus in his "Cosmographia," published in 1509, to say of the discovery of the different parts of the globe: "*Alia quarta pars per Americū Vesputium ... inuenta est: qua non video cur quis iure vetet ab Americo inventatore ... Amerigen quasi Americi terram, siue Americam dicendam.*"[2] Thus it comes that a third of the land of the globe bears the name of a man who had no claim to be considered as of any particular importance on the ship which bore the first Spanish explorers who set foot in Venezuela.

Meanwhile, close behind Ojeda there was travelling an expedition including Pedro Alonso Niño, Luis Guerra, and Christobal Guerra, who visited Margarita and the adjacent islands of Cubagua, where they had some intercourse with the natives and obtained from them by barter a number of pearls. Next they touched the Cumanagoto coast, not far from where Barcelona now stands, and sailed from there to the Coro district. Here again they were well received by the natives, and exchanged European trinkets with them for gold and pearls. They continued their voyage as far as the Goajira Peninsula, but found the people there of a fierce and menacing aspect, so they returned to Spain, bearing news of the wealth of the West.

Had those natives only kept their pearls and golden trinkets from the sight of these first genuine explorers, the history of Venezuela might have been very different. The white men who next visited Venezuela were little, if anything, more than rapacious brigands, consumed with a lust for gain, before which any shreds of morality or good feeling they may once have possessed went for nothing.

In the year 1500 some fifty adventurers, sailing from Hispaniola, established a settlement on Cubagua for the pearl fisheries, and soon a horde of nondescripts from all the countries of Europe flocked to this source of easily won treasure, which under their uncontrolled and extravagant exploitation began to fail rapidly. With appetites whetted, these spoilt children of fortune turned to look for other means of acquiring wealth, always provided these did not entail any honest toil, and from this time begins the long black record of Spanish cruelties in the Indies, with the fabricated excuses of cannibalism and ferocity among the Indians.

To appreciate the position we must recall the infamous decree of Charles V. of Spain, which permitted the Europeans in the Indies to capture and enslave the natives who in any way opposed the "colonisation" of the new countries, or who practised cannibalism. The Indians being found most reprehensibly innocent of either of these crimes, the Cubaguans pronounced their very presence an evidence of opposition, and further assumed that they must all be cannibals. Carefully avoiding the possibility of arousing the wrath of the fine and stalwart Guaiquerias of Margarita, who lived in uncomfortable proximity to their town, they took steps to enslave some of the more remote Indians of the mainland.

While the world, the flesh, and the devil had been having things to themselves on Cubagua, the Church had been entering upon the new field of missionary work on the mainland, and three Franciscan monks settled on the Cumaná coast in 1513, while some Dominicans established a little community at Manjar, near Píritu. At both places the monks were on the most friendly terms with the natives, on whom, at that date, their influence was wholly for good.

The Franciscans of Cumaná received one day a visit from a few of the adventurers of Cubagua, who had previously, for obvious reasons, ignored the existence of the missionaries. Notwithstanding, they were hospitably treated, and entertained as well as might be by the monks and their Indian friends for several days; then the most catholic and Christian *conquistadores* revealed themselves in their true colours. The cacique of the district (christened Don Alonso by the friars) was invited with his family to dine on board; he accepted, unsuspecting, and found himself, his wife and children, captives on a ship making sail for Santo Domingo. At sight of this treachery, the Indians naturally seized the monks as partly responsible, but acceded to their request that before taking summary vengeance they should allow time for a messenger to go to Hispaniola and return with the cacique in safety; for this purpose four months was granted. But justice in Santo Domingo was non-existent, and legal decisions bought and sold. The pleas of the friars and their superiors in the island were of no avail, and at the termination of the stipulated period the monks of Cumaná were put to death by the mourning Indians. The region remained abandoned by Spaniards till 1518, when a new Franciscan community was established.

THE CHAMA VALLEY ABOVE MÉRIDA.

MOUNTAIN STREAM BETWEEN CUMANACOA AND CUMANÁ.

In 1520 the Dominicans of Chichirivichi, near Barcelona, also fell victims to Spanish treachery; the Indians had previously recognised their innocence of any possible complicity in the Cumaná affair, but their turn came on this wise. One of the Cubagua colonists, Alonso de Ojeda, said to have been the unworthy father of the author of the name Venezuela, crossed to Chichirivichi, and was well received by friars and Indians alike. Being, like most of his confrères, neither a gentleman himself nor able to recognise one when he met him, he insulted one of his hosts, the cacique of Maraguey, by asking whether any of his people ate human flesh; the chief replied with some feeling that they did not, and withdrew, recognising the motive of the question, as seeking the sanction under the *codicia* to enslave all cannibals. Ojeda departed, we may believe unregretted, and sailed along the coast to Maracapana, where he was well received by the cacique (christened Gil Gonzalez). Ojeda was, or pretended to be, short of corn, and accordingly Gonzalez gave him guides for ten or twelve miles inland to enable him to buy maize from the Tageres Indians, while these lent him fifty men to carry the grain to Maracapana. By way of return for the various favours received, Ojeda's men fell on the porters as they rested in the market-place and carried them off to the caravel. On this occasion retribution fell, in part at least, on the heads of those who deserved it, for Ojeda landed again farther down the coast, where Gil Gonzalez met and killed him with six of his fellow-scoundrels. Unfortunately, the reception accorded to their countrymen by the friars of Chichirivichi made them appear privy to the plot against the Indians, and they, too, fell victims to the vengeance of Maraguey.

The Audiencia Real of Hispaniola, by way of brazening out the crimes of the Cubaguans, now dispatched Gonzalez de Ocampo with an armed force to settle the country. The leader of the expedition appears to have been temperate and wise in his dealings, and succeeded in establishing peace, founding a city where Cumaná now stands under the name of Nueva Toledo (1520). Shortly afterwards, Bartolomé de las Casas, a noble figure in the history of the period, reached these shores, and discovering for himself the true history of what had been described as unprovoked attacks by the Indians, suggested that a fortress should be built opposite New Toledo, with a garrison under such control that it should protect the Indians from the lawless gangs of Cubagua, and keep in check any unprovoked manifestation of hostility on the part of the natives towards well-intentioned Spaniards. As might be expected, the Cubaguans were extremely hostile to such a project, and so hampered Las Casas that he resolved to return to Hispaniola and thence to Spain, to lay before the authorities a true account of the condition of affairs in the west.

Francisco de Soto was left in charge of affairs in New Toledo, and no sooner was the good influence of Las Casas withdrawn than he recommenced the slave traffic, which had been the cause of all the previous trouble, and now resulted in the destruction of the new city after the massacre of inhabitants and missionaries and an invasion of Cubagua by the Indians of the mainland. A second semi-military expedition from Hispaniola in 1521, under the leadership of Jacome Castellon, built the castle of Araya in spite of the Cubaguans, and founded the city of *la gloriosa Santa Ines de Nueva Córdoba*, the modern Cumaná. The fortress was reduced to ruins by an earthquake in 1530.

In the meantime, orders had been received from Spain to name the already existing city on Cubagua, Nueva Cadiz, and three years later, in 1524, La

Asunción was founded on the island of Margarita, while in 1527 the inhabitants of New Cadiz received the right to elect annually an alcalde, the Emperor giving 500 pesos for rebuilding the church there. Thus we have three cities founded in Venezuela territory within the first twenty-five years of the sixteenth century.

With the year 1527 the history of Venezuela as a colony, or rather a group of colonies, under Spanish dominion, may be said to commence. We have already seen a form of government established in Cubagua, which for a time appears to have existed more or less irregularly apart from the other provinces into which Venezuela, with Trinidad, was shortly divided, namely, Nueva Andalusia in the east, Venezuela or Coro in the west, and Trinidad and the Orinoco in the south.

Attracted by the reports of the first expedition, various merchants and adventurers had settled in the Coro country, and lived on good terms with the Caiquetia nation of Indians. Now, however, some of these colonists, losing taste for a civilised life, made attempts to commence the nefarious trade which was at that time disgracing all the countries of the Old World in Africa and America. Having learned wisdom from the disasters in Nueva Andalusia, the audience of Santo Domingo dispatched a splendid man in Juan de Ampies to nip the evil in the bud; as a first step he founded the city of Santa Ana de Coro on that Saint's day in 1527, and in his administration sought steadily to foster the spirit of amity between the Caiquetias (under their cacique Manaure) and the Europeans. His good work was soon, however, destined to be ignored and frustrated by the selfish policy of the King of Spain.

Charles V. had at various times raised heavy loans from the *Welser*, the bankers of Augsburg, and now in part payment he handed over to them the administration and exploitation of the newly-acquired province of Venezuela. Ambrosius Alfinger was appointed first Governor of Coro, with jurisdiction over all the country between the Gulf of Coquibacoa and the western end of the Peninsula of Paria. He arrived at the seat of his government with three hundred Spaniards, many of them of noble blood, and fifty German miners, and found Juan de Ampies too patriotic to raise difficulties on account of the ingratitude of a worthless king. The man who had founded Coro and started administration on sound lines spent the remainder of his days in retirement in Santo Domingo, though at a later date the barren island of Curaçao was given to him as some return for his services.

The following year saw Nueva Andalusia constituted a definite province, under Don Diego de Ordaz as first Governor, who was given authority to explore and conquer all the territory to the south. Sedeño was appointed Governor of Trinidad, but as yet the Orinoco region was ignored or by implication included in New Andalusia, and it was therefore Ordaz who, upon his arrival, journeyed up the Orinoco as far as the rapids of Carichana, near the mouth of the Meta, where he heard stories of the gold and emeralds to be found in the country whence that river flowed. The success of the voyage proved his death, however, for Sedeño was jealous of his fame and in league with Matienza, then commander-in-chief in Cubagua, managed to poison Ordaz in Nueva Cadiz on his return.

In the west Alfinger undertook a long journey of discovery towards what is now Colombia, and in his greed for gold and precious stones committed all manner of atrocities on the Indians who had none, or who refused to be robbed. Making a permanent camp in the country to the west of the Lake of Maracaibo, after founding the city of that name in 1529, he sent a party of Spaniards and Germans to Coro for fresh supplies and reinforcements. The party lost themselves in the forest-clad mountains at the south end of the lake, and in their privations some of the members turned cannibals, killing and eating their Indian servants. Apparently the taste for human flesh, once acquired, was not easily overcome, for the survivors, when given food by some Indians on the banks of the Chama, fell upon their benefactors and devoured them! The few that reached Coro found that Alfinger had been killed in his camp in 1531, and his expedition had accomplished nothing beyond outraging the Indians.

Georg von Speyer (Jorge de Spira) was the next Governor, appointed in 1533, and with him came Alonso de Pacheco, and ancestors of many of the modern Venezuelan families. Before his death, in 1540, von Speyer and his equally energetic lieutenant, Nicolaus Federmann, carried out extensive journeys in western and southern Venezuela, and the former reached the banks of the Guaviare, which were never again visited by Europeans until the middle of the nineteenth century. In the meantime Coro was made the seat of a bishopric, and Don Rodrigo de Bastidas arrived as first occupant of the see in 1536. The Bishop acted as interim Governor after Speyer's death until the new Governor, Philip von Huten (Felipe de Urre), arrived in 1541. The latter also made extensive journeys into the Llanos in search of El Dorado, but was killed in 1545 by Juan de Carvajal, the founder of Nuestra Señora de la Concepción de el Tocuyo. With his death the rule of the Welsers practically came to an end, though the King of Spain only finally removed all claim to power on their part in 1558. Their energy in exploration is indisputable, but their dominion was marked throughout by cruelty and extravagance.

In Nueva Andalusia the new Governor after Ordaz, Gerónimo Ortal, and after him Sedeño, Governor of Trinidad, were also exploring the Llanos and endeavouring to settle that region, but the previous evil deeds of the Cubaguans had made the task very difficult, if not impossible. Before long these received a just reward for their crimes, in a succession of natural catastrophes, which ultimately drove the remnant from the island. In 1530 an earthquake shook the town and destroyed many buildings, not without loss of life, and in 1543 earthquake and hurricane together wrought so much havoc to life and property that only a few lingered on, persisting in the slave trade, for which New Cadiz was notorious, until at last the population decreased to nil in 1550; even the exact site of the city is now unknown. One important man appears on the scene from Margarita, about 1555, in Francisco Faxardo, the son of a Spaniard of noble birth who had wedded a princess of the Guaiquerias. Crossing to the coasts of the Carácas, he established friendly relations with the Teques and other Indians, and in 1560 built the Villa de San Francisco, approximately where the capital of Venezuela now stands, together with the Villa de El Collado (Pablo Collado being the Governor in Coro), afterwards Caraballeda, about eight miles east of La Guaira.

Under the Spanish Governors who succeeded the Welsers, the already evident tendency to leave the barren plains of Coro for the more fruitful territory to the east and south became more marked. Mérida had been founded in 1542, Borburata (Puerto Cabello) in 1549, Nueva Segovia (Barquisimeto) in 1552, and Nueva Valencia, on the shores of Lake Tacarigua, in 1555, with Trujillo in 1556, while the mines of San Felipe and Nirgua had been known and worked for some years.

In 1561 occurred the rebellion of the mad "traitor" Lope de Aguirre. After journeying down the Amazon from Peru, he sailed up to Margarita, and there robbed the treasury. With his booty he crossed to Borburata, sacked the port, and climbed the mountain road to Valencia, from which town he wrote his famous letter to Philip II. In this he upbraided the monarch for his lack of practical interest in the colonists' welfare, in lands won by Spaniards for his father, while the latter lived at his ease in Castile; the officials and priests sent out to guide them sought, he said, only their own ends. The monkish historian Oviedo y Baños, incensed by the reference to the laziness of the Churchmen, calls him *aquel bruto* ("that brute"), but it is probable that most of his complaints were fully justified, though he was hardly fitted to found a new and better order of things. He marched on Barquisimeto and took it, and, hearing that the Governor was approaching with troops from the direction of Tocuyo, wrote him a letter, the humour of which can best be appreciated after reading the early writers' accounts of the poltroonery of Pablo Collado, for which he was subsequently deposed by the Audience of Santo Domingo.

The letter opens: *"Muy magnífico Señor,—Entre otros papeles que de V. md. en este Pueblo se han hallado, estaba una carta suya a mi dirigida, con mas ofrecimientos, y preambulos, que Estrellas ay en el Cielo."*[3]

These offers he rejects because, he says, he has thrown off his allegiance to Spain and therefore needs no pardon for rebellion; then he closes with the sarcastic farewell:—

"Nuestro Señor la muy magnífica persona de V. md. guarde,

"Su Servidor,

"Lope de Aguirre."[4]

The Governor wept with vexation on reading this epistle, and, after the manner of men of his stamp, said what he would do to Aguirre, were they able to fight the matter out in single combat. Meanwhile the troops surprised and took the town from the rebel, who fled towards San Felipe. He met his daughter there, and killed her to save her from the disgrace she might expect as the child of "the traitor." Oviedo y Baños declaims at length against the murder as the crowning act of cruelty of his life, but while he was undoubtedly guilty during his career of many acts of wild savagery, this final deed seems to an unbiased mind to be creditable rather than otherwise. Be that as it may, he was captured and killed, and his body was quartered and thrown to the dogs on the various roads leading away from Barquisimeto.

Whether as a result of Aguirre's protest or no, it is impossible to say, but in 1564 Philip II. took steps to adequately reward one man who had worked to develop his Caribbean colonies, in conferring upon Faxardo the title of Don, and offering him the governorship of the lands he had been so instrumental in opening to commerce. Unfortunately, before the messenger arrived, Faxardo had been treacherously killed by Cobos, alcalde of Cumaná, who was jealous of his exploits in the west.

The work of this first traveller in the Carácas was not entirely lost, however, for three years later, during the governorship of Don Diego Ponce de Leon, Diego de Losada, a native of Tocuyo, travelled across through Villa Rica (Nirgua) to the Llanos, where his efforts, in spite of many battles with the Indians, were directed rather towards settlement than conquest. Returned to the Villa de San Francisco (of Faxardo), he founded there—presumably in the latter part of 1567, though, strangely enough, the exact date is not recorded—the city of Santiago de Leon de Carácas. As he had on his travels adopted San Sebastian as his patron and protector against the poisoned arrows of the Indians, that saint's day has been celebrated in a special manner in Carácas since its foundation.

Ten years later Don Juan Pimentel, the newly appointed Governor, moved his seat from Coro to Carácas, and that city has remained since, with one short break, the capital of Venezuela. For some years at this time there seems to have been no Governor of Nueva Andalusia, and a captain of considerable energy and tact, named Garcia-Gonzalez, was dispatched by Pimentel to settle the countries near the boundaries of the two provinces.

Carácas is splendidly situated for defence, the steep range of the coast making a natural 5,000-foot rampart against invaders from the sea. It was taken once, however, and the story of its capture has, for some reason, been wrongly described by nearly every writer on Venezuela, though Kingsley's reference in "Westward Ho!" avoids the current inaccuracies. Generally it is briefly stated that Drake, or El Draque, took the city at the beginning of June, 1595; but Sir Francis was then in England preparing for what proved to be his last voyage, during which he died at sea off Porto Bello in Panama, a place confused by an American writer on Venezuela with Puerto Cabello. The true account may be read in Hakluyt's "Voyages" as it was given by one of the members of the party.

Briefly, Captain (afterwards Sir Amyas) Preston and Captain Sommers, after putting Cumaná to ransom, landed on the Carácas coast and captured a small fort, presumably near Naiguatá. Finding the Governor of the fort asleep in the forest, they learned that the inhabitants of Carácas had heard of the arrival of the corsairs, and were preparing to meet them on the main road over the mountains from La Guaira. The fugitive, whose name is given as Villalpando, was induced to act as guide along the "Indian Way" to the city, which Preston entered on May 29th, after a difficult journey through forests and over mountains. The only Spaniard found in the place was an old gentleman, Don Alonso Andrea de Ledesma, who gallantly tried to repel the invaders single-handed. The Englishmen had orders to spare him for his chivalry, but his refusal to accept defeat led to his death, and he was interred with honour by his foes. Meanwhile messengers were carrying the news to the troops in the pass on the La Guaira road, who returned to find such valuables as they had left in the city gone with the invaders by the supposedly unknown Indian way. Preston continued his way to Coro, found nothing there and burned the town, and finally returned to England on September 10, 1595.

Here we must go back for a year or two to follow the course of events in the east and south. In 1591 Don Antonio de Berrio y Oruña was appointed Governor of Trinidad and the Orinoco, and very shortly after his arrival he gave evidence of his energetic spirit by crossing to the mainland and founding there the city of San Thomé de la Guayana, east of the mouth of the Caroni, where the castle of Guayana Vieja stands to this day.[5] In 1595 Sir Walter Raleigh first visited these regions of Guayana or Guiana, described so fully in his famous book. On his way he took Berrio prisoner in Trinidad, but afterwards released him.

BARQUISIMETO.

Both men, clever and energetic as they were, rapidly became fascinated by the stories of Manoa, the city of El Dorado, which were being handed on from one narrator to another, and losing nothing, by repetition; the fabled wealth of the Golden Inca was eventually the cause of the death of both. In 1615 Berrio led an expedition southward from San Thomé, but he at length returned unsuccessful, with only thirty of his three hundred men, and himself died of fever shortly afterwards. His son, Don Fernando de Berrio, took charge temporarily, but was soon removed to Santa Fé de Bogotá, as Viceroy of the New Kingdom of Granada, into which Venezuela was now incorporated.

Raleigh's final expedition in 1618 captured the fortress of San Thomé, but this and other encounters with the Spanish colonists, who, owing to a misunderstanding, appear to have commenced the attacks, led to his execution by the poltroon James I. to appease the wrath of Spain. Thus the fable of Manoa remained alive for two centuries more till finally exposed by Humboldt.

The province of Venezuela by this time was completely conquered, but New Andalusia, or Cumaná, which again had a Governor of its own, still continued to be the scene of strife; and Vides, as Governor, did not improve matters by his encouragement of the slave trade. At length, in 1652, the suggestion of one Francisco Rodriguez Liete to the bishops of Puerto Rico, made four years previously, was adopted, and, all military operations against the Indians were forbidden, with a view to carrying out organised attempts to civilise them through the missions, and in 1656 a station was again founded at Barcelona by Franciscan monks. As an indication of the success of these new methods it may be observed that within 150 years (before 1799) the Franciscans founded 38 towns with 25,000 Indian inhabitants, while the previous equal period of aggression and oppression had effected no settlement of a lasting nature. In 1686 missions were established round Cumaná and south of the Delta by the Capuchins, while the Jesuits undertook to civilise the Orinoco. The latter were obliged on account of ill-health to abandon their first stations within a very short time, but returned again in 1725 to meet with increased success. The inhuman cruelty which their creed allowed some of them to practise towards the pagan Indians undid much of the good they may have at first accomplished, and in the nineteenth century their missions became deserted, with one or two exceptions, while the last of the missionaries after the revolution seem to have been as licentious and lazy as their predecessors had been cruel and energetic.

The founding of the University of Carácas by Philip V. in 1721 seemed to promise development of the colony on sound lines, but three years later a monopoly of trade was granted to the Compañía Guipuzcoana, a step which probably did more than any other single act to bring about disaffection towards Spain. The province was separated from New Granada in 1731, when the whole of what is now Venezuela (with the exception of the Maracaibo region, incorporated in 1777) was included in a new *Capitania-General* of that name. The first Captain-General was Colonel Don Sebastian Garcia de la Torre.

As a result of the evident discontent among the colonists the privileges of the Guipuzcoana Company were taken away from them in 1778, but the disregard by the mother country of Venezuela's best interests could not be atoned for by a negative act only, and nineteen years later, in 1797, occurred the first definite attempt at revolt. Under the influence of the French Revolution, some of the colonists banded themselves together with the purpose of forming an independent Republic of Venezuela; the leading spirits appear to have been Don Manuel Gual and Don José Maria España, but one of the other leaders in his zeal to multiply adherents disclosed the schemes to his barber, who straightway communicated the fact to the authorities, Carbonell being Captain-General. Six of the leaders were hanged, drawn, and quartered, many having voluntarily given themselves up as their best hope of safety. Gual and España fled, but the latter, returning from Trinidad in 1799 to visit his wife in La Guaira, was captured, executed, and his body mutilated by order of the new Captain-General, Manuel Guevara Vasconcelos.

The revolution of Gual and España thus being ended, nothing of special note occurred in Venezuela for six years, but in the meantime a Venezuelan, Don Francisco Miranda, who had relations in Europe and had travelled in many lands, fighting in the American War of Independence, and for France in the wars with Prussia in 1792-5, was conferring with Pitt in England. From the British statesman he obtained promises of help, but finally got practical assistance in America, and at last invaded the colony at Ocumare oh March 25, 1806. Vasconcelos had been warned of his arrival, and repulsed him without difficulty; Miranda retired to Trinidad, but continued to work for his purpose there, and made an unsuccessful landing in Coro some five months later. His resources were exhausted, however, and he finally returned to Trinidad and thence to Europe.

In the following year Vasconcelos died, and the interim Captain, Juan de las Casas, recognised Prince Murat as regent in place of Charles IV., the Prince's commissioners reaching La Guaira in July, 1808. The colonists, however, compelled him to swear allegiance to Prince Ferdinand as Ferdinand VII., then captive in Bayonne. In May of the following year Vicente Emparan arrived as new Captain-General, appointed by the Supreme Junta of Spain, but finding the people unwilling to acknowledge that authority, he was easily led by Madariaga, a Chilian, then canon of the cathedral of Carácas, to appeal to them as to whether they wished him to carry out his duties as Governor. It is said that Emparan came out on a balcony to put the question to the crowd, and Madariaga, behind him, signed to them to reply to him in the negative, "*No lo queremos*" ("We do not wish it"), in answer to which Emparan said, "*Yo tampoco quiero mandar*" ("Nor do I wish to command"), and so retired from the captaincy, which he was the last to fill. He was finally deposed by a local Junta formed to act in the name of Ferdinand VII. on April 19, 1810.

While this new Government had sworn allegiance to the rightful occupant of the throne of Spain, it was inevitable, in view of the disturbed state of that country and the insecurity of the reigning dynasty, that sooner or later the colonies would break away completely. The Junta sent Simon Bolivar to England to appeal for protection and to ask the Government to urge Spain to avoid war with the colonists. Our statesmen, however, were not then able to resist the temptation to secure the utmost from Venezuela in return for such passive assistance as they might render, even to the point of asking for a monopoly of trade, and negotiations fell through. Spain declared Venezuela under blockade conditionally, and appointed Miyares, Governor of Maracaibo, to be Captain-General, an office which he never filled.

Later Miranda returned from Europe, being sent by Bolivar, and was refused a landing by the Junta, in view of his avowed republican principles. The people of La Guaira, however, insisted on his landing and brought him ashore.

In 1811 forty-four deputies were elected by the seven provinces which recognised the Junta (Carácas, Barinas, Barcelona, Cumaná, Margarita, Mérida, and Trujillo), and they met on March 2nd. The names of the first Congress of Venezuela (as it subsequently became) included, besides Miranda, the Marquis del Toro, Martin Tovar, Fernando de Peñalver, and many gentlemen of rank and standing in the colony. Miranda was elected President of the Junta, and the combined effect of the inaction of Miyares, a man of more vanity than talent, and such incidents as the massacre of persons of republican inclinations by royalists in Cabruta on April 2nd, led finally to the Declaration of Independence by the deputies on July 5, 1811.

The seven provinces were declared to be a confederation of free, sovereign, and independent States, governed in accordance with the will of the inhabitants, and thus ended, in name at least, the long period of Spain's misrule. From this time onward, whatever has been the internal policy of the country, the inhabitants, in theory if not in fact, have had the government they chose for themselves.

CHAPTER V
THE REPUBLIC, 1811-1911

Local character of revolution—Declaration of a Constitution—Centralised government—Troubles of the young republic—The Church and the patriots—Miranda—Dictatorship and downfall—Drastic measures of Monteverde—Youth and parentage of Simon Bolivar—The *guerra a muerte*—Dictatorship of Bolivar—Monteverde murders four prisoners—The *Mestizos*—Massacre of Spaniards—Murmurings—Retirement of Bolivar—Royalist victories and reinforcements—Morillo's barbarities—Return of Bolivar to Venezuela—Indecisive campaign—Renewed discontent—Bolivar withdraws to Haiti, but returns—Mariño's insubordination—Massacre of Barcelona—Campaign in the Llanos—Arrival of the British Legion—Congress of Angostura—The march to Bogotá—The republic of Great Colombia—Change of allegiance of the *Mestizos*—Armistice of Trujillo—Negotiations with Spain—Recommencement of hostilities—Battle of Carabobo—End of Spanish power in Venezuela—Position of Venezuela in Colombia—Separatist movement—Death of Bolivar—Páez first President of Venezuela—Vargas—Folly of Mariño—Progress of the country—Public honours to Bolivar—Recognition of republic by France and Spain—Commerce and prosperity of the country—Tyranny of Tadeo Monágas—Gregorio Monágas—Abolition of slavery—Revolution of Julian Castro—Capital temporarily removed to Valencia—Federalists and Centralists—Falcón—*Convenio de Coche*—Federal Constitution—Guzman Blanco—Development under his government—Revolution of Crespo—British Guiana boundary dispute—Cipriano Castro—The Matos revolution—*Coup d'état* of General Gomez—Centenary celebrations—Present prospects.

Even though subsequent events proved that the Declaration of July 5, 1811, marked in reality the beginning of the independence of Venezuela, that end was far from being attained as yet. The revolution itself had begun, not amongst the people but with a few of the more intelligent and patriotic members of the aristocracy of the country; and even the open breach with Spain found popular feeling about equally divided, or, if anything, on the side of Spain and the royalists. While the movement had thus little staying power within the colony, there were many foreign sympathisers, notable amongst whom was William Burke, an Irish Catholic.

The Declaration of Independence was followed almost immediately by disturbances in Los Teques and Valencia, instigated mainly by colonists from the Canary Islands; but though the provinces of Coro, Maracaibo, and Guayana held aloof, the leaders of the Revolution were sufficiently strong to declare a Constitution on December 21, 1811.

One of the main features of this first Constitution was the power given to the Central Government to revise the Constitutions of the provinces. The national power was divided under three heads—Legislative, Executive, and Judicial. The Legislature was to consist of two Chambers—one of Representatives, the other of Senators, the first to be elected by popular vote, the second by the Provincial Governments; the qualifications for membership of the Lower Chamber were: to be over twenty-one years of age, five years a citizen, and a property-owner; the Senators were to be over thirty years of age, ten years citizens, and to possess 6,000 pesos. A National Guard was provided, to be controlled by the Legislature. The Executive was vested in a Junta of three persons, who were to have been in Venezuela on July 5th or to be natives of the "Colombian Continent" (*i.e.*, South America); they held office for four years. Judicial power was exercised by a Supreme Court, subaltern Courts, and inferior tribunals, under control of Congress. The royalists who had been responsible for the risings in Valencia were pardoned and released.

In 1812 the troubles of the young republic began. Early in the year Don Domingo de Monteverde landed in Coro and marched inland, capturing Siquisique and Carora, finally directing his steps towards Carácas via Barquisimeto and San Carlos. On Holy Thursday (March 26th), while thousands were gathered in the churches, a terrible earthquake destroyed Carácas, La Guaira, San Felipe, Barquisimeto, Tocuyo, and Mérida; in Carácas alone 10,000 people were killed. The ecclesiastics, recognising their interests to be largely bound up with the royalist cause, attributed these disasters to the wrath of Heaven at the revolution, and one who preached in this strain in Carácas is said to have been threatened with death by Bolivar, who exclaimed, "If Nature opposes us we will fight her and make her obey us!" For his antagonism to the new régime the Archbishop of Carácas was expelled and Madariaga put in charge in his place. An expedition to Guayana had been planned, but was abandoned after the earthquake, when Miranda was made Dictator by Congress. The royalist leader Monteverde reached La Victoria in June, and some four weeks later, for obscure and, it was widely suggested, discreditable pecuniary reasons, Miranda, with 4,000 men, capitulated to the Spanish force of 3,000 on July 25th. Monteverde sent him to Puerto Rico, but for which Bolivar and others would have shot him as a traitor at the first opportunity. He finally died in prison in Spain in 1816.

Had Monteverde shown more discretion and mercy this reverse of the patriots would probably have had far more lasting results, but he speedily showed himself treacherous, and, in direct violation of the terms agreed upon with Miranda, he sent eight of the revolutionary leaders, including Madariaga, to Spain. He imprisoned 1,500 more, and, refusing to apply any part of the new Spanish Constitution to Venezuela, proclaimed martial law; as a result, war to the death was declared by the patriots in the following year.

The Simon Bolivar who has been referred to above was the direct descendant, six generations removed, from Simon de Bolivar, a Biscayan of noble rank who reached Venezuela in 1588. This man entered the service of his adopted land immediately upon his arrival, for he was the special commissioner dispatched in 1589 by the then Governor to Spain to urge the need of reforms and to obtain permission for the initiation of projects calculated to open up and settle the country. The Simon Bolivar of the revolution was born on July 24, 1783, in Carácas; he went to the Court of Madrid as a youth, and there acquitted himself well, but, shortly after his return to his native country in 1802, lost his young wife. Possibly this bereavement helped to harden his character, and so to acquire for him that reputation for cruelty and obstinacy which marred the early history of his work as liberator of his native country and of half of South America.

The young soldier found himself in Cúcuta (southward of the Lake of Maracaibo) early in 1813, and was instructed by the revolutionary Government in Santa Fé de Bogotá to proceed with the conflict, but to wage war against armed Spaniards only. On June 8th he declared a war of vengeance to the death against Spain in Mérida, and marching northwards, won victories at Niquitao, Los Horcones, and Taguanes, finally reaching and taking Carácas. Meanwhile, Juan Bautista Arismendi had taken the Island of Margarita; and Mariño, Bermudez, Piar and Sucre took Maturín and Cumaná in August, leaving only Coro, Maracaibo, Guayana, part of Barinas, and the plaza of Puerto Cabello in the hands of the royalists.

Following these successes, Bolivar was made Dictator, with legislative and executive powers, and arrangements were made for the formation of a Congress similar to that of New Granada. Later in the year the Dictator marched on Puerto Cabello, where his proposal for an exchange of prisoners met with an offer of two Spaniards for one Venezuelan, with the exception of one Jalon, whom Monteverde refused to release; at the same time the Spanish leader killed four of the prisoners. Reinforcements reached him from Cadiz about this time, but they were defeated by the patriots, who later in the year gained other victories over Ceballos.

Early in 1814 Monteverde was compelled by his officers to give up his command and retire to the Antilles; but to counterbalance this, just after the meeting of the popular assembly in Carácas came the rising of the *Mestizos*, or half-breeds of the Llanos, under Tomas Boves, on behalf of the royalists, a new factor which delayed the settlement of the struggle for years. After Boves's victory over the patriots at La Puerta, when another force was advancing on Ocumare, Bolivar was guilty of the barbarity of massacring all the Spaniards in Puerto Cabello. After several battles, the total results of which were indecisive, Boves finally defeated Bolivar and Mariño by sheer force of numbers in the Aragua valley and forced them to fly to Carácas. On July 6th Bolivar evacuated the town, and with its inhabitants retreated to Barcelona overland, where upon the royalists and llaneros entered it two days later and Boves claimed the supreme power in Venezuela, although this had been vested by the Spanish Government in Cajil. Murmurings against Bolivar now made themselves heard, and Ribas and others of his generals wished to assassinate him in revenge for their defeats; he was, however, permitted to retire in safety to the Antilles. Later Boves occupied Cumaná with massacre and defeated the patriot leaders in Urica, sending his lieutenant, Morales, to Maturín. Meanwhile, after the restoration of Ferdinand VII., an expedition of 15,000 men was sent from Spain under Morillo; with the capitulation to him of Margarita early in 1815 the outlook for the republic was black indeed.

STATUE IN PLAZA BOLIVAR: CARÁCAS.

Once again the barbarities of the new Spanish leader acted as a goad to the jaded spirits of the patriots, for after breaking his promises of amnesty in Margarita he proceeded to show no mercy to any patriot families met with in Carácas or on his way to New Granada, where also his barbarous conduct brought him an unenviable notoriety. Bolivar had recaptured Santa Fé with the remnant of the Venezuelan patriot army, but the beginning of 1816 found him in Jamaica planning his great campaign, with a view to forming fifteen independent republics in South America, including the Great Colombia, which afterwards became for a short time a reality.

With a view to the fulfilment of these dreams he secured help in Haiti, and later in the year reached Margarita. His associates included MacGregor and Ducoudray-Holstein, Crossing to Carúpano, he sent Mariño to Guaira, Piar to Maturín, and with Anzoátegui and other leaders he himself marched to Ocumare; here, however, he was cut off by royalist forces, and, retreating, joined Zaraza and Monágas with their guerilla troops in the Llanos, and finally with Piar defeated the royalists in the battle of El Juncal, near Barcelona. The net result of the campaign in the earlier part of the year was, however, adverse, and when, after joining Bermudez in Bonaire, he crossed again to Paria, he was threatened with death by the newly arrived leader and Mariño. As a result he returned to Haiti on August 22nd, but came back later in the year at the request of Piar and other generals.

Early in 1817 Mariño and Bermudez again came to an agreement with Bolivar, but when he and Arismendi were defeated at Clarines, on their way to Carácas, Mariño again became subordinate, and, to his lasting disgrace, left General Freites without support in Barcelona, where he and 300 refugees were massacred in the *Casa Fuerte* on April 7th by the royalists. Shortly after these events a Congress was formed in Cariaco, by which Bolivar was made one of the Executive, but Mariño Commander-in-Chief; the latter was at this time in Margarita, which was now first named Nueva Esparta.

Meanwhile, Bolivar had moved southward to Guayana, and a fresh invasion of royalists soon drove the other leaders in Cariaco to join him there. After a victory at San Felix by Piar the prisoners and monks were massacred, but by whose orders could not be definitely ascertained. The city of Angostura was evacuated by the Spanish on July 17th, and Guayana Vieja on August 3rd. During the succeeding months Páez was fighting with Morillo in the plains of Barinas; Mariño, by the intervention of Sucre, finally acknowledged Bolivar as commander-in-chief, and Piar, for insubordination and ostensibly also for the massacre of San Felix, was condemned by court-martial. On September 3rd an order was issued for the sequestration of royalist property to pay for the war, and in November Bolivar left Angostura for Calabozo. After one reverse he retired into the province of Barinas, where Páez joined him; and finally, early in 1818, he defeated Morillo at Calabozo, though Páez was in April forced back on San Fernando de Apure with a few men.

With insubordination and murmurings among his own generals, decreased troops and depleted treasure, and without the encouragement of decisive victories to make good these deficiencies, the outlook for Bolivar and for the cause in which he was fighting might well have disheartened him at this time. In March, however, Colonel Daniel O'Leary had arrived with the troops raised by Colonel Wilson in London, consisting largely of veterans of the Napoleonic wars. These tried soldiers, afterwards known as the British Legion, were destined to play an all-important part in the liberation of Venezuela, and Bolivar soon recognised their value, spending the time till December in distributing these new forces to the best advantage.

Elections were arranged in the autumn, and on February 15, 1819, Congress was installed in Angostura. Bolivar took the British Constitution as his model, with the substitute of an elected president for an hereditary king, and was himself proclaimed provisional holder of the office. The hereditary form of the Senate was, however, soon given up.

The early part of the year was spent in local marchings and counter-marchings, but in June Bolivar set out, accompanied by Colonel James Rook and the British Legion, on his famous march to New Granada. Pushing through swamps and forests and marching over interminable plains, they met and defeated the advance guard of the enemy in the defile of Paya. The first week in July found them crossing the Páramo of Pisva on the road to Bogotá, where many men perished from the cold. The rest of the month saw them victorious in many battles, in which the British Legion and the llaneros made themselves conspicuous. With 2,000 patriots Bolivar defeated 3,000 royalists in the battle of Boyacá on August 7th, taking many prisoners. On reaching Bogotá he made Santander vice-president of New Granada and left the prisoners in his charge, a confidence which the latter abused by shooting the most prominent, on pretext of an attempted escape. In the meantime there was the normal disaffection in the east, where Arismendi had been made vice-president, in the place of Zea, in Angostura. On hearing of Bolivar's successes, he immediately wanted to resign; Bolivar, however, ignored his attempted insubordination, and made him commander-in-chief in the east.

On December 17, 1819, Bolivar formally inaugurated the Great Colombian republic, consisting of the three Departments of Venezuela, Cundinamarca, and Quito. A new capital with the name of Bolivar was to be built near the boundary of Cundinamarca and Venezuela, and the first united Congress was to assemble in Rosario de Cúcuta. Although this Declaration was not formally ratified for two years in Quito, 1820 marks the close of the first period of Venezuela's independence, from the Declaration of July 5, 1811, to its inclusion in the Great Colombia, a part of which it remained till 1830.

With the commencement of the second period we come to an entirely new condition of affairs. While Spain was desirous of attempting a reconciliation with the northern colony, she did not realise that the Mestizos, and therefore the population of Venezuela generally, were now in favour of independence, and after their period of successful fighting, were not willing to accept less than a recognition of their freedom in some part, at least, of the territory. While the attitude of the Spanish authorities was thus foolishly lacking in appreciation of all that had happened in the last ten years, their general in command in Venezuela, Morillo, showed himself most conciliatory and even magnanimous. On November 25th, owing to his efforts, the armistice of Trujillo was declared. On the following day came the "regularisation" of the campaign, by which it was determined that hostilities should not recommence till April 28th of the next year, and on the 27th of the month the opposing leaders met in the little village of Santa Ana, north of Trujillo.

By the beginning of 1821 Bolivar had returned to Bogotá, and there he nominated a plenipotentiary to carry on negotiations with Spain, claiming for his part recognition of the absolute independence, either of Colombia with its three divisions or of the part of the territory which had now been liberated. He authorised the republic's representative, however, to give up the recognition of Quito, if necessary, but either that or Panama was to be included. Finally, the republic asserted its willingness to enter into an alliance with Spain, but its unalterable opposition to union or to the rule of any European sovereign.

Spain, in spite of this clear statement of the case of the republic, persisted in regarding the revolution as a mere insurrection, and the first negotiations broke down. Meanwhile, in January, the province of Maracaibo had declared itself independent and part of Colombia. Later, one of Bolivar's generals occupied the town of Gibraltar, on the Lake of Maracaibo, an act of zeal on his part which was nevertheless a violation of the terms of the armistice of Trujillo. Bolivar wished to submit this matter to arbitration, but before anything had been arranged the date for resumption of hostilities came round, and the last stage of the struggle began.

The royalists, at this time held the province of Cumaná, and Carácas between the towns of Unare and Guanare, and at both ends of the region they were attacked simultaneously. They succeeded in driving Bermudez out of the capital, but Bolivar was in Tinaquillo, not far to the west, with 6,500 men, his generals being Páez, in command of the Bravos de Apure and Británico battalions; Cedeño, with one brigade of the La Guardia, and the Tiradores, Boyacá and Vargas battalions; Playa, with the other brigade of the La

Guardia, a regiment of English Rifles, the Granaderos, and Vencedores de Boyacá; and Anzoátegui, with one cavalry regiment under a Llanero leader. Mariño was Bolivar's chief-of-staff.

On June 24, 1821, the Spanish leader, La Torre, occupied the plain of Carabobo with 5,000 men (six columns of infantry and three of cavalry). The patriot army, in order to reach them, had to follow a narrow mountain path over the Alto de Buenavista, under the fire of the royalists, and Páez was dispatched on a flanking movement to the right. Meanwhile Bolivar, having descended this exposed path, had to defile a second time to cross a small stream between the two hills. The enemy descended to dispute his passage, which was effected under cover of a hot fire from the infantry on both sides. The Apure battalion crossed first and were nearly driven back, but the British crossed just in time to allow them to re-form, while the Tiradores speedily came over to their assistance, the hollow square formed by our countrymen having held the ground at the critical moment of the day. By this time the cavalry were across and the field was won, for the Spanish troops were unable to withstand the attack of the llaneros, once these were in their natural element in the open plains. La Torre and Morales made good their escape, owing to the gallant stand made by the first Valencey battalion, while of the patriots, Bolivar wrote that only 200 were killed or wounded. La Torre fled to Puerto Cabello, and Bolivar marched on to Carácas.

Casual fighting continued for two years more, but the power of Spain was finally broken at Carabobo, and the last royalist adherents capitulated in Puerto Cabello on October 8, 1823.

In the meantime the Constitution of Great Colombia had been adopted by the Congress of Cúcuta in August, 1821, but before long Venezuela found her position in the Union far from satisfactory. The discontent found voice in the municipality of Valencia in 1826, Páez being one of the leaders of the separatists. Bolivar arrived in Puerto Cabello from the west in 1827, having previously written to Páez, whose loyalty to his old chief made him bow to his opinion. This, however, would not suffice to make up for the bad state of agricultural industries and of the country generally, and the murmurings broke out afresh. In 1828 Bolivar was given dictatorial power by the Congress of Colombia, while on the other hand plots were formed by the malcontents to assassinate him. In the following year, during Colombia's squabbles with Peru, Carácas and Valencia repudiated Bolivar, and on January 13, 1830, Páez declared Venezuela independent of Colombia.

The last Colombian Congress met in the "conference of Cúcuta," and Bolivar finally retired from power on March 1st. Valencia even demanded his expulsion. The sentimental attempt, carried through in spite of practical opposition, to form so large a single State of three groups of settlements, separated by wide areas without roads or other means of communication, seems but another instance of the frequent inability of a gallant soldier to play a worthy part in the politics of the land he has served. It was, nevertheless, a melancholy period of the history of Venezuela when the liberator of half of South America, as well as of his own land, was left to retire broken-hearted to Santa Marta in New Granada, where he died of phthisis on December 17, 1830, and was buried in the little church of the town.

But though Bolivar was unhonoured in his death, the main object to which he had devoted his life was attained, and, as we shall see, after twelve years his services were duly recognised by the country and town which gave him birth. The next period of Venezuelan history lasts to 1864, during which the centralist Constitution was in force, to be changed afterwards to the federal type which exists to-day.

One of his generals, Monágas, still remained loyal to Bolivar's views, and for some years continued his efforts to persuade the powers that were in Venezuela to join themselves again with Colombia. In April, 1831, however, the new Congress assembled and formally elected General José Antonio Páez as President of the republic; an embassy was dispatched to Bogotá, and Carácas was declared the capital on May 25th. Early in the following year their independence was formally recognised by Colombia, and measures were taken to provide for the efficient administration of the country, which was divided into three districts, the Oriente, Centro, and Occidente, the supreme courts of each being at Cumaná, Valencia, and Maracaibo respectively.

The third Venezuelan Congress met in January, 1833, and proceeded to incorporate the wandering soldiers of the revolution into a regular army, and to arrange the division of the public debt and other agreements with Colombia and Ecuador.

At the end of 1834 there were four candidates for the presidency, of whom Doctor José Maria Vargas was elected in 1835; a good omen for the country, inasmuch as Vargas was a scholar, not a soldier, and his claim to the confidence of his country rested on more solid grounds than those of his military opponents. He was only prevailed upon with difficulty to stand, or to act when elected, but displayed a praiseworthy loftiness of motive while in office. Mariño, however, showed his shallow and selfish nature once more in raising discontent amongst those who considered that might should triumph over right rather than the reverse; Vargas resigned early in 1836, and for the rest of this presidential term the vice-president carried out the duties of the office.

In 1839 Páez was again elected President, and in that year did much to increase the prosperity of the country and to raise its position in South America. The cart-road from La Guaira to Carácas was opened, and another commenced between Puerto Cabello and Valencia. The liberty of the press was so far increased that A. L. Guzman was able to start the journal *El Venezolano* in opposition to the existing Government, and in support of the Federal ideal of the newly formed Liberal party, the Centralists being known as the Oligarca. In the following year a colonisation scheme was put forward, and a national college for girls opened, while an attempt was made to found a national bank in 1841. This year also saw authority given to the executive to take measures for the education and civilisation of the aborigines, and to put in hand the standard works on the geography and history of Venezuela by Codazzi and Baralt.

In 1842, the last year of Páez's second presidency, the gradually increasing appreciation of Bolivar's services to his country culminated on April 30th in a decree of public honours to the "Libertador," as he was now styled, and burial in state in Carácas. The Venezuelan boats *Constitucion* and *Carácas*, H.M.S. *Albatross*, the Dutch warship *La Venus*, and the French frigate *Circe*, accordingly left La Guaira, bearing a deputation of influential men, including Vargas, and reached Santa Marta on November 16th. The people of Nueva Granada recognised willingly the prior claims of Carácas, as Bolivar's birthplace, and his body was borne back on the *Constitucion*. A permanent triumphal arch had been erected in his honour at the foot of El Calvario, and the remains were laid to rest in the chapel of the Holy Trinity in Carácas Cathedral, being transferred later to the Pantheon.

General Carlos Soublette was elected President in 1843, in which year France formally recognised the republic, while Spain followed in March, 1845. A further honour was done to the Liberator by renaming Angostura Ciudad Bolivar on May 31, 1845.

The foreign trade of Venezuela had tripled since 1830, the debt had been reduced from 9,372,448.44 pesos to 2,085,595.72 pesos, and General Urdaneta was in London, endeavouring to raise a loan to enable the Government to free the slaves. The country was, therefore, in a fair way of prosperity, but opposition to the centralist form of government was not decreasing. It would seem, notwithstanding, that under wise rulers this grievance could have been redressed without the first of that series of revolutions which, beginning not many years later, made Venezuela a byword in the latter half of the nineteenth century.

In 1847 General José Tadeo Monágas was elected President, and commenced his period of office by sentencing Guzman, the editor of *El Venezolano*, to death, subsequently commuting the penalty to banishment. For this act of tyranny he was censured by Congress in the following year, and retaliated by dissolving the Assembly with armed force, not without bloodshed. As a not unnatural result, Páez attempted to start an insurrection against him in Calabozo, but was forced to fly to Colombia, and a similar rising in Maracaibo died out. The death penalty for political offences was abolished by Congress, but Páez, on landing in Coro in an attempt to continue his revolt, was overpowered and capitulated; he broke his terms, however, and was imprisoned in the fortress of Cumaná.

THE UNIVERSITY: CARÁCAS.

By the end of 1850 Tadeo Monágas, having acquired power as a member of the Oligarca, avowed himself a Liberal at the end of his presidency. General José Gregorio Monágas was elected to succeed him, a man of whom Tejera says that he was affable in temper, of a generous spirit, and capable of noble actions. In 1854 he promulgated the decree abolishing slavery within Venezuelan territory, March 24th.

The year 1855 saw J. T. Monágas re-elected. In this term the country was divided into provinces identical with the States of to-day, though in some cases the names differed. In 1857 it was reported that Guayana had been sold by the President, and this rumour, with his repeated abuses of power, led to the revolution of Valencia under General Julian Castro, Governor of Carabobo, March 5, 1858.

This was the first serious internal dissension in Venezuela, but here we have only the revolt of the people against a tyrant, not the attempt of an individual to make himself master of the country on selfish grounds. Taking as their motto *Union de los partidos, y olvido de lo pasado*, the revolutionaries forced Monágas to take refuge in the French Legation, Julian Castro being acclaimed Provisional President. Unfortunately, despite the motto, one of his earliest acts was to imprison Monágas, in direct violation of the promises given to the French and British Legations, which led to an imbroglio with the two countries.

Meanwhile the seat of government was removed to Valencia, though Carácas again became the capital after a few weeks, when, following the success of Julian Castro's rising, he being a Conservative, the Liberals, with Zamora and Falcón as leaders, landed in Coro on July 24th. Castro was shortly afterwards captured and imprisoned, but the Conservatives proclaimed Pedro Gual President, with Manuel Felipe Tovar as Vice-President. Battles were fought between the Centralists and Federalists in the streets of Carácas, and at Santa Ines and San Carlos, but finally Falcón was defeated on March 17, 1860, and Tovar elected as constitutional President. Throughout 1861, however, Páez was actively working against him, and finally, in 1862, was declared dictator.

In 1863, after a conference between the dictator's secretary and General Guzman Blanco, leader of the Federals of the Centro, the *"convenio de Coche"* allowed the National Assembly to nominate Falcón President and Guzman Blanco Vice-President, while Páez left for the United States. After the elections public works of some magnitude were authorised and a £1,500,000 European loan. Finally, on March 28, 1864, the new Federal Constitution was adopted, whereby the United States of Venezuela came into being, consisting of twenty sovereign States, with a Federal two-chamber Legislature, an Executive of President and six ministers, and judicial power in the hands of a high Federal court holding jurisdiction in international affairs. The death penalty was abolished, with imprisonment for debt, the rights of meeting and of a free press were established, and in other respects the Constitution took the general form which it has to-day.

At the close of Falcón's presidency the Centralists again attempted forcibly to gain power under the leadership of the changeable J. T. Monágas, by whom Carácas was occupied in June. He died in November, and J. R. Monágas was chosen provisional President in 1869. The Federalists meanwhile were endeavouring to regain their position by force of arms, with the result that Monágas was never elected, and on April 27, 1870, Guzman Blanco was able to call together a Congress which nominated him provisional President. Owing to continued disturbances he was only formally elected towards the end of 1872. In 1874 an Act was passed reducing the presidential period from four years to two, and Francisco Linares Alcantara was elected in 1877, but the fatal series of individual revolutions now begins with Gregorio Cedeño, by whom Carácas was occupied in February, 1879.

Guzman Blanco was immediately recalled from Europe and hailed as *Director Supremo de la Revindicacion Nacional*, being made provisional President by the new Congress, and formally elected in 1880, and again in 1882, doing much to advance the reputation of his country during these years. General Joaquin Crespo, a llanero, who had been Minister of War since 1870, succeeded him for the period 1884-6, but in the latter year Guzman Blanco, again President, was dispatched by Congress to Europe as plenipotentiary. Doctor Rojas Paul and R. A. Palacio successively occupied the presidential chair till 1892, by which time Venezuela's trade had reached an amount never touched before or since, and the country was generally in a prosperous condition.

Despite the advance made by Venezuela during the period from 1880 to 1892, throughout which Guzman Blanco was either actually or virtually President, his rule was at times unduly autocratic, and his affection for statues of himself and for high-sounding titles, such as "*El Ilustre Americano*," seems strange in a man with so great business ability both on behalf of his country and himself. In time he might have raised Venezuela to a position comparable to that of Mexico under Diaz, but as it was the less attractive and dignified side of his character began, for the time being, to undermine the affection and esteem in which he had been held by his countrymen, and a desire for a change of control became general. It is hardly necessary to add that the Venezuelans of to-day remember only the beneficent aspects of his periods of office.

Unfortunately, the example of Cedeño, and the successful internal revolutions of earlier days, had not been forgotten, and now Crespo secured his re-election by force, his first act being to restore the presidential period to four years. In 1898 he was succeeded by José Andrade, formerly Venezuelan Minister at Washington, and though his period of office was short it was important as marking the settlement of a dispute which, after lasting for over sixty years, nearly led to a rupture between this country and the United States.

From the early days of the independence of Venezuela continual protests had been made by the representatives of the republic against the alleged encroachments of residents and officials from British Guiana. Briefly, the contentions raised by the two parties were: on the part of Venezuela, that the Dutch, to whom we were successors, had only claimed jurisdiction on the east side of the Essequibo River; on the part of Great Britain, that the Dutch had in 1759 and 1769 put forward the claim that their territory included, not merely the Essequibo River but the whole of the basin drained by that river and its tributaries. This claim was never rebutted by the authorities in Madrid.

So the dispute dragged on, the British Government refusing to consent to arbitration of the boundary unless it was previously agreed by Venezuela that such parts of the Essequibo Valley as had been effectively occupied by British colonists were recognised as their territory. In April, 1895, the arrest by the Venezuelan authorities of two inspectors of the British Guiana Police on the Cuyuni River brought matters to a crisis. The inspectors were soon released, but Crespo appealed to Washington for protection against any claim for indemnity. President Cleveland took up the cause of Venezuela on the ground that any action by Great Britain would constitute an infringement of the Monroe Doctrine, and in December, 1895, sent his two famous messages to Congress, in which he declared that any forcible action by this country would constitute a *casus belli* with the United States. For a time great excitement prevailed in Carácas, associations being formed for the boycott of British goods and for national defence. Fortunately, wiser counsels prevailed on both sides and diplomatic relations were resumed in 1897, the matter being submitted to arbitration, and finally settled by the award of the tribunal of Paris on October 3, 1899.

Hardly had this long-standing and vexatious external dispute been cleared up when the prosperity of Venezuela was once again threatened by internal dissension. Cipriano Castro, a Tachiran, had in May declared his intention of avenging a real or intended slight received from the Government, and, after marching through the Andes at the head of the so-called *Ejercito Restaurador*, fighting several successful battles on the way, he entered Carácas late in October. The executive power, which he immediately assumed, was only confirmed by an *Asamblea Constituyente* in February, 1901.

In March of that year a new Constitution was decreed, whereby the presidential period was extended to six years, and Castro was duly elected to the office. In 1902 the "Matos" revolution broke out, under the general of that name; this appears to have been a genuine popular revolt, and almost proved successful when in the autumn of the year a tactical mistake on the part of the revolutionists left Castro master of the country.

No attempt was made to compensate foreigners for the damage to property suffered by them during these various revolutions, and in view of the accumulation of claims the powers chiefly concerned—Great Britain, Germany, and Italy—declared a blockade of the ports of Venezuela in January, 1903, which had the desired effect of persuading Castro's Government to agree to the arbitration of the various claims by third parties. Though the allied Powers demanded that their claims should be settled first, the counter-demand of Venezuela, that all the Powers, peaceful and otherwise, should be treated alike, was upheld by the Hague Tribunal, and protocols with all the countries were signed within a few months.

A second change of the Constitution was decreed in April, 1904, whereby it was made possible for Castro to be again declared provisional President, and in June of the following year he was elected for the term 1905-11, with General Gomez again as one of the Vice-Presidents, the other being José Antonio Velutini.

Once securely possessed of the presidency, Castro's rule became that of a Dictator, and though his strength of purpose might well have made him a national hero had he been animated by love of country, his selfish abuse of power rendered his period of office a time of retrogression throughout the republic. Vicious reprisals for real or fancied slights and equally capricious distribution of rewards to those who obeyed his behests, while they produced as much satisfaction as discontent amongst individuals, left the thoughtful man with a feeling of insecurity which was fatal to any real advance in commercial or general prosperity. An equally whimsical expenditure of money on public works of questionable utility tended only to aggravate the dissatisfaction amongst the wiser heads of the community.

When, after nearly five years of despotism, he started for Europe in 1909, leaving, it was said, secret instructions to assassinate General Gomez, of whose popularity he was jealous, the discontent found vent in a general acclamation of the latter's *coup d'état*, whereby he secured his safety, the admiration of the soldiery, and the presidential power, without deliberately shedding Venezuelan blood, A new Constitution was promulgated in November, 1909, reverting in general to the form of 1864, and in April, 1910, the elections established General Juan Vicente Gomez as Constitutional President for the current term.

Since that time the centenary of the independence of the republic has been celebrated in Carácas, at which period the ex-Dictator's carefully planned attempt to occupy the country was frustrated by the seizure of his ships as piratical vessels in Haiti. The new President has shown himself eager to promote the welfare of the country and to encourage commerce, Consuls have been appointed to stations where, since the time of Guzman Blanco, there have been none; the application of foreign capital to the development of the resources of the country has been encouraged, with due regard to the rights of the inhabitants; and, more than all, the spirit of the country at large, wearied with the fifty revolutions of the last eighty years, is opposed to further civil strife, and inclined to maintain that internal peace the benefits of which are already being enjoyed.

CHAPTER VI
MODERN VENEZUELA

Boundaries—Frontier with Brazil—Colombia—British Guiana—Internal subdivision—States and territories with their capitals—Density of population—Constitution—Departments of the executive—*Jefes Civiles*—Legislature—Senators and deputies—Administration of Justice—Laws relating to foreigners—Marriage—Public health—Philanthropic institutions—Education—Coinage—Multiplicity of terms—Towns—Typical houses—Furniture—Hospitality—Food—Clothing—Army and Navy—Insignia—*Busto de Bolivar*—The Press.

The United States of Venezuela, as constituted to-day, are bounded on the north by the Caribbean Sea, on the south by the United States of Brazil, on the east by the Gulf of Paria, the Atlantic Ocean, and British Guiana, on the west by the republic of Colombia.

The boundary between Brazil and Venezuela was determined by a Joint Commission in 1880 as follows: From Mount Roraima, south and west along the watershed of the Sierra Pacaraima, to Cerro Mashiati, thence southwards along the Sierra Parima, and the Sierras de Curupira, Tapira Peco, and Imeri to the bifurcation of the Rivers Baria and Cauapury on the Rio Negro.

The Colombia-Venezuelan frontier was submitted to arbitration in 1891, and the King of Spain made the award thus: From Los Mogotes or Los Frailes islands to the highest point of the Oca Mountain separating the Valley of Upar, the province of Mairacaibo, and Rio del Hacha, thence along the watershed of the sierras of Perija and Motilones to the source of the Rio de Oro. Thence across the Rivers Catatumbo, Sardinata, and Tarra to the mouth of the La Grita on the Rio Zulia; from that point along the previously recognised line to the junction of the Quebrada de Don Pedro with the Táchira, and up that river to its source. Thence across the range and Páramo of Tama to the River Oira; down this to its junction with the Sarare, and along the latter, through the Laguna de Desparramadero, to the junction with the Arauca, down that river to a point equidistant from Arauca and the meridian of the junction of the Masparro and Apure. Thence in a straight line to Antiguo Apostadero, and down the Meta to the Orinoco. Then down the mid-stream of the Orinoco, reserving a right of way for Venezuelans on the left bank between Atures and the Maipures rapids to the mouth of the Guaviare, up the latter to the junction with the Atabapo; then up this to a point 36 kilometres west of Pimichin, and so across to the Guainia (or Rio Negro), following this down to Cocuhy.

The British Guiana boundary was submitted to arbitration in 1897, and the Paris tribunal, in 1899, awarded as follows: From the coast at Punta Playa in a straight line to the junction of the Barima and Mururuma; thence along mid-stream of the latter to its source. From this point to the junction of the Rio Haiowa and the Amacura, and along mid-stream of the latter to its source in the Sierra Imataca. Then south-west along the spur to the main range of the sierra opposite the source of the Barima; then along the watershed south-east to the source of the Acarabisi and down it to the Cuyuni, westward along this river to its junction with the Wenamu (Venamo) and up the latter to its most westerly course. Thence in a straight line to the summit of Mount Roraima.

The political divisions of the country established in 1856 were adopted, with some slight changes, in the Constitution of November, 1909, when General Gomez assumed the presidency. The divisions for which these were substituted were less convenient for administrative purposes, but were in general form the same—that is to say, States divided into districts, a Federal District and Territories. There are now twenty States with their own Legislatures, the Federal District of Carácas under the Central Government, and two Territories. The population of these is given in Appendix A.

The Federal District includes the country round Carácas, and the coastal region between Naiguatá and Cabo Blanco, with the islands to the north. The States are distributed as follows:—

Zulia (capital, Maracaibo), includes all the lake region; Táchira (capital, San Cristobal), Mérida, and Trujillo are the Andine States; Lara (capital, Barquisimeto), Falcón (Coro), and Yaracuy (San Felipe) include the Segovia highlands and the coastal regions in front; Carabobo (Valencia), Aragua (La Victoria), Miranda (Ocumare), and Sucre (Cumaná) are in the Caribbean hills; Nueva Esparta includes Margarita and the other islands immediately to the north and east (capital, Asunción); Monágas (Maturín), Anzoátegui (Barcelona), Guárico (Calabozo), Cojedes (San Carlos), Portuguesa (Guanare), Zamora (Barinas), and Apure (San Fernando) are wholly or mainly Llano States; and nearly half the territory south of the Orinoco is comprised within the State of Bolivar and governed from the city of the same name. The Delta-Amacuro Territory includes the delta proper and the similar region to the south of it; its capital is Tucupita, on the Caño Macareo: the Amazonas Territory, with its capital on the Orinoco at San Fernando de Atabapo, includes the Upper Orinoco basin and the adjacent districts, an enormous, almost unknown area.

THE FEDERAL PALACE: CARÁCAS.

The density of the population in the country as a whole (according to the *Anuario Estadístico*, 1910, census of 1891) is 2·27 per square kilometre, or 5·88 to the square mile. Some idea of the meaning of these figures may be gathered from a comparison of the population of Monágas, where there are 6·68 inhabitants to the square mile, over an area almost equal to that of Belgium, with that of the latter country, Monágas having 74,500 inhabitants and Belgium nearly 7,500,000. The Federal district stands highest, with 151·94 to the square mile; and, making due allowance for the greater density of the population in the higher lands, the figures decrease in proportion to the distance from this centre. Thus the coast States adjoining the Federal districts, with the island of Margarita, are the most thickly populated, the Segovia highlands, Andine States, and region of Paria next, with the northern lowlands and the Llanos, having a density of population approximately equal to that of the whole country, while the Guayana region and the Delta territory range as low as 0·41 to the square mile. It should be remembered, however, that no exact figures are available for the nomadic tribes who people the remoter districts of Venezuela.

The Constitution of the Republic is modelled upon that of the United States of America; the President, elected by a college of fourteen members of Congress for a term of four years, is the head of the nation; under him are the three great departments of the administration—executive, legislative, and judicial, these being again regarded as National, Federal, and Municipal, according to their powers. Each State of the Union has its own Legislature and President, who is a Federal officer, while the territories are governed directly by the national Executive.

The national Executive exercises its functions through the following departments: Ministry of the Interior, for Home Affairs; Ministry of Hacienda (Finance); Ministry of War and Marine; Ministry of Fomento (National Development, Agriculture, Commerce, and Industry); Public Works Department; Ministry of Education; the special province of each being sufficiently indicated by the name. There is also a Government Council of ten members appointed to advise the President, who has his State Secretary and Chaplain; the presiding officer of this Council takes charge during the absence, or in case of the death, of the President. The executives of the State Governments are similarly constituted, but here both President and Government Councillors are Federal officers, while the District *Jefaturas Civiles* are also supported at Federal charges. It should be explained that there are *Jefes Civiles* (Commissioners of Police and Chief Magistrates) for each district, while under these as municipal officers are the *Jefes Civiles* of rural districts and towns (*municipios*).

The legislative power is vested in the National and State Legislatures and the Municipal Councils. The Congress of the United States of Venezuela consists of two Chambers—one of Senators and the other of Deputies. The Deputies (1 to 35,000 of the population, or portion of this number greater than half) are elected by the citizens of each State and serve a term of four years; they must be Venezuelan by birth and over twenty-one years of age. Two Senators are elected by each State Legislative Assembly, and they also remain in office for four years; the Constitution requires all to be Venezuelan by birth and over thirty years of age. In case of dispute a joint session is provided for, and Bills finally sanctioned by both Chambers become law, and are thereupon communicated to the President as head of the Executive for publication in the *Gaceta Oficial* and administration by his officers.

Justice is administered by the *Corte Federal y de Casacion*, whose members are appointed by Congress, and by lower courts and tribunals throughout the country; the territorial judges are national functionaries, but judicial powers in the State are wielded by Federal officers, while the municipal courts are the same throughout the country.

The law prohibits foreigners from taking any part in politics, but in other matters they have equal rights with Venezuelans, as regards personal liberty, free correspondence, safety of life and limb, &c. There are three principal general codes—civil, criminal, and commercial, the last named including special regulations for foreign companies. A new revised mining code was sanctioned on June 29, 1910.

The laws make marriage a civil contract with or without a religious ceremony, but in the country districts the people seem to prefer no ceremony at all to one not conducted by a priest; and as the latter are few and their fees often exorbitant, it results that more than two-thirds of the births in any year are (most unjustly) recorded as illegitimate.

While sanitation and hygiene have not as yet received sufficient attention to reduce the death rate in what appears to be a naturally healthy country to its possible level (see p. 36), a large number of officials are employed in the departments of public health, and the authorities are now in possession of data which have made them thoroughly alive to the needs of the country in this particular. Arrangements have already been made with a British firm for an up-to-date system of sanitation of the capital. There were, in 1908, 52 philanthropic institutions in the republic under Government control, consisting of the following: 27 hospitals, 2 leper asylums, 2 lunatic asylums, 9 homes for blind and aged persons, and 12 orphanages. The number of inmates at the close of that year was 3,244, but, as might be expected, the remoter regions of the country are absolutely unprovided for, and many parts of the central and western regions are as yet without establishments for public assistance.

In a similar manner provision is made, more or less adequately, for education in the central area, and, in fact, throughout the old province of Venezuela; but outside this the number of establishments decreases to nil in the Amazonas territory, while in the 40,000 square miles of the Delta there are only 2 municipal schools. There are in the republic 1,404 elementary schools with 48,869 pupils, 102 institutions for secondary education with 2,189 pupils; and for higher and technical education there are 31 institutions with 2,441 students, including 2 Universities (Carácas and Mérida), 1 school of engineering, 6 seminaries of philosophy and divinity, 8 schools of fine arts, and 14 of arts and crafts. Of all these establishments rather less than nine-tenths are supported by public money, though more than half of the secondary schools are private. The proportion of males to females is in general about as 10 is to 8; but there is no provision for women in the Universities, and save for the schools of fine arts the proportion of females to males in the higher departments is below the average for all classes of instruction.

The currency of Venezuela is established upon a gold standard, with the result that there is none of the depreciated coinage which constitutes one of the curses of the neighbouring State of Colombia. The monetary unit is the *bolivar*, equivalent to the French franc, the London rate of exchange being generally 25.25; this is divided into 100 centimos, and the system is therefore in theory extremely simple; since, however, there is in practice a multiplicity of terms and coins, it is a matter of time for the visiting foreigner to become sufficiently familiar with both to carry on business with promptitude and confidence. The coins issued by the Government of Venezuela are of gold, silver, and nickel, in the following values: gold, 100 bolivars, 25 bolivars, and 20 bolivars; silver, 5, 2½, and 2 bolivars, 1, ½, ¼, and ⅕ bolivar, the limit of legal payments in silver being restricted to sums under 50 bolivars; nickel, 12½ centimos and 5 centimos, with which sums may be paid not exceeding 20 bolivars. The three principal banks, *i.e.*, the Banco de Venezuela, Banco Carácas, and Banco de Maracaibo, have the right at present to issue notes, but these, though current at par in the region where the banks are situated, are often refused in more remote districts. The following gold coins are also current in practice; American gold pieces of 20, 10, and 5 dollars, the dollar being reckoned as 5 bolivars; old Spanish onzas; and those issued by different Latin-American States both before and after secession from Spain, at the nominal value of 80 bolivars, but in both cases there is a premium on gold coin which renders the 20-dollar piece worth 104 bolivars and the onza 82 bolivars. Finally, the English sovereign is readily accepted in Carácas, the premium varying from 4 to 10 per cent. according to circumstances.

As an outcome of this condition of affairs the ordinary traveller in Venezuela has, for the purpose of petty commerce, to be acquainted with three methods of reckoning. In La Guaira and Carácas and other towns affected by commerce with the United States and the West Indies dollars and centavos represent respectively 5 bolivars and 5 centimos, and English-speaking Venezuelans always use American monetary terms; in the towns, however, the bolivar is often voluntarily used as the unit in speaking, and will always be so used on request. In the country the old Spanish nomenclature is everywhere employed, having the *real* as the unit, equivalent to 25 centimos, with its subdivisions the *medio* (12½ centimos) and the *cuartillo* (6¼ centimos). In Maracaibo and the Andine States, for large sums, the *onza* is employed as a unit, or more commonly the *morrocota* (20-dollar gold piece). Finally, in commerce on a large scale and for all accounts, pesos and centavos are employed, representing respectively 4 bolivars and 4 centimos; there are no coins corresponding to these sums, and in writing the dollar sign is used, a practice bound to lead to some confusion when the sign is occasionally used in the correct way. Thus, a tradesman will present a bill for $12.50—*i.e.*, 12½ pesos or 50 bolivars, the proper market price for the article supplied, and will receive from a new-comer (who may think the figure dear, but remembers that he is buying goods imported under a heavy tariff) the sum of $12½, which gives an unscrupulous seller an extra profit of 12.50 bolivars. Throughout the country, however, people know the Venezuelan terms, and can be asked to explain any account, verbal or otherwise, in bolivars or centimos.

The metric system is in general use throughout the civilised parts of the country.

As in all Spanish and most American cities, the towns of Venezuela are regularly laid out, with a *plaza* or square as centre, from which roads diverge towards the four cardinal points. Round the plaza are generally the Government offices, the church, and other principal buildings or private houses; the ground within the square is either occupied by gardens or trees or (in the smaller towns and villages) is grass-covered. Away from the centre the streets show little sign of arrangement in the buildings, old Spanish houses of imposing design standing out here and there, conspicuous among the smaller, more modern edifices.

The doors of the houses open directly on to the pavement, if there is one, and a wall with a few windows, and sometimes none, is all that meets the eye of the passer-by. Inside, however, in all the older and better-built modern residences the short passage opens into a patio, generally full of palms, trees, and flowers, and having a fountain in the centre. Round the patio there is a covered veranda with doors opening into living-rooms and bedrooms on the different sides. From beautiful and elegant courts like this there is every grade to the bare yard, with perhaps only one or two banana-plants. At the back are the kitchens, and in general a second patio, without trees or shrubs, and having stalls for the horses or mules on one side; there are generally several pigs and numerous chickens running about here.

In the country places the furniture of the houses is very simple: a few chairs, some or all of which may be home-made and of hide stretched over wooden frames of all shapes, tables, and one or two stands for glasses, &c., complete the inventory for the ordinary rooms; pictures are rare and not infrequently are limited to lithograph calendars and coloured advertisements received from the more advanced business houses.

The stranger is not as a rule invited to join the family circle, but if he is admitted, on account of introductions from mutual friends, he will find the traditions of Spanish hospitality carried out to the full, and all that the house affords is at his disposal. The elaborate lace edging of the linen, particularly of the pillow-cases, is another characteristic shared in common with other Spanish peoples.

Maize forms the staple grain of the country, though in the east especially cassava is an equally important foodstuff, and sometimes entirely replaces corn, for a large proportion of the people. The maize flour is generally made with water into cakes (*arepa*), rather like curling-stones in shape, about 4 inches in diameter, which are lightly baked and brought to the table warm: a variation of these, generally considered somewhat of a luxury, are known as *bollas*, which are sausage-shaped rolls of fine maize flour. In the Andes dark-coloured bread (*pan de trigo*) of native wheat flour is generally eaten, and in every large town white bread made from imported flour can be had. The cassava root has its poisonous juices extracted in a long straw tube which contracts in diameter as it is extended in length, thus providing the necessary pressure; the dry material is ground to the consistency of oatmeal, and made into large flat cakes, which, when baked, are often two feet across and extremely hard. The broken cake as placed on the table is often soaked in water to soften it. Cassava bread, like arepa, is of more than one quality, according to the fineness to which the material is ground.

In the coast regions *carne seca* (dried beef) forms an important item in general diet, while *carne de chivo* (goat's flesh) is a staple in Coro. Fresh meat is of course the rule in the towns, and fowls are everywhere abundant; the *sancoche de gallina*, a kind of rich stew made of chicken with herbs and oil, is very good if properly prepared. For other articles of diet, yams and *frijoles* (beans) are the commonest vegetables, with potatoes in the Andes, while fruit preserves and similar sweets are found everywhere. Last, but not least, the cheeses of the Llanos and foothills (of which *queso de mano* is perhaps the best) and the ubiquitous *papelon* (brown unrefined sugar) are an important item in the country fare.

OVEN: LA RAYA.

AN ANDINE POSADA: LA RAYA.

A refreshing and sustaining drink known as guarapo also consists of raw sugar and water, and this with the aguardiente, distilled from the fermented syrup, and coffee are to be seen everywhere. Cacao is less common, but is naturally largely drunk in the neighbourhood of the plantations. A light beer is made at the Carácas and Maracaibo breweries, and there is a multitude of sweet non-alcoholic drinks manufactured from fruits.

The meals are in general as follows: *Café*, coffee, with or without solid food, on first rising; *almuerzo*, like the *déjeuner* of Europe, at midday; and *comida* or dinner, at sunset. As far as order and number of meals are concerned, Carácas is like the rest of the country, but the remarks above made relative to food apply in the main only to the provinces.

As for food, so for clothing, Carácas and the large towns need no special mention, since the imported weaving material here is mainly European or American. The country towns, however, frequently depend, not only for workmanship but also for materials, on the products of the country. The poorer people wear simple white or blue garments, with broad-brimmed straw hats, and generally go barefoot or wear leather sandals (*alpargatas*). Everywhere, however, both men and women turn out on feast days in their finest and gaudiest apparel.

A country protected as regards great world powers by the Monroe Doctrine and their own international jealousy, and surrounded by States where the density of population is even less than in its own underpeopled lands, has naturally no need of great and expensive establishments for national defence, and the army and navy are merely of a size sufficient for the settlement of possible petty disputes with neighbours. The land force consists of 5,632 officers and men, and the navy employs only 457 combatants. These figures represent men under national control only, though there are also a small number of militiamen and Federal Guards distributed through the States, paid by the Ministry of War and Marine. This department controls also the pilots and lighthouses round the coast, and is responsible for the execution of the surveys for the military maps of Venezuela. The total expenditure in all branches for 1908-9 was Bs. 9,113,534.86, or about £361,000.

The insignia of the republic, as adopted in 1836 and modified by decree of July 29, 1863, consist of a flag and coat of arms. The flag is a tricolour of yellow, blue, and red, in equal bands, one above the other in the order mentioned, and having in the blue seven white stars, representing the seven original provinces of Venezuela, grouped in a circle of six round the seventh. The shield has three quarterings; the right red with a sheaf of corn, as many ears being indicated as there are States; the left yellow, with a group of arms and flags, crowned with a laurel as a token of triumph; the third, occupying the whole of the bottom part of the shield, is blue, and bears a white horse rampant, symbolising independence and liberty. Above the shield there are two horns of plenty, and below an olive-branch and a palm-leaf, tied with blue and yellow ribbons, which are inscribed *Dios y Federación* in the centre, *5 de julio de 1811* and *Independencia* on the left; and the date of the Constitution of the United States of Venezuela (*13 de Abril 1864*) and *Libertad* on the right.

There is one decoration in Venezuela, given to prominent men in the country and, in its lower classes, to foreigners whom the nation delights to honour. This is the *Busto de Bolivar*, the medal showing the head of the liberator and the ribbon the national colours.

There are in all 237 periodicals published in the country, including, besides the official gazettes of the capitals, one or more of general interest in every State, and a considerable number devoted to scientific, literary, masonic, and other special subjects. The State of Lara had in 1908, according to the Venezuelan Year-Book, the largest number of periodical publications in the Union.

CHAPTER VII
THE ABORIGINES

The Goajiros—Lake dwellings—Appearance—Territory—Villages—Government—Burial customs—Religion—Medicine-men—The Caribs—A fine race—Cannibalism—Headless man of the Caura—The Amazons—Industries—Religion—Marriage customs—The aborigines of Guayana—Tavera-Acosta on languages—The Warraus—Appearance—Houses—Food—Clothing—Marriage customs—Birth—Death—Religion—Treatment of sick—The Banibas—Appearance—Customs—Religion—Celebration of puberty of girls—Marriage customs—The Arawaks—Religion—Early missions amongst Indians—Wanted, a twentieth-century apostle.

The aboriginal inhabitants of Venezuela preserve their habits and racial customs unchanged only in two regions of the republic, namely, along the north-west frontier and in the vast forests of Guayana. Elsewhere, a few families remain in the less accessible and more barren regions, but the "Indians" have been in general absorbed by intermarriage into the Spanish-speaking Venezuela nation, slowly emerging from the mixture of races which have at various times occupied the territory.

A powerful tribe occupy the mountains and forests along the Colombian frontier, and these are generally known as the Goajiros. Some of their villages are on the shores of Lake Maracaibo, as at Sinamaica, and are of the pile-dwelling type which first gave rise to the name of the country; most of the tribe, however, live as an independent nation within recognised boundaries.

Both men and women may be seen in Maracaibo on market days, clothed then in the white or blue garments which all keep for contact with civilisation. In their own villages they wear a less elaborate costume. The men are well built, light and agile, with keen and intelligent faces, but the women have the amorphous figures and dull, heavy faces which come of centuries of slavery and drudgery for their menkind. Apparently they are ethnologically a branch of the great Carib group of which we shall have more to say later. As might be surmised from the fact of their independence, the Goajiros are vigorous and warlike, and incidentally excellent horsemen.

Their territory extends from Rio Hacha, in Colombia, down into the Goajira peninsula, and across the Venezuelan border to within eight or ten miles of Sinamaica. The boundary is guarded by military pickets, and most of their trading is done on the frontier, merchants travelling to this point from all sides.

They live in small villages made up of round thatched houses, which at a distance look like so many ant-hills; the floor inside is strewn with grass, and on this the women and children work and sleep; the men spend much of their time in hammocks slung from the rafters. They are more fond of fighting than of working, but in civilised regions they are peaceable, and make excellent boatmen, while from their secluded homes they go out hunting and fishing, and are famous for the horses and mules which they breed. Their fields are tended by the womenfolk or by the slaves taken from neighbouring tribes in battle, and are of exceptionally large size, sown with yuca or manioc, potatoes and maize; they have banana plantations, but apparently have never cultivated cocoa or coffee.

In their homes the less wealthy members of the tribe wear the *guayuco*, or small apron, of different patterns, common to all the Venezuelan Indians, but some have good cloth clothing, trousers and jacket, with embroidered white shawls or blankets for the men and long mantles or knee-high tunics for the women. Nearly all the men carry firearms of modern patterns.

Each village has its cacique or headman, but they acknowledge the suzerainty of a temporal chief or king living in Tunja, and a supreme spiritual prince or pope in Iraca. Like the ancient Incas, who possibly influenced them and helped to make them what they are, they worship the sun, but little is known of their modes of worship or religious festivals.

If one of the tribe dies at home his body is buried in his cattle-pen, or where he may have been most frequently found in his lifetime, his clothing and weapons being interred with him for use in the happy hunting grounds to which he is shortly to depart. Their belief is, however, that for about twenty-four hours after death the spirit remains near its dwelling, and therefore they keep up a kind of lyke-wake all day, not to mourn for the departed but to wish him good hunting and to speed him on his way to the next world. At sunset his spirit departs, no more to return.

Along with their sun-worship is a belief in a good and evil principle in Nature, residing in the spirits of the wood, streams, rain, thunder, and so forth. Probably this represents the original animism of the nation before their contact with the Incas. From this animism arises the custom of exorcising evil spirits from the bodies of the sick. The sufferer is shielded by a curtain from the rest of the hut, and the medicine-man, clothed in a long white mantle or blanket, first massages the patient till both perspire freely, then flagellates himself till the blood flows, and finally, casting a powder into the fire, which sends up clouds of blue smoke, dances himself into convulsions, until from sheer exhaustion he sinks to the ground, covered with the white mantle; the fire is allowed to die down, and the sick man and his doctor are left alone in the darkness and silence.

As we have said, these Goajiros appear to be a family of the Carib group, but while they remain where they were at the time of the conquest, their relations eastward have been driven southwards or absorbed by the white races, just as they themselves at an earlier date drove back the aborigines, who now, with them, people the forests of Guayana.

The Caribs probably spoke more than one dialect when they first invaded the mainland from the islands of the Caribbean, but now the number of the tribes and languages considered by Señor Tavera-Acosta to belong to the group is about thirty, including the following: Caribe, Tamanaco, Otomak, Maquiritare or Uayungomo (also spelt Guayungomo and Waiomgomo. In every case for names beginning with U there is the alternative spelling with the unsounded Spanish G, and B and V are interchangeable), Maco or Macapure, Cuacua or Mapoyo, Taparita, Uiquire or Uiquiare, Pauare, Pareca, Uayamara, Cadupinapo, Curasicana, Yabarana, Arecuna, Macusi, Uaica, and others of minor importance.

The members of these tribes were those who, like the Goajiros, fought most stoutly for their independence when they saw it menaced by the *conquistadores*. These patriots, superior in many respects, as we have seen, to their foes, were characterised by the European invaders as cannibals, vicious and degraded, and the Jesuits later, in their holy zeal for souls (*conquista espiritual*) were no less harsh in their judgments on those who naturally resented the separation of parents from children and husband from wife and the general atrocities of the self-styled Christians who thus endeavoured to forcibly convert them.

In reality they were then, what they still are where unspoilt by "civilisation," a fine race physically, brave and intelligent, possessing, no doubt, the vices of savagery, but also its virtues. The charges of cannibalism brought by the European exploiters of the New World (who had the vices of civilisation and barbarism combined, without the virtues of either) were either entirely baseless, or due to the ignorance which mistook the limbs of monkeys, which the Indians were always accustomed to eat, for those of men. As we have seen (Chapter IV.), the only substantiated cases of cannibalism occurred among the *conquistadores* themselves.

As an instance of the unintentional perversion of facts, it is interesting to recall the sixteenth and seventeenth century fables of the headless men of the Caura, the *Ewaipanomo*. The banks of the Caura are, in point of fact, inhabited by the Uayungomo branch of the Caribs, a name sufficiently like to be possibly the same. Whether that be so or no, a perusal of Raleigh's and other original accounts gives the impression that some member of one of the shorter aboriginal tribes told the white men, by signs, that in the direction of the Caura were men whose shoulders were above their heads (*i.e.*, the heads of the speakers). I put this forward as a plausible hypothesis for the origin of the fable, which may not commend itself to all, but may be compared with that advanced by various writers to explain the legend of the Amazon communities of this region.

The story of manless villages and tribes was told (and doubtless is still told) to nearly all travellers in Guayana and Brazil, and it has been suggested that the statements are founded upon actual attempts at emancipation on the part of small groups of women intelligent enough to realise the light esteem in which they were held in the social organisation of the Indians, and their worthiness of better treatment. These banded themselves together in free villages in remote parts of the forest, were seen at times by, or perhaps fought with, members of the normal tribes, and so gave rise to a legend of a nation of warlike independent women living somewhere, but no man knew where.

To return to the Caribs, we find these peoples at the present day inhabiting the forests along the banks of the Caroni, Parana, and Caura almost entirely, and particular regions on the Upper Orinoco and its tributaries, notably the Ventuari. They are still among the best formed and most intelligent natives of Venezuela, and retain in their native haunts the many industries by which they long ago learned to support themselves upon the produce of the forest lands.

These industries include cultivation of corn and manioc, the manufacture of fibres from the *moriche*-palm for cloth, of simple earthenware, often decorated with hieroglyphics in colour, of pigments for this and for painting their bodies in wartime. Their arrows are often poisoned with *curare*, the concentrated and congealed sap of the *mavacure* creeper, sometimes also with the extracted juice of the poisonous manioc. From the pith of the moriche-palm they obtain a kind of sago-meal, and this, with maize flour, bitter and sweet manioc or cassava-bread, and fish-paste or meat from their hunting expeditions, forms their staple diet. Their canoes are of bark or dug out of the solid trunk with the aid of stone or flint hatchets or fire. For hunting and war they had in early times good bows and arrows, spears of hard, heavy wood, shields of plaited creepers covered with hides of manati, tapir, or jaguar. Nor were they without musical (?) instruments, of which the *maracas* or rattles of small dried calabashes are used all over Venezuela in the country districts to-day.

Their religious beliefs appear to be, generally speaking, those of the Goajiros without the sun-worship, and birth, marriage, and death customs are much alike amongst all the tribes, whether Carib or no. The only difference here is that, in place of the usual marriage by consent without any religious ceremony, at the time of their conquest of the mainland, they adopted in part a marriage by capture, which has otherwise never been their custom.

The principal tribes of the aborigines of Guayana are thus enumerated, with their distribution and general characteristics, by Tavera Acosta, the spelling of the names being changed in some cases.

(1) The Warraus or Guaraunos (see note, p. 122) of the Delta; dull, unintelligent, and dirty.

(2) Arawaks, south of the Delta; intelligent, gentle, and exceptionally cleanly.

(3) Banibas, a branch of the Quichua nation living on the Guainia or Rio Negro and Atabapo; intelligent, gentle, and of a sedentary mode of life, excellent boatmen and hammock-makers.

(4) Guahibos or Uajibas, on the Vichada; dirty.

(5) Barias, on the Baria, Casiquiare, and Rio Negro; good workers and boatmen.

(6) Yaviteras, at Yavita; like the Barias.

(7) Piaroas, including the Maipures and Atures; living on the Sipapo, Cataniapo and Mataveni; timid and agricultural.

(8) Puinabi or Guaipunavi, on the Inirida; intelligent, but fierce.

(9) Caruzana or Marapizanos; on the Guainia, and neighbouring rivers, cultivators of manioc.

(10) Wareca or Guareca, at San Miguel and Baltazar; intelligent and industrious.

(11) Piapocos and Salibas, on the Guaviare, &c.; agricultural.

(12) Guaharibos, round the head-waters of the Orinoco; savage.

(13, 14, and 15) Guaicas, Pasimonabis, and Mandawaks, on the Casiquiare, &c.; agricultural.

(16) Yaruros.

Of these the Piaroas, Guarecas, Piapocos and Salibas, Pasimonabis, and Mandawaks are becoming extinct or are leaving Venezuela for neighbouring countries. It may be noted that many place-names, such as Guárico, Achaguas, Apure, Mucuchíes, are those of extinct tribes or of branches of those given above.

Tavera-Acosta finds the languages spoken by these people divisible into three main groups, but some appear to have an admixture of Parian or Carib words. It is interesting to note his statement that the common Chinese root *chi* abounds in all the dialects of Guayana, and the system of counting is

Mongolian. In addition, he states that the languages show some Malayan affinities.

The most numerous tribes appear to be the Warraus or Guaraunos, the Banibas (a branch of the ancient Quichua stock of the Rio Negro), and the Arawaks; these last, however, are chiefly to be found in British Guiana.

The Warraus occupy the Delta of the Orinoco, and extend into the lowlands of British Guiana, having everywhere retained their racial characters to an unusual extent. Their language appears to be akin to the Carib group on the one hand and the Arawak on the other, while the people themselves have at times been considered as an offshoot of the Carib nation.

They are dark copper in colour, well set up, and strong, though not as a rule tall, and with low foreheads, long and fine black hair, and the usual high cheek-bones and wide nostrils of the South American "Indians." Where they have not come into contact with civilisation they are particularly shy and reticent, but they soon lose this character, and some are said to show considerable aptitude as workmen.

Living as they do mainly in the Delta, their houses are of necessity near water and are raised from the ground as a protection against floods, being sometimes, it is said, even placed on platforms in trees. The roof is supported in the middle by two vertical posts and a ridge pole, and is composed of palm-leaves, supported at the corners by stakes. The sides of this simple hut consist of light palm-leaf curtains, and the floor is of palm-planks. The hammocks are slung on the ridge pole, and the bows and arrows of the occupants fixed in the roof, while their household furniture, consisting of home-made earthenware pots, calabashes of various sizes, &c., lie promiscuously about the floor. Some of the Warraus are nomadic and live in canoes, but the majority are grouped in villages of these huts, with captains responsible to the Venezuelan local government authorities.

The staple diet of these people is manioc and sago, with *chicha* (a mixture of manioc meal and water). For clothing they dispense with everything in their homes, except the *buja* or *guayuco*, a tiny apron of palm-fibre or ordinary cloth, held in position by a belt of palm-fibre or hair. That worn by women is triangular, and often ornamented with feathers or pearls. Among the whites the men always wear a long strip of blue cloth, one end of which passes round the waist, the other over the shoulder, hanging down in front; the women have a kind of long-sleeveless gown. For ornament they wear necklaces of pearls, or more frequently of red, blue, and white beads, and tight bracelets and bangles of hair or *curagua* (palm-fibre); some pierce ears, nose, and lower lips for the insertion of pieces of reed, feathers, or berries on fête days. The characteristic dull red paint on their bodies is intended to act as a preventive against mosquitoes, and it is made by boiling the powdered bark and wood of a creeper in turtle or alligator fat. All hair is removed from the body by the simple but painful process of pulling each one out with a split reed.

Marriage, as is usual among savage races, takes place at a very early age, the husband being often only fourteen, the wife ten or twelve years of age. Polygamy is common, but not universal; where a chief or rich man has several wives the first, or the earliest to become a mother, takes charge of the establishment during the absence of the owner on his hunting or fishing expeditions. The girls are sometimes betrothed at the age of five or six years, living in the house of the future husband from that time on.

At birth the mother is left in a separate house alone, where all food that she may need is placed for her, though she remains unvisited by any of her companions throughout the day; meanwhile the father remains in his hammock for several days, apparently owing to a belief that some evil may befall the child; there he receives the congratulations of the villagers, who bring him presents of the best game caught on their expeditions. This male child-bed or *couvade* is common to many of the Indian tribes.

The dead are mourned with elaborate ceremony—shouting, weeping, and slow, monotonous music; the nearest relatives of the defunct cut their hair. The body is placed in leaves and tied up in the hammock used by the owner during life, and then placed in a hollow tree-trunk or in his canoe. This rude coffin is then generally placed on a small support, consisting of bamboo trestles, and so left in the deserted house of the dead man.

LA GUAIRA HARBOUR.

The beliefs of the Warraus have been somewhat modified by contact with foreigners, and perhaps on this account they speak, according to Plassard, of one Supreme Being, the *Gébu*, superior to all the lesser spirits of plenty, famine, fire, and all phenomena of Nature. Earthquakes are looked upon as good signs, indicating the presence of a healthy, invigorating spirit in the earth; a belief not so strange when it is remembered that in the alluvial plains where the Warraus live earthquakes have seldom been sufficiently violent to do harm.

The religious rites of the communities are presided over by the *Wicidatu*, like the piache, a mixture of priest and medicine-man. Their worship includes invocations against disease and famine, and prayers for good hunting. To Gébu and the lesser spirits they offer the first-fruits of their harvest, vegetable and animal alike, at the one great festival of the year, for which elaborate preparations are made. All the previous day is spent in preparing provisions, and at dawn on the feast day, their bodies decorated with lines in blue and red, they surround the house of the wicidatu. The priest shortly comes forth, a crown of feathers on his head, and holding a pair of maracas. Shaking these, he leads the crowd to the *rancho*, or hut, set apart for the offerings, and there, sitting on the trunk of a tree, smokes and chants (accompanying himself with the maracas) to Gébu, in whose name he presently takes the offerings. After this he holds a maraca in the air at the length of his arm, shaking it, and after a time bringing it down to his mouth. Then, in a disguised voice, supposed to be that of Gébu, he asks why he is called; in reply the wicidatu salutes and offers the first-fruits, which are accepted. This acceptance is the signal for a general chant of the assembly recounting their petitions, which Gébu, speaking as before through the priest, promises to consider. Finally, the priest alone sings a song of farewell, and Gébu returns to his heaven. The ceremonies over, the wicidatu takes the best of the food and drink, and the remainder provides refreshment during the dancing and revels which occupy the rest of the day.

In addition to conducting this public worship the wicidatu acts as doctor in times of sickness, making use of certain simples and invocations to the spirits of the disease. Religious ceremonies are performed round the hut by night, and the medicine-man enters with a cigar of tobacco and herbs and blows the smoke on to the abdomen and chest of the patient. After the fumigation he is left alone for some time, until the wicidatu returns, dances and prostrates himself round the hut, performs the fumigation once more, and finally retires, leaving the sick man to recover or die, according to the manner in which the spirit has been affected by the supplications.

Not only are the Banibas probably the most numerous of the many tribes of the hinterland of Guayana, but they are considered by Tavera-Acosta to be the most advanced of them all. A description, therefore, of their principal customs may be taken as a sufficient indication of the tendency of the beliefs and practices of other aborigines of the interior.

The Banibas are found chiefly along the Guainia and the Atabapo Rivers, their villages extending into Brazil and Colombia. They are said to be intelligent and peaceable, of a sedentary mode of life, excellent boatmen and hammock-makers. Tavera-Acosta, adopting the view that they are a branch of the ancient Quichua nation, gives d'Orbigny's description of the latter thus: "The head is oblong, nose long, slightly aquiline, eyes horizontal, profile almost European, though the cheek-bones are higher. They are serious, somewhat melancholy, industrious, with an intelligent expression, but reserved. Neither red nor copper in colour, but bronze. The foot is small, but instep rather high."

Their villages are composed of round conical huts, built of poles covered with palm-leaves, each hut containing twenty or thirty of the same family. All the work is done by the young men and women, the elders living a life of absolute idleness; the men hunt and collect the rubber and other produce of the forest, travelling about in canoes; the women attend to the household duties, fish, and sow the small fields with maize and manioc. The hammocks made by the Banibas are especially noted, some being beautifully interwoven with feathers; the best have been known to fetch as much as £40.

Their staple foods are maize flour, manioc meal, and the cakes of arepa or cassava made therefrom; the meal they preserve by treating it with a preparation of bitter yuca, known as *murujui*; fish, smoked and dried tapir meat, and small game vary their diet, and in default of other beverages they drink *yucuta*, the chicha of the Warraus.

Their religious beliefs and customs have been considerably affected by the presence in the region of Jesuits and other missionaries from an early period in the Spanish occupation; hence Roman scapularies and pagan fetiches are found side by side, and their form of worship, as well as their faith, is a similar mixture of pagan and heathen dogmas.

Their customs as regards birth, sickness, and death are sufficiently similar to the rest of the aborigines to render description unnecessary, but the marriage ceremony is bound up with the celebration of the pubescence of the girls, which is extraordinarily barbarous in view of the high standard of their morals and general character.

When a maiden of the tribe attains the age of puberty her mother communicates the fact to the elders of the village, and her daughter is shut up alone in a hut, where she is expected to lie in a hammock, eating and drinking only a little manioc and water. Notice being given, the eligible youths of the community apply to her father for the girl, who is promised to him who shall bring as a present the best piece of curare, the finest hammock, or certain kinds of fish or game. The bridegroom having been thus selected, the girl's seclusion is over. She is led forth, with eyes bandaged and head covered with a kind of bonnet, to a stake in the centre of the village, where the elders tie up and beat the unfortunate damsel with whips of cord or fish-skin, sometimes studded with sharp stones; the proceedings are accompanied by the blowing of conches. The two senior elders then advance inside the revolving circle and command the supposed demon in the girl to leave her and enter the stake to which she is tied, and presently, at a given signal, the flagellation ceases. The girl, often fainting from pain and weakness, is released and taken away to a distance; her wounds are washed and soothing herbs applied, while the youngest elder present is dispatched to advise the bridegroom that his future wife has been freed from the demon and is to be found in such and such a place. Then he goes from house to house shouting, "Come and burn the demon which would have taken possession of such and such a girl!"

Meanwhile the bridegroom has found the bride and taken her to his father's house, and the rest of the population is collected round the stake, which is surrounded with faggots; the women, wearing fringed belts and holding one another by the waist, dance round in a ring execrating the demon; the men shout and sing and drink strong liquors prepared previously by the girl's parents. The bridegroom, having left the bride with his mother, approaches with a torch to fire the pile, and apostrophises the demon, telling him that the girl he wished to harm is now his wife, paid for with curare (or whatever the present may have been), and finally, in token of their vengeance, he lights the faggots to the sound of a fearful din from the conches, tambourines, and maracas. All the people dance up to the fire and back again, the men lined up on one side, the women on the other, finally circling round till everything is consumed. In this way the safety of the bride from evil influences is secured, and she is recognised henceforth as the wife of her purchaser.

Sir Everard im Thurn described the Arawaks, of whom there are many families, as one of the most advanced groups in British Guiana, whence they extend into Venezuela. They build the cleanest and best houses, sometimes square and sometimes round, especially on the savannahs. Their standard of morality is high, and their religious belief, where untouched by those of the colonists, is a pure animism. He notes, however, that they use one general term very frequently in apostrophising a heavy rain, severe thunderstorm, or other unpleasant display of the powers of the air, without any definite idea of one being. This term, *Oenicidu*, he suggests, represents an approach to recognition of a single force behind all the phenomena of Nature, which might grow into a belief in a Supreme Spirit. Those who wish to know the folklore of these and neighbouring peoples should turn to Sir Everard's book on the Indians of Guiana.

We have already seen that, while the early Romish missionaries in the north of Venezuela did much good in civilising and settling the Indians there, who have since become amalgamated with the Castilian element, in Guiana the atrocities perpetrated by the Jesuits far outweighed any good effect produced by the lessons of industry inculcated in the mission settlements. It is not surprising, therefore, in view of the early opposition of some of even the better ecclesiastics to the republic, that foreign priests and monks of all denominations were prohibited from entering the republic. There has been absolute freedom for all beliefs within the country since 1854, however, and the State contributes to the support of the Catholic churches throughout the land, while reserving the right to make all ecclesiastical appointments and to admit or reject papal bulls as it sees fit.

These remarks are made here in partial explanation of the absence of any recent attempts on the part of any branch of the Christian Church to convert or civilise the natives of Guayana. There is little inducement for the 409 priests who serve the 547 churches of the country to penetrate the unattractive regions of Guayana, and no Protestant missionaries have been found willing to sacrifice their nationality in order to take up the work. Yet these Indians are fine material for a sincere apostle to work upon, and were they given an incentive to use their time well, the talents of the best among them might soon lessen the distance between that visionary prosperous future of Guayana and the present day, when both land and inhabitants are standing still amid the progress of the world.

CHAPTER VIII
THE STATES OF THE "CENTRO"

La Guaira—Heat—Port works—The Brighton of Venezuela—Sugar plantations—Streets and *botiquins*—*Guarapo*—La Guaira-Carácas Railway—A great engineering feat—Carácas—Climate—Population—Streets—Buildings—The Salón Elíptico—El Calvario—El Paraiso—"La India"—Water-supply—Trams and telephones—Lighting—Industries—The Guaire Valley—Coffee—Miranda—Ocumare del Tuy—Petare—Central Railway—Vegetable snow—Carenero Railway—Rio Chico—Los Teques—Great Venezuelan Railway—La Victoria—Sixteen-fold wheatfields—Maracay—Grazing lands—Cheese—President Gomez's country house—Villa de Cura—An epitome of the State—Lake of Valencia—Cotton—Carabobo—Valencia—Cotton-mills—Montalbán—Deserted vineyards—Wild rubber—Puerto Cabello Railway—The port—Meat syndicate—Club—Ocumare de la Costa—What is bad for man may be good for cocoa—Mineral resources.

For obvious reasons the central region of Venezuela, round about the capital, is that most frequently visited by Europeans, and generally even those travellers who, at the call of science, commerce, or pleasure, penetrate to other parts of the country first come into contact with it at La Guaira, the chief port of the republic.

The first settlement in the neighbourhood was established some eight miles to the westward, and was known as Caraballeda, the present town being founded in 1588, shortly after the seat of government was removed from Coro to Carácas. Standing as it does on a narrow strip of more or less level land, at the foot of the cordillera which here rises from the water's edge to the height of about 5,000 feet, and extending up the precipitous slopes of the bare mountain, the town is terribly hot at times. In early days the roadstead must have been very unsafe, for the swell running on this coast at all seasons prevents secure anchorage outside the harbour.

The existing port works belong to an English company, and cost £980,000 to complete; and even so, the rise and fall from the swell is merely reduced, not neutralised. The contract for the La Guaira harbour was given to Messrs. Punchard & Co., who decided, in view of the fact that the roadstead was open to the waves to north and east only, that a straight east and west breakwater would prove most effective. The length of this was to be 2,050 feet, and the design allowed for the enclosure of 90 acres of water of an average depth of 30 feet, 3,100 feet of quays, and 18 acres of reclaimed land. There are seldom severe wind-storms, and the strong swell with the resulting huge waves which break upon the coast were the principal difficulties to be met. Unfortunately, as we have said, the movement is not entirely kept back by the breakwater. The work was commenced in December, 1885, but the first breakwater was destroyed by a particularly heavy swell in December, 1887; the second was commenced in July, 1888, and finally completed, more or less as it stands to-day, in July, 1891.

A railway runs through the town from the suburb of Maiquetia, about a mile and a half westwards, to the fashionable watering-place of Macuto, three miles in the opposite direction. Here there is an esplanade, gardens, and sea-baths, and as the coast, in contrast to La Guaira, faces the direction of the prevalent winds, climatic conditions are pleasant. In the season this Brighton of Venezuela is full of visitors.

Through La Guaira passes out the greater part of the produce of the "Centro," and much from other parts of the country, the principal exports being coffee, cacao, cotton, hides, gold, rubber, pearls, feathers (egrets'), and *alpargatas* (sandals). There are factories turning out cigars, cigarettes, hats, boots, and other articles for home consumption; and at La Guaira the French cable enters the sea. Near Punta Caraballeda there is the big Juan Diaz sugar-mill of Messrs. Boulton, surrounded by bright green cane plantations; but save coconut-palms, little of value grows along the greater part of this coast near the shore.

The narrow street behind the quay is chiefly occupied by *botiquins*, some with abundant tropical and temperate fruits of which cooling *refrescos* can be made, with green milk-coconuts and barrels of diluted *guarapo* (sugar syrup) at a centimo a tumbler—not the pleasantest to an unaccustomed palate but probably the most effective of Venezuelan thirst-quenchers. After the hot sun on the quay the little tables under the trees look particularly inviting, though it is only fair to say that the unkempt appearance of this small fore street is more likely to strike the new-comer than the more pleasant matters.

Communication with the capital is carried on by rail and road, the former carrying the express freight, though the loaded donkeys and mules leaving Maiquetia before sunrise show that the railway is not without competition. The road is well engineered, and is about twenty-five miles in length; the unmacadamised surface is, however, little used for wheel-traffic. In a straight line Carácas is about eight miles from La Guaira, but stands 3,000 feet above the port, and is separated from it by a mountain range 5,000 feet high, over which climbs the old Spanish paved road.

The British-built and owned La Guaira-Carácas railway accomplishes the climb in about 23 miles, the ruling gradient being 1 in 27 to the head of the pass at 3,200 feet, whence it descends 200 feet to the city. The chief feature of the line is the small radius of the curves, some of which are so sharp that it has been said that the guard at the rear of the train can whisper to the driver. For much of the distance there is a splendid view over the Caribbean, and as the line climbs higher up into the gorge the train is often only a few feet from the edge of precipices, with a vertical drop in some cases of over a thousand feet. De Lesseps said that there was only one dangerous part of the line, but that that extended from La Guaira to Carácas. The whole is a fine piece of engineering, and, notwithstanding the theoretical risks, there has never been an accident to a passenger train, thanks to the energetic management and splendid system of *vigilantes*, or watchmen, ever on the lookout for landslips as well as for faults in the permanent way.

Carácas stands on the north bank of the River Guaire, on the inner slope of the coastal cordillera. The northern part of the city is thus higher than the southern. Founded in 1567 by Diego de Losada, its equable climate at the elevation of 3,000 feet and the fertile valley in which it lay soon attracted the Government away from Coro, on the hot, barren plains near the Gulf of Venezuela. The minimum temperature recorded in an average year may be as low as 48° F. (this, of course, at night), but, in general, days and nights are mild, and only in the middle of the year is the air uncomfortably warm at any time of the day. The population was estimated as 90,000 in 1904, and suburbs bring the total to over 100,000. It would be obviously unfair to institute a comparison between a city of this size and any of the better known capitals of Spanish-American republics, but, considered purely on its own merits, the capital of Venezuela has much to commend it, and undoubtedly exerts a peculiar fascination over most of those who visit it.

PLAZA BOLIVAR: VALENCIA.

The streets are narrow, though the one-storey buildings make this hardly noticeable, and are paved in the outer parts of the city with cobbles, in the centre with cement. Though most of the private or business houses have one storey only, this does not apply to the public edifices, and the distribution of these is as casual as in London. As is usual, the principal square or plaza occupies the centre of the town, and round it are grouped the cathedral, Federal Government offices, Palace of Justice, Archbishop's palace, the Casa Amarilla (containing the archives), the G.P.O., and the principal hotel (the Klindt) of the city. The centre of the plaza gardens is occupied by an equestrian statue of Bolivar in bronze. The Capitol is south-west of the Plaza Bolivar, and is a large building in semi-Moorish style, divided by a central patio into two main portions. The southern part is occupied by the two Chambers of the Legislature, while the northern houses the Executive. Part of the Executive Palace, as it is called, is occupied by the Salón Elíptico, containing portraits of famous patriots and statesmen of Venezuela, conspicuous among the dark-haired Spanish or Venezuelan types being the Irishman O'Leary. The dome is decorated with a picture of the battle of Carabobo, and the roofs of the wings with representations of those of Pinchincha and Boyacá, while to the east is a large picture of the Congress of Angostura. The offices of the various departments are on the first floor. Among the remaining buildings of note we may mention the University, an imitation-freestone gothic structure south of the Capitol, the Municipal Theatre, the Pantheon, and the presidential residence (Miraflores).

On the hill of El Calvario west of the city is the Observatory and the Independencia Park, from which a fine view of the city can be had in the afternoon. On the south of the Guaire, which is crossed by two bridges, is the Paraiso drive, with the villas of some of the wealthier residents. Here the society of Carácas drives just before sunset, and we may note, in passing, that the cabs (generally hooded victorias or small landaus) are remarkably cheap and good. One carries a walking-stick when driving to con the coachman, a tap on the right arm meaning a turn in that direction, a poke in the middle of the back "stop," and so on. Not far from the plaza on the one hand and the Municipal Theatre on the other is the restaurant "La India," where the youth of Carácas indulge in cakes and ale in the mornings, and chocolate (which is excellent), or less innocuous liquids after the theatre. Tea, or at least afternoon tea, is uncommon in Carácas as yet, though a growing British colony may change matters in that respect. An enumeration of the plazas and monuments could be of little service, and still less a list of the various hospitals and charitable institutions, of which there are many. On the practical side, however, it is worth noting that Carácas has two public slaughterhouses in different parts of the city.

The water supply is mainly derived from the River Macarao, about fifteen miles west of the town, whence it is brought by an aqueduct to El Calvario and there filtered; there are also reservoirs for the north of the city, deriving their supply from the streams of the Silla de Carácas. There is an excellent service of trams and telephones, both started and controlled by Britishers, and the electric supply for the former as well as for lighting the city is derived from the falls of El Encantado and Los Naranjos, on the Guaire below Carácas. A new plant is shortly to be erected at Mamo. The city also boasts a brewery, foundry, and factories for furniture-making, cigarettes, matches, &c. The remarks made in reference to the trade of La Guaira apply equally to the capital, for practically all the merchandise of the one passes first through the other.

The bottom of the Guaire Valley near Carácas constitutes economically the most important part of the Federal district, for the inner slope of the

Cordillera here supports only small forest or grass, while the more accessible parts of the seaward flank are barren and useless. The sugar plantations of Juan Diaz have already been mentioned, but in the neighbourhood of Carácas there are, or were, many of these, even though the climate is sufficiently cool to have allowed the cultivation of wheat in earlier days, when the Spaniards found it, as might the Venezuelans, less costly than importation. There are fine coffee plantations also in the neighbourhood of Carácas, and the elevation would point to this as one of the best coffee districts of the country; indeed, the yield obtained on some haciendas here is said to have been as much as twenty pounds to the tree.

East and south of the Federal District lies the State of Miranda, including all the hills to Cape Codera and the edge of the Llanos as far as Uchire. The capital is Ocumare del Tuy, though this is not the largest town. Its name at the time of its foundation in 1692 was Sabana de Ocumare, but its proximity to the River Tuy led to the adoption of the present name as a distinction from Ocumare de la Costa. Coffee is grown on the hills in the neighbourhood, with cacao lower down, and sugar and beans in the valleys. The importance of the town is rather political than commercial at present, though the Central Railway may some time reach it and make a centre for the traffic from the Llanos, which lie southward.

Petare was the largest town in Miranda at the last census, having then a population of nearly 7,000. It was founded on the Guaire, some seven miles east of Carácas, in 1704, and is a locally important manufacturing town, turning out principally *alpargatas*, cigarettes, and starch, the last named made from yuca or manioc.

This town was the first terminus of the Central Railway of Venezuela, which was projected by Guzman Blanco to travel south-eastward from Carácas down the Guaire to its junction with the Tuy, then up the larger river westwards and down the Aragua to Valencia. At present it has only reached Santa Lucia, rather more than thirty miles from Carácas, and the direct German line has done away with the necessity of carrying it through to Valencia. The prosperous nature of the country under Guzman Blanco made the enterprise extremely promising, but the long series of revolutions and counter-revolutions since his day have kept the freight down to a minimum. Better days may be in store for the line, however, when the owners of the rich coffee, cocoa, and sugar lands which it taps rise to their opportunities, and an extension to Ocumare should bring it an ever-increasing amount of traffic in the produce of the Llanos.

All the way along the Valley of the Guaire the hills are, in the season, white with the coffee-bloom, and the small patches of yuca, maize, and bananas may yet become big and profitable plantations. Beyond Santa Lucia the

Guaire joins the Tuy, and here, in a broad, flat-bottomed valley full of sugar and cacao, stands Santa Teresa.

If we follow down the fertile valley of the Tuy we come at length to the barren, sandy stretch along the coast and its fringe of mangroves, where we encounter the second railway (a rather primitive affair) in the State.

The line crosses the river at right angles, and connects the port of Carenero with the little town of Higuerote, a few miles to the south, and with the flourishing manufacturing town of Rio Chico, south of the Tuy; beyond them it is continued to Guapo, on the way to the Llanos of Guárico. Rio Chico is therefore about twenty-four miles by rail from its port, even though the open sea is but four miles away. Here we are down at sea-level, and the mean annual temperature is 82° F. Its position at the edge of the rich alluvium of the Tuy brings it large quantities of coffee, cocoa, beans, and maize, which are easily transmitted by rail to Carenero, and thence conveyed in little schooners or steamers to La Guaira for use in the country or for export. More important to its welfare are the cattle of the Llanos, whose hides are similarly passed on through Carenero to La Guaira, while the carcasses provide the raw material for the manufacture of soap and candles, which, with the making of alpargatas, constitutes the chief industry of the town.

Returning to Santa Teresa, we can traverse the plantations to Ocumare, the capital, and beyond to Cúa, named after a famous Indian cacique. Beyond this there are no towns of importance east of the State boundary, but a road over the watershed leads to Los Teques, at the head of the Guaire. This stands at a considerably greater altitude than Carácas, and is chiefly of importance to-day as a health resort, though when Faxardo first visited the Indians after whom the place is named, in the sixteenth century, he was attracted by the copper-mines of the district, now no longer worked.

Los Teques is the first town of importance on the Great Venezuelan Railway (a German line) west of Carácas, but it is the last in the State of Miranda. The train climbs up a picturesque gorge to Los Teques, then passes through a tunnel, and begins to cross by equally picturesque loops and zigzags the head of the Tuy, finally dropping down into the fertile valley of Aragua, from which the next State takes its name. The western terminus of the line is Valencia, but the first large town reached is La Victoria (much beloved of ex-President Castro), the capital of Aragua.

All along the line are evidences of the agriculture and sylvan wealth of the land, in coffee and sugar-plantations, and patches of forest of valuable timber. La Victoria is a well-built, handsome town. It was founded in 1593 and had a population of over 14,000 at the last census. The barracks form an imposing block of buildings, and there are factories on a small scale for cigarettes, paper, sandals, boots and shoes, and candles. The tobacco and wood for the two first come from plantations and forests close at hand, and the considerable traffic from the Llanos, as well as the pasture-lands of the Aragua Valley farther west, supply the raw materials for the other articles. There is a mill here also which uses the cotton of the drier parts of the valley, near the Lake of Valencia. The railway, both before and after La Victoria, passes many cane plantations with small refineries and distilleries, turning out the raw sugar and spirit which constitute an important part of the trade of the town. A good deal of wheat used to be grown here, the fields producing as much as 3,000 pounds to the acre, a sixteen-fold return, which would surely pay well to-day, when the heavy duty on imported flour (about 1d. per lb.) is considered.

Maracay, also on the railway, near the east end of the Lake of Valencia, is in a splendid farming and stock-breeding country. There are rich grazing lands planted with pará grass, forest for timber, and coffee, sugar, indigo of excellent quality, and tobacco, as well as cotton, can be grown in the vicinity. The dairies of Maracay produce a famous cream-cheese, known by the name of the town throughout Venezuela, and the hogs of Maracay are very different from the skinny animals generally seen in the tropics. President Gomez has a ranch here, to which he retires whenever allowed a respite from cares of State.

South of Maracay at a distance of about fifteen miles is the main pass across the Serrania Interior to the Llanos, and in this pass stands the important town of Villa de Cura, founded in 1730. It is a well-built town, standing between two rivers flowing in opposite directions; the valley itself is dry compared to that of Aragua, but has many big cattle-ranches, so that here, as at Maracay, cheese and hides form the principal articles of commerce. Since it derives a certain amount of profit from the cacao and coffee of the mills near by, it forms in itself an epitome of the wealth of the State of Aragua, which, with its fertile valleys, combines the products of the hills and forests with those of the neighbouring Llanos.

The beautiful Lake of Valencia, with its many islands, lies partly in Aragua and partly in the neighbouring State of Carabobo. The dry, sandy shores are mainly utilised for cotton-growing, an industry which, like many others in Venezuela, has never received the attention which it deserves, because an ample return on capital can be had in a multitude of enterprises for a minimum expenditure of labour and forethought.

In Carabobo we begin to leave the more densely populated region of the Centro, and find something of the wildness of virgin territory away from the towns. Thus we have timber and dye-woods and uncultivated rubber exported as well as the products of the pastoral and agricultural industries.

The capital of the State is Valencia, once greater and more important than it is now, much of the produce of Aragua which formerly passed through the city being carried eastward by the Great Venezuelan Railway, while the Bolivar Railway now carries direct to and from Barquisimeto goods which in earlier days came in and passed out through Valencia. The industry of the inhabitants has saved the place from absolute decay, and the population at the last census was over 54,000.

As we have already seen, Valencia is connected with the capital by rail, and there is a cart-road for slow traffic, while the Telephone Company has a line as far as Puerto Cabello, passing through Valencia. For its internal comfort, the city has a good supply of water brought by aqueduct from the hills, tramways, electric light, hotels, and plazas. The public buildings include the State Capitol and Municipal Theatre, and there is a column in the Plaza Bolivar commemorating the battle on the *campo* from which the State takes its name. The large cotton-mills testify to an attempt to develop the resources of the neighbourhood; flour-mills and cigarette-factories deal with some of the produce of the fertile valleys to the west. Coffee, sugar, alcohol, live beasts and hides, with other agricultural products, all find their way to the markets of Valencia; nor should the marble quarries of the hills be forgotten, since the country may one day use more of its own ornamental stones in place of importing them over the high tariff wall.

Twenty-three miles westward from Valencia (which by the way, is unusually hot for its elevation) is the town of Montalbán, higher up in the hills, with a population of nearly 9,000. It was named after Montalbán in Aragon, and rejoices in a mean annual temperature of 73°F. On the fertile river banks the Montalbanians used once to grow excellent grapes, as well as wheat and indigo of fine quality. With the introduction of coffee in 1813, it was found more profitable to devote the land to that, and the cultivation of the fruit, for which it was formerly famous, has died out.

The river-valleys and mountain-slopes of Carabobo are often forest-covered, and wild rubber is sufficiently common to be collected. From all the western region of the State the produce of field and farm is brought by road to Valencia, and thence, if intended for export, sent down the English railway to Puerto Cabello.

This line was begun during the construction of that from La Guaira to Carácas, but presented in some respects a less difficult task, since the highest point to which it must rise to cross the watershed of the coastal cordillera is only 1,950 feet above the sea. The original scheme of ordinary traction was changed to include a short piece of 8 per cent. grade with a rack engine, working on a cogged centre rail, the rest of the descent is then easily accomplished.

Puerto Cabello has one of the best harbours in Venezuela, which possesses the additional merit of being entirely natural. The name is a witness to the excellence of the shelter, since the Spaniards changed Borburata to Cabello in token of the fact that in calm waters of the harbour a ship would be held with a hair (Sp. *Cabello*). On the outer side are the red iron-roofed buildings of the Venezuela Naval Dockyard, next door to the fortress, the submarine dungeons of which have too often been occupied by innocent men, both in colonial and republican times. Through Puerto Cabello is exported most of the produce of Carabobo, Yaracuy, and the Llano States of Cojedes and Portuguesa, with some from Lara, Trujillo, and Mérida. The new buildings of the Venezuela Meat Syndicate are near the station, an enterprise which seems likely, when once fairly started, to give Puerto Cabello an increasing importance, in addition to encouraging improvement in stock-farming. The various members of the staff make up a small English colony, who are largely responsible for the presence of English papers in the waterside club, a pleasant place to spend the sultry evenings.

Round about the port there are numbers of attractive villas and plantations, but the most fruitful land is in the neighbourhood of Ocumare, some twenty miles eastward along the coast. The town is situated near the mouth of a deep valley, and, but for the sea breezes, would be unbearably hot. As it is, the climate which would, untempered, be so unpleasant for men, is excellent for cocoa, and that of Ocumare has a deserved fame. From the higher lands behind come cattle and cereals to swell the trade of the town, whose population has increased greatly since the last census.

The agricultural resources of the "Centro" have received, as we have seen, a moderate share of attention, and if they are not developed to anything approaching a full extent, the region is nevertheless one in which less remains to be done than elsewhere in the republic. There are said to be "mines" of all manner of metals unworked as yet, particularly in the west, but without months of work by a mining engineer it would be impossible to verify such a statement. At present all that can be said is that it may be true, and perhaps some day the copper, silver, iron, and gold of the Centro will be established realities, and not mere words in "accusations" of territory for mining purposes.

MARACAIBO BAY.

SAN TIMOTEO: LAKE OF MARACAIBO.

CHAPTER IX
ZULIA

The Lake of Coquibacoa in the sixteenth century and now—Wealth and importance of the State—Area and population—Waterways—Forests—Mineral wealth—Savannahs—Maracaibo—Harbour and dredging schemes—Cojoro—Wharves and warehouses of Maracaibo—Exports—Population—German colony—Buildings—Industries—Tramways—*Coches*—Lake steamers—Ancient craft—The comedy of the bar—Railways—Communication with Colombia—Altagracia—Santa Rita—A western Gibraltar—An eventful history—San Carlos de Zulia—Sinamaica—Vegetable milk—Timber—Copaiba—Fisheries—The "Maracaibo lights."

When Alonso de Ojeda, first of all Europeans, entered what was then the Lake of Coquibacoa, he was chiefly struck by the unusual appearance of the Indian huts, built on platforms over the shallow waters, and were it possible for any one to-day to cruise round the "lake" without observing the port of Maracaibo, he might come away with the impression that the greater part of the State of Zulia has not changed since the sixteenth century. Strangely enough, this impression would not be far from the truth as regards the extent of cultivation and settlement, and yet, thanks to the great fertility of the soil in these steaming lowlands, and to the commercial importance of the capital, the State of Zulia is already one of the most important and wealthy in the Union of Venezuela.

The area within its boundaries amounts to some 23,000 square miles, the greater part of which is inhabited (if we except the concentrated populations of Maracaibo and the Goajira territory) by about 56,000 souls. Even if we take the total population the density is but 6·4 to the square mile, in a State whose resources might support with ease ten times that number, while its death-rate is one of the lowest in the republic.

Among the most valuable assets of the State are its abundant waterways. Not only is the central part occupied by a brackish-water lake on which small *goletas* or schooners and steamers can ply, but through the level plains around flow innumerable rivers, most of which are navigable for the greater part of their length. The forests which cover much of the area are at once a benefit and a hindrance to progress, the valuable timber and natural products to be found there being only in part a compensation for the obstacle they present to the increase of the much more valuable cultivated fruits. It would be a matter for regret were the forests to be indiscriminately cut down, but the absence of clearings is not due to any prudential reasons of this sort.

While the other resources of Zulia have received more or less attention, its mines, for one reason or another, have never been developed. Yet indications of petroleum or asphalt and outcrops of coal are to be met with all round the lake. The *salinas* near Maracaibo are not mines in the normal sense of the word, but in so far as their product is a mineral, it may be said that this is an exception to the rule, the salt of Zulia being well known in the Andes and Colombia.

The savannahs which here and there break the forest on both sides of the lake, and especially on the lower slopes of the Serrania del Empalado to the east, provide pasturage for many head of cattle, and in the north goat-farming is extensively carried on.

The port through which all these products are, or might be, transmitted to the outside world was first founded by Alfinger in 1529, but the original town fell into decay, and the present city dates back to 1571, when Don Alonso Pacheco founded it as Nueva Zamora; as usual, the Indian name soon ousted the Spanish title. To-day it is the second port of the republic, and has a larger export trade than La Guaira.

The beautiful bay, with its wharves and smooth roadstead, makes a splendid harbour, but the difficult navigation of the mouth of the lake presents a hindrance ever increasing in magnitude with the silting up of the bar. Schemes have been advanced for dredging one of the four channels and so providing a permanent entrance for the kind of steamer which at present reaches Maracaibo. The alternative idea of utilising the fine natural harbour of Cojoro on the Gulf of Venezuela and connecting this with the capital by means of a railway, appears much more satisfactory, since in this way the increasing volume of exports from Zulia and the Andes could be brought to a port capable of accommodating the largest of ocean-going steamers. The length of this line would be some 100 miles.

The foreign trade of Maracaibo is at present carried by the National boat *Venezuela* or by the boats of the American Red D Line, which in many cases transfer them to other lines in Curaçao; the greater part of the exported produce is carried by sailing-boats. The wharves and warehouses are under public control, and there is a fixed scale of charges from 65 centimos per 100 kilos. for exported goods to B12.0 for imported goods destined for merchants in Maracaibo or in transit to Colombia. The last-named trade is very considerable, as all the foreign goods consumed in the province of Santander enter through Maracaibo. The chief exports are coffee, cocoa, quinine, copaiba-balsam, dye-woods, sugar, and hides.

If one ignores the fact that the great majority of the streets of Maracaibo are as Nature made them, it is possible to admire the extent of the city and flourishing aspect of the port, but on a hot afternoon (and this is worse than

La Guaira for heat) the dusty walk or drive to one's hotel does not add to the pleasure of the first experience of the place. The city had a population of 34,740 at the last census, but there must now be nearly half as many again living in the capital.

There are no Anglo-Saxons at present in Maracaibo, the larger business houses being entirely managed, though not always owned, by Germans, from all of whom, including the British Vice-Consul, Mr. Schröder, our party met with the greatest kindness. The town being built for use rather than ornament, there are no public buildings of particularly striking appearance. The Legislative and Municipal Palaces in the Plaza Bolivar and the spired church of the Immaculate Conception are among the most noticeable buildings. There are hospitals and two clubs, and the Teatro and Plaza Baralt, with many statues, keep in memory the name of one of Maracaibo's most famous citizens, who wrote the first comprehensive history of Venezuela.

Factories for candles, soap, hats, boots, tanneries, and saw-mills are among the more prominent industries of Maracaibo, whose products command a sale in Colombia as well as in Venezuela.

The town has a well-equipped electric light plant, a tramway to the south of the town, which is shortly to be electrified, another out to the Bella Vista suburb, worked by steam, a more or less efficient water supply, and restaurants, shops, and other means of administration to the public comfort, not to mention *coches* equal to those of Carácas. The chief needs of the city are really efficient water supply, paving and drainage systems; with these it ought to be, though hot, one of the healthiest cities of the republic; as it is, the death-rate is high.

From Maracaibo steamers and sailing craft of all kinds travel to points of the lake shore, and in some cases far up the larger rivers to the ports of the Andine States and Colombia. The steamers plying on the lake include some venerable hulks, whose passage through the water is accompanied by painful groans and sobs from the ancient engines; one of those which still makes the trip to Encontrados, on the Catatumbo, is mentioned by Dr. Sievers as working when he visited the region in 1884. The charges for freight and passengers are in inverse proportion to the efficiency of the boats.

There are two main lines of steamers from the capital, one travelling along the western side of the lake and then up the Catatumbo to Encontrados, the port of Táchira; the other crossing diagonally to La Ceiba, where the railway from Motatán in Trujillo reaches the shore. A smaller boat travels round the southern end of the lake, connecting the mouth of the Catatumbo and La Ceiba with Santa Barbara on the Escalante, where a railway was once built part of the way to Mérida. There is a bar at the mouth of the Catatumbo, and in consequence of this the smaller steamer is always there awaiting the arrival of the large boat from Maracaibo. If there is much cargo, some of it is transhipped outside the bar and reloaded when the lightened vessel has successfully navigated the shallow water. Often a whole day is wasted over this performance, and one cannot help thinking that if the dredging of a channel would be more expensive it would at least be less ludicrous.

Of the railways mentioned in connection with the lines of steamers, that from La Ceiba is wholly in the State of Trujillo, but the others traverse a considerable extent of the forests of Zulia before entering the Andine States. The metre-gauge line from Santa Barbara was originally intended to reach Mérida by way of the Chama Valley, but it only reached El Vigia, on that river, and has now fallen into disrepair. The Encontrados line or Gran Ferrocarril del Táchira, also a Venezuelan concern, has a 1·07-metre track, and is intended ultimately to reach San Cristobal; passing as it does through great stretches of virgin forest on the banks of the Zulia, it has already done much to open up this country to cultivation, and ends at present in the coffee-bearing foothills of the Andes. From Encontrados a line of small steamers carries merchandise on up the Zulia River to the Colombian port of Villamizar.

While the majority of settlements round the lake consist of a few palm-leaf huts, or houses on piles in the ancient fashion of the Indians, there are several towns of more or less importance. Altagracia, immediately opposite Maracaibo on the eastern shore, is the largest of these, and has a considerable importance on account of the agricultural products of its surroundings, with a fleet of fishing-boats, whose catches are sold in the town and thence shipped into the interior. Santa Rita, not far to the south, is in the midst of a fine goat-farming district, and the coco-palms along the lake shores are cultivated with great profit.

At the extreme south-east corner of the lake there is a hamlet which bears a famous name, and has itself been of note in Venezuelan history. This is Gibraltar, founded by Gonzalo Piña Lidueña, afterwards Governor of the province, in 1597. It is said that during the night when he camped at this spot there was a total eclipse of the moon, reminding him of a bivouac at Gibraltar in Spain, where he had last seen the phenomenon; as a result he named the new settlement after the famous rock. The fertile lands around were so excellent for cacao and tobacco that the place soon became important, and substantial buildings were erected to accommodate the increasing population. Before long it was sacked and reduced to ruins by the Motilones Indians, but in 1666 was again so flourishing that the pirate Henry Morgan considered it worth taking, and the town, which had again grown up in 1678, was sacked a third time by Gramont. From one cause and another, chiefly the disturbances during the revolution against Spain, the place became deserted, and now only a few huts amid the ruins of the old stone buildings mark the site of the city, while the cacao and tobacco plantations have, through neglect, lost their prestige or been swallowed up by forest.

San Carlos de Zulia, on the Escalante, is important by virtue of the through traffic from the haciendas in the interior to the shores of the lake, but it is not attractive, being, like the port of Encontrados, an insanitary, unhealthy, riverside village rather than a town.

North of the cultivated lands on the west shore near Maracaibo, opposite the entrance of the lake, we have open, dry lands where the salt-pans are to be found, and on a lagoon in these plains stands Sinamaica, interesting for the Goajiro population, who preserve their primitive customs alongside the civilisation of the town.

In the forests south-west of the capital occurs the peculiar *arbol de leche*, whose sap can be used in every way like cow's milk, though it is slightly thicker. Here and elsewhere the woods are full of valuable timber (mahogany, ebony, lignum-vitæ) and of useful creepers and trees like that which furnishes the copaiba-balsam. These represent to a great extent the undeveloped resources of the State, and side by side with them must be considered the many varieties of fishes inhabiting the waters of the gulf and lake, only a few of which are caught at the present time.

No account of the Zulian region could omit a reference to the famous "Maracaibo lights," or *farol de Maracaibo*, the flash of which can be seen far out at sea and is used by mariners out of range of any of the lighthouses. This vivid and continuous lightning is to be seen nightly over the south end of the lake, and is generally described as visible over the mouth of the Catatumbo. The flashes seem, however, rather to extend all along the line of the mountains, which rise a few miles from the lake to a height of fourteen or fifteen thousand feet. A possible explanation seems to be the following: As the atmosphere over the bare mountains cools rapidly at sunset the heavily-charged hot air of the basin-like depression of Maracaibo rises, so that masses of air at different potentials meet at a great height and emit huge sparks visible for hundreds of miles. Whether this be so or not, it is a fact that the flashes are visible nightly from sunset until sunrise, with little variation in brilliance.

CHAPTER X
THE ANDINE STATES
Táchira, Mérida, and Trujillo

Access—Roads versus railways—Mineral wealth—Maracaibo coffee—
Forests—San Cristobal—Water supply—Industries—Roads—Rubio—
Táchira Petroleum Company—San Antonio—Lobatera—Colón—
Interrupted communications—Pregonero—El Cobre—Old mines—La
Grita—Seboruco copper—Mérida—The Bishop and the Bible—Eternal
snows—Earthquakes—Electric light—Road schemes—Gold and silver—
Lagunillas—*Urao*—Wayside hospitality—Puente Real—Primitive modes of
transport—Las Laderas—The Mucuties Valley—Tovar—Mucuchíes—The
highest town in Venezuela—The *páramos*—Timotes—Trujillo—Valera—
Water supply—La Ceiba Railway—Betijoque and Escuque—Boconó—
Santa Ana—Carache—Unknown regions—Possibilities of the Andes.

Were I asked which of all the regions of Venezuela I thought the most
attractive and interesting to the general traveller, I should have little
hesitation in replying, "The Andes." The three mountain States constitute a
territory where, along with an appreciable extent of development, there is a
complete absence of the commonplace both in the country and its people.
The deep valleys and gorges and snow-clad peaks, with towns and cities
perched on mountain-sides and gravel plateaux, might be paralleled
elsewhere in South America but not in this republic, and though the
inhabitants of the towns have often travelled in America and Europe on
modern steamers and trains, to reach their homes they have, like their less
aspiring countrymen, to jog on mule-back for many leagues over rough
mountain paths which lead them frequently along precipices and through all
but unfordable rivers, and are marked by crosses commemorating the violent
deaths of previous travellers. It is a region where, a few miles from the towns,
are great stretches of unknown uplands and forest-clad slopes, unexplored
territory side by side with the habitation of some of the most industrious
communities of the republic.

The Andes may be reached from the north via the Bolivar Railway and from
Maracaibo either by way of La Ceiba, whence the railway brings the traveller
into the foothills of Trujillo at the north end, or by Encontrados, when he
enters Táchira, the most southerly of the trio of States. There is a fourth
route along the disused railway from Santa Barbara, on the Escalante, up the
valley of the Chama and so into Mérida, but this is best avoided by those
who do not hanker after unnecessary discomforts and the less pleasant type
of adventure. Within the Andes proper everything is carried on mules, and
on the narrow paths one has continually to pass or be passed by trains of

laden beasts, bearing the produce of the hills and valleys or the imported wares of Europe and America.

Over the swiftest and deepest rivers there are generally bridges, but a stream flooded by heavy rain may hold one up for a week or more, and where the track is along the sides of precipitous ravines wash-outs and landslides are often serious obstacles. Despite the industry of the inhabitants, the primitive character of the roads in the Andes is a great hindrance to adequate development of the country, and when one hears of machinery for use in Mérida taking a year to get there from the terminus of the La Ceiba Railway one wonders that the prominence of the Andinos in politics has not secured for their States some beginning of a system of adequate roads suitable for wheel traffic. Railways have been projected, but the cost of building these in virgin country generally renders the freights so high that they do little or nothing for development. Roads may appeal less to the imagination than the more modern means of communication, but there can be little doubt that the often despised road in a country like Venezuela would for a time be a better investment for public, if not for private, capital.

A STREET IN LA GRITA.

PUENTE REAL: GORGE OF THE CHAMA.

The mineral wealth of the Andes is as yet practically untouched, yet copper and silver are known to occur in Táchira and Mérida; gold is said to have been found in the latter, and coal and petroleum occur in all three States.

The Andine States include some of the best coffee-lands in the republic, and Maracaibo coffee, as it is called, enjoys great favour in the United States. In the warmer regions good cocoa can be grown, while wheat is common in the upper temperate zones. Tobacco also flourishes in Mérida and Trujillo.

The forests of the mountain-flanks add to the botanic wealth of the region mahogany, ebony, lignum-vitæ, quinine, dividive, and many other valuable products hardly exploited as yet.

For population and revenue Trujillo stands first of the Andine States, Táchira second, and Mérida, though the largest in area, third. For convenience of description we will consider them in geographical order, beginning from the south.

The capital of Táchira is San Cristobal, founded on the left bank of the River Torbes by Juan Maldonado in 1561. Although, in approaching the town, the traveller who does not trace his route on a map would consider himself still on the Maracaibo side of the watershed, the waters of the Torbes flow round the mountains behind the town to join the Uribante, a sub-tributary of the Orinoco. The main watershed of the Venezuelan Andes at this point is probably less than 4,000 feet above the sea, and San Cristobal is well situated in respect of through traffic from the western Llanos to Zulia or Colombia. Despite its political importance, therefore, its aspect is in the main that of a busy commercial town situated in a fruitful valley.

As in all the Andine towns, the question of water supply is settled with comparative ease by leading water down from a spring or stream above and allowing this to follow stone channels in the centre of the cobbled streets, while side channels behind and under the houses provide continuously flushed drains emptying into the river. The system is not always as well or elaborately worked as in San Cristobal, but in essentials it is the same throughout the region. In addition to its through trade the town has several flourishing industries, not least of which is the manufacture of vermicelli, or *fideos*, used extensively, if not perpetually, in the soups of this part of the country; the beasts and stock products from the Llanos provide in addition raw materials for making candles and soap, as well as for the tanneries in the neighbourhood.

From San Cristobal roads lead to San Antonio on the Colombian frontier; to the Llanos down the Torbes and Quinimari valleys; to Uracá, the terminus of the Táchira Railway; and to Mérida.

San Cristobal being built on the slope of a steep range of hills, with a river flowing in a semicircle in front, it is impossible to leave the town on any of the main routes without crossing water, somewhat of a difficulty when unbridged streams are flooded. On the road which leads to Colombia, however, there is a bridge over the Torbes, which enables communications to be maintained at all seasons.

Fifteen miles down the valley to the south is the flourishing little town of Rubio, surrounded by some of the biggest and best coffee estates in the country, fitted with modern plant for handling the beans. Coal and, it is said, silver are to be found near by, and the Táchira Petroleum Company, a local affair, has produced and sold small quantities of illuminating oil in the neighbourhood for many years.

A good deal of the produce of these parts is shipped through Colombia in bond to avoid the additional, and often difficult, length of road to Uracá. San Antonio is the frontier town on the River Táchira, both river and State taking their name from a frontier Indian tribe; here is the terminus of the English railway which runs through Cúcuta to Puerto Villamizar. Once cocoa, coffee, and indigo were the chief products of the neighbourhood, but now, with the growth of Cúcuta and San Cristobal, it has been found more profitable to use the lands for grazing or for sugar.

The other main export route from the capital of Táchira passes through the small towns of Lobatera and Colón to Uracá, the terminus of the Táchira Railway leading to Encontrados in Zulia. Lobatera itself is something over 3,000 feet above the sea, on the Maracaibo side of the watershed, up to which the white road zigzags behind the town. Its productions are said to have decreased of late years, but I have pleasant recollections of the agreeable impression produced by these clean and apparently prosperous towns of Táchira, on first arriving there from the lowlands of Zulia, with their miserable huts and muddy, insanitary villages. People, housing, and food alike seemed vastly improved. Colón is the half-way house for arrivals from Uracá, and as a result has several *hoteles*. It is a neat, well-built little town, the surrounding hills and plateaux being chiefly devoted to stock-farming. Some ten miles to the north is the railway terminus in the small town of Uracá, on the edge of the hot lands and very damp in consequence, the mists banking up in the narrow valley nightly; coffee and cocoa seem to be the chief products of the neighbourhood.

Both the Encontrados road and that to Mérida pass through the little town of Táriba, about three miles east of San Cristobal, on the north bank of the Torbes. There are no bridges here over the stream, and as a result in time of floods would-be travellers are penned up in San Cristobal, for on both roads one must ford the stream below the town, and on the way to Mérida, a second ford is necessary immediately above; at the latter there is a foot bridge, and when the Torbes is in flood the mules are fairly hauled across the stream on a rope; the strong currents would otherwise carry them down over the rocks. It is interesting to watch and follow a man who knows these fords as he pricks his way along through the shallows, but they are a great hindrance to traffic.

Up the Torbes Valley and across the páramo of El Zumbador (8,000 feet), a day's ride brings one to La Grita (I shall have to refer to páramos again later on). Near the watershed a road branches off to the east to Pregonero, capital of the Uribante district, in a valley whose products range from potatoes and wheat at the top to coffee and sugar at the bottom; out on the plains, too, there are big cattle-ranches whence comes much of the meat consumed in the Andine towns. The district needs roads for its development, and at present is rather an isolated, unvisited region.

Vargas or El Cobre is a pleasant little village on the northern or western side of the pass, and its alternative name is said to refer to mines of copper in the hills near by worked by the Spaniards, who made the bells of the little church from the metal.

Forty miles is the estimated distance from Táriba to La Grita, but the road is sufficiently good to make it seem shorter, and the view up the valley, with mountains rising tier upon tier into the clouds, is superb. The town was founded in 1576, on a gravel *mesa* or tableland, necessitated a steep climb before actually entering the town. Its position makes it peculiarly subject to earthquake shocks, but in spite of this the old churches and Government buildings are still standing. The many stores are an indication of the importance of La Grita as a market town, and on Sunday one finds the streets full of countrymen in charge of mules laden with the wheat, wool, tobacco, and cotton of the surrounding country. At 6,000 feet above the sea, the town has the reputation of being one of the healthiest in Venezuela, and certainly the apples, apricots, and peaches in the patios, with roses and violets beneath them, are a pleasant sight to the man from the north, who has found the "luscious fruits" and gorgeous flowers of the tropics a snare and delusion. A few miles down the river towards Uracá is Seboruco, with its copper-mines, soon, it is said, to be worked again. Not far above the town is the Pass of Portachuelo, which marks the boundary with Mérida, the central of the three Andine States.

Mérida is the mountain State *par excellence* of Venezuela, including within its boundaries the highest peaks and some of the hottest valleys in the country. With this variety of climate it is natural that the range of products should be wide, but bad roads and resulting high cost of transport have kept the country largely undeveloped.

The capital was founded in 1542 under the lengthy appellation of Santiago de los Caballeros de Mérida, and it has long been the seat of the Bishop of the Andes. A colporteur having recently been found in the diocese selling Bibles, the energetic occupant of the see promptly excommunicated him and all who had purchased the forbidden books; his zeal, however, seems merely to have rendered more marked the indifference of the male portion of the population to public religion of any kind.

The city is built on a high plateau like that of La Grita between the Rivers Mucujun and Chama, and towering above it to the east is the white-topped Sierra Nevada, while a lower but equally steep range bounds the valley to the west. The snow on the Sierras is said to have been retreating of recent years, but there are still perpetual snow-fields and glaciers round the summits, the permanent line being now at about 15,000 feet. The city has often suffered severe damage from earthquakes, but new buildings have always quickly taken the place of those destroyed. Partly, probably, on account of the humidity of the atmosphere of the valley, Mérida has a somewhat deserted look with its grass-grown streets, yet there are looms turning out cotton and woollen cloth, and it is an important market centre for the coffee, wheat, and sugar from the various zones in its neighbourhood.

The torrent of the Chama immediately above Mérida has been requisitioned to supply power for an electric lighting system in the city. The turbines were brought at great trouble and expense over the mountain track from La Ceiba, the journey occupying about a year, but in view of the determination which carried through such an enterprise, it is to be regretted that the results are not more impressive. Strings of three or four bulbs each across the street at regular intervals might provide an efficient light, but as a matter of fact they do not, the total number of lamps being far in excess of the capabilities of the present turbine installation, though much below the available water-power. As a result, while one may have the electric light in the house, it is better to resort to the homely candle for reading or writing after sunset.

What is chiefly needed for Mérida to-day is a good road to connect it with the lake, across which all the produce of the region has to travel to the sea. Long ago the project was formed of building a railway along the Chama Valley to connect with Santa Barbara on the Escalante, but the engineering difficulties in the gorges would probably prevent the carrying out of any such scheme just yet; a second idea, which has never received much attention, was to carry a line up the Mucujun, and so over the pass of the outer range of the Cordillera to Bobures, on the lake, a feasible scheme enough, though at the present stage a road would better supply the need of the place.

There have, from time to time, been reports of mines in the Sierra, but the best authenticated occurrence is that of gold and silver, near Estanques, on the main road to the lowlands; these deposits have never been worked, as far as I could ascertain. The chief assets of the district are at present the fertile lands of the Chama and tributary valleys. Down the former, on the way to Ejido, about seven miles from the capital, the road passes all the way through coffee and cacao plantations, with some open pasture-lands; beyond Ejido the valley becomes more and more barren towards Lagunillas, famed for its mineral lake, containing large quantities of *urao* or trona. The view over this little town to the snow-clad peaks above Mérida is very fine in the early morning, but the place seems to have little commerce. I must not omit mention of a pleasant incident which occurred near Lagunillas, showing the hospitable temper of the Andinos. We asked at a wayside store (empty of goods) if we might buy some of the oranges growing profusely in their garden. "With great pleasure," said the proprietor, and brought us chairs that we might dismount and rest. Presently came plates of oranges cut up into a salad, a very welcome dish in these hot valleys. "And the charge?" we asked. "Nada, señores." Nor would our kind hosts accept a centimo. We knew they would not have eaten the fruit themselves, but the spirit of hospitality was the same.

Two or three miles below Lagunillas is one of the worst bits of road in the Andes, and yet it is on the main route to the south. First, a descent down a steep zigzag brings one to a picturesque wooden bridge over the torrent of the Chama, giving the name to the group of houses near by of Puente Real. Not many years ago travellers and their baggage were taken over the stream in a sort of breeches-buoy, while their mules were dragged through the swift current below, and often only landed with difficulty far down on the opposite bank; the bridge is at least an advance on this primitive mode of transit.

The bottom of the bare steep-sided ravine is hot and dusty, and on the far side, after a mile or two, the road begins to follow the nearly vertical side, finally narrowing down to a mere path, with a precipice into the torrent below. This lasts for some four or five miles, and the whole stretch takes its name from the most unpleasant part of all, *Las Laderas*, or "the steeps," just before the San Pablo tributary enters from the south. Here the height of the road above the stream gradually increases, until at length the descent to the side valley is accomplished in a short distance by what is practically a staircase of loose rock, buttressed with logs, while there is a sheer drop on the offside into the foaming torrent beneath; not a pleasant place on a dry day, and almost impassable on a wet one. Once at the bottom, the rest of the way, until more open valleys are reached, is a precipice road, generally, but not always, wide enough for two mules to pass.

Beyond Estanques the main valley narrows down to a gorge, but the road climbs over the hills to the side, and at length descends past a tile and brick making yard to the hot valley of the Mucuties with its cacao plantations. A picturesque bridge across the river leads to the parting of the roads, one going up the Mucuties to Tovar, the other down the Chama Valley to El Vigia, and so to the Zulia plains.

Tovar forms a local market-centre for the produce of the cocoa and coffee plantations of the valley, but beyond it Bailadores marks the downward limit of the wheatfields which make the top of the Mucuties ravine almost like a European landscape in time of harvest.

Northward of Mérida, the Chama Valley has some coffee plantations, but the road soon leaves these, and at Mucuchíes, the highest town in Venezuela (10,000 feet), we are in the region of pasture-land and potatoes, even wheat being absent in these high altitudes. There are a few scattered houses above Mucuchíes, one of which is a small inn known as Los Apartaderos, the best stopping-place to ensure a calm crossing of the pass next day, the winds rising normally towards midday.

These high exposed passes are known in Venezuela as *páramos*, a word as to whose precise meaning some doubt appears to exist, though Humboldt's definition as "all passes above 1,800-2,200 Toises above the sea, where inclement rough weather prevails," seems to cover the present use of the word. The páramo of Mucuchíes or Timotes over which passes the main road between Mérida and Trujillo is the highest in the Venezuelan Andes, the big wooden cross at the summit being about 14,500 feet above the sea. In the rainy season, owing to the dense mass of clouds on the pass, it is often deep in snow, and woe betide the unlucky traveller whose mule becomes *paramada* then! The verb derived from the generic name of these high passes is often applied jokingly to an individual who has merely got wet through and is cold and uncomfortable.

At Timotes, the first town on the north side of the pass, the tropical plants begin again to make their appearance, but the valley is chiefly occupied by grazing land, as far, at least, as the boundary of Trujillo.

The most northerly State of the trio is far more temperate in its general aspect than Mérida, though in Trujillo also there are páramos as well as tropical lowlands. The chief products are coffee and sugar, and while Mérida has its metallic ores, the most notable minerals here are coal and petroleum.

The capital dates back to 1556, and has been the scene of many notable events in the history of Venezuela, while its commercial prosperity tempted Gramont to march from La Ceiba and sack the town in 1678. It stands in a valley alone, surrounded by coffee plantations and canefields, which provide the principal articles of commerce in its markets. As is the case with San Cristobal, a ford on the main road to its port makes communications uncertain, although there is a second but difficult track over the hills which can be used in emergencies; either route means about twenty-five miles to Motatán and the same distance on a branch road to Valera, an important town on the road to Mérida.

THE SIERRA NEVADA AND CATHEDRAL OF MÉRIDA.

Although Trujillo is the capital of the State and Motatán the present terminus of the La Ceiba Railway, it is in Valera that most of the important commerce of the State is carried on, a fact due, on the one hand, to the more advantageous position of the town in regard to the fertile valley of the foothills, on the other, to its age in comparison with Motatán, regarded as only the temporary terminus. Sugar and coffee estates, bearing evidence of prosperity in their appearance, occupy the valley in which the town of Valera lies, and the produce of these, as well as that from the regions around, passes through the hands of the merchants of the place on its way to Maracaibo. There are some hot springs near by, but so far Valera has acquired no fame as a health resort. There is a good water supply from mountain streams far up the valley, brought to the town through cisterns and mains, arranged by its energetic citizen Señor Antonio Braschi, who, like many of the prospering merchants and professional men of Trujillo, Zulia, and Mérida, claims Italy as his mother country.

The La Ceiba Railway was built with the aid of Venezuelan capital, and is controlled by a local board of directors, though the actual construction of the line was carried out by French engineers. It is proposed to replace the wooden bridges by those of iron and to effect other improvements in the permanent way which will tend to avoid the occasional stoppages of the past.

Not far to the west of Valera are the towns of Betijoque and Escuque, both of considerable antiquity, situated in richly fertile valleys; near the former there are well-known oil-springs, so far not exploited, while the coffee of Escuque is of specially fine quality.

From the streets of Trujillo the hills can be followed with the eye to a pass, of threatening appearance when covered with heavy clouds, far to the south-east the Páramo de la Cristalina. Over this lies the way to Boconó, one of the most picturesquely situated towns in Venezuela in its fertile valley, which produces at different altitudes sugar, coffee, and wheat.

Following the road northward from Trujillo, down the valley and then up the *cuestas* (sharply zigzag roads up steep ascents), we come to Santa Ana, or Santana, a place famous in the history of the revolution as the meeting-place of Bolivar and Morillo after the declaration of the armistice. A column outside the town commemorates the event. It has little attraction to-day, save as a half-way house to Carache, being a small village situated on a cold and misty limestone ridge between two deep valleys.

Carache, beyond it, is near the north-east boundary of the State, and near also to the northern end of the Andine region proper. The dry valley in which the well-built little town stands seems fit to support only goats, a few cattle, and some cotton, but the hills and valleys round grow wheat, sugar, and coffee, giving business to more than one merchant in the town. From the bare hills behind the town a glimpse may often be obtained through the clouds of the Lake of Maracaibo far below the west, while over the clouds to the south are the peaks of the Cordillera, a splendid prospect on a suitable day.

North-west of Carache is an almost unexplored area, extending down the flanks of the Sierra del Empalado to the lake shore, one day, perhaps, to be visited and developed, but as yet hardly known save to those who cut dividive in the forests.

There must be great possibilities for such a region as that of the Andes, where much territory remains unexplored, while it includes, as it were, all the climates of the globe. Many plants have already been acclimatised, and of those whose cultivation is already carried on on a larger scale much more might be made; the coffee and cocoa of the moister tropical valleys, the wheat of the open higher zones, the possible cotton of the Chama, Carache, and other valleys are among their number. The possible culture of fruits of all kinds for which a demand might be expected in Venezuela generally as the country develops, and the less permanent resources of mines and forests, make an increasing prosperity for the Andine States almost assured, but adequate and permanent means of transport are required before they can be developed to their full extent. The long mule-trains on the mountain roads are picturesque, but roads fit for wheel traffic would leave these where desirable and yet provide the means of quicker and cheaper transit for the produce of the fertile valleys of the Cordillera.

CHAPTER XI
LARA, YARACUY, AND FALCÓN

The original Venezuela—Ancient cities—Communications—Barquisimeto—Fortified stores—Productions—The Bolivar Railway—Duaca—Aroa copper-mines—A precarious house-site—In the mine—Bats and cockroaches—"*El Purgatorio*"—Blue and green stalactites—San Felipe—The Yaracuy Valley—Nirgua—Yaritagua—Tocuyo—The "coach" to Barquisimeto—Quíbor—*Minas*—Carora—An ill-advised scheme—Siquisique—Steamboats on the Tocuyo—San Luis—Coro—The first cathedral of South America—Goat-farms—Fibre—La Vela—Capatárida tobacco—Curaçao—A fragment of Holland—A mixed language—Trade—Sanitation—The islands.

The three States whose boundaries include to-day the Segovia Highlands and the Coro Lowlands represent the greater part of the original province of Venezuela, as known to the Welser Governors. The region is for the most part high, with no exceptional peaks, and therefore may be considered as an elevated plateau, separated from the sea by a belt of plains. In Yaracuy there are fertile valleys, as well as in the northern part of Lara and the south of Falcón; in Lara, too, round Carora, we have llanos for cattle-grazing, and Barquisimeto receives much wheat from the surrounding country. The Coro plains are mostly dry and barren, covered with cactus, which nourishes thousands of goats.

The towns and cities of this region are, almost without exception, of sixteenth-century foundation, and include, therefore, the majority of the earliest settlements in Venezuela. Despite the fact that a railway connects Barquisimeto with the coast, communication with much of Lara is only carried out by primitive means. A projected branch line to San Felipe, capital of Yaracuy, will further open up that fertile valley, and the products of northern Falcón are mainly shipped through La Vela and Curaçao. Both upland and lowland plains are very suitable for wheel traffic, and natural carreteras there contrast favourably with the bridle paths of the hills, though little labour has been expended upon them.

Barquisimeto was founded in 1552, at the northern edge of the plain, which extends thence to Tocuyo, in appearance like the dry bed of an ancient lake. As the centre for the produce of the northern Andes, as well as Lara, the town has a busy aspect, busier even than Maracaibo. In the recent troublous years the conflicting parties seem to have met in and around Barquisimeto, and as a result one is struck by the heavy iron doors, often pitted with bullet marks, of the big commercial houses, which were thus at times turned into fortresses. The plains and valleys of Lara sent to the markets of Barquisimeto their wheat, coffee, cocoa, beans, sugar, and sugar-spirit, while the aloes of this region furnish not only *cocui* (a spirit distilled from cocuiza) but also fibre for the manufacture of sacks, bridles, and hammocks, for which the town is celebrated.

The British built and owned Bolivar Railway connects Barquisimeto with its port of Tucacas, and a steamer of the Company carries goods and passengers thence to Puerto Cabello, Tucacas being only an internal port without a custom-house. The gauge of the line is only two feet, but a considerable amount of traffic is carried. Leaving the open and dry plains of Barquisimeto, it climbs through scrub (probably excellent cotton land) to Duaca, and then begins the ascent of the humid coastal slope, along a valley full of coffee, sugar, and cacao plantations, but little cultivation has been carried on away from the line, the country on either side being as wild and as unknown as any in Venezuela. Near Tucacas the swampy forest gives place to open sandy plains, as on much of the northern coast of Venezuela.

Below Duaca, a well-built and picturesque but apparently sleepy little town, the railway enters the State of Yaracuy, and so continues to beyond the important junction of El Hacha, where the Barquisimeto line joins that from the copper-mines of Aroa. Originally the line was built from Tucacas to Aroa, the El Hacha-Barquisimeto extension being known as the South-Western of Venezuela; now both are united, and El Hacha to Aroa is regarded as a branch line.

The copper-mines of Aroa have been known from early colonial days, and even in 1800 some ore was exported. The greatest output was recorded after the concern was conceded to an English Company in 1880, and in 1891 (the maximum year) 38,341 tons of ore, with a smaller quantity of 25 per cent. regulus, was shipped from Tucacas. Three years later the production began to decrease greatly, and smelting-works and mines alike fall into disuse. They have now been reopened by an English syndicate, and, under Mr. Scrutton's energetic management, have already commenced to pay well. In the eighties the mines of Aroa sent to Swansea so much ore and regulus that in the statistics they ranged next to Chile.

The mines, or the entrances to them, are in a beautiful limestone gorge, full of the blue and green tinted pebbles and boulders which led the pioneers to search for the source of the mineral. On the left bank there are some cottages situated under an overhanging rock which would give a nervous inmate qualms, but presumably here as elsewhere familiarity breeds contempt. The manager's and other white houses up the valley look charming with their girdles of orange-trees, bananas, and papayas.

Wash-outs in the gorge sometimes cause considerable damage, and at the time of our visit the mine was temporarily closed owing to the disablement of the centrifugal pumps buried under the debris brought down by exceptionally heavy rains; four inches in an hour was, I think, the fall during part of the downpour, which also carried away or buried big pieces of the Bolivar Railway.

As one walks through the galleries with a little acetylene lamp clouds of bats brush past, and the floor is alive, where dry, with cockroaches. The most recently opened parts develop a very high temperature owing to the oxidation of the copper pyrites, and in "El Purgatorio," as it is called, one finds it difficult to breathe for a moment until a slight effort of will forces the lungs to take in the hot air. In many of the older workings there are quantities of beautiful stalactites and stalagmites in all shades of blue and green. Unfortunately, the copper-salts which colour them also make them brittle, and it would be difficult to bring one away without injury. After these the ore looks very black and dingy, though the freshly broken surface glitters brightly enough.

Near the edge of the forest on the Bolivar Railway is the station of Palma Sola, whence a branch is now being surveyed across the Aroa and up the Yaracuy Valley to San Felipe, a great boon to the agricultural interests of the State. There is a road from the town to Puerto Cabello, along which the merchandise now travels, but it is often impassable in the rains; the comparatively easy task of engineering a railway here to connect with the nearer port of Tucacas will probably enable it to be carried out profitably at the same time that it provides a cheap and rapid mode of transit for the coffee, cocoa, and hides of these rich agricultural and pastoral valleys.

In the State of Yaracuy, but south of the watershed at the western extremity of the coastal cordillera, lies Nirgua, founded in 1628 in the picturesque alluvial plain of the Buria. Copper-mines have been known and worked here from very early times, but I believe they are quiescent now; there are also, it is said, deposits of sulphur in the neighbourhood. The fertile plains and the surrounding hills send to the markets of Nirgua coffee, cocoa, beans, sugar, alcohol, cotton, and wheat, a goodly list for one small town.

Twenty miles away from Nirgua to the west in a straight line, though very much more by existing roads, is Yaritagua, the only other town of note in Yaracuy, connected by road with Barquisimeto. This is a good place for tobacco, and cigarettes used to be manufactured in considerable quantities from the local leaf; also it has its share of the ubiquitous coffee and sugar.

A natural cart-road enables the produce of Yaritagua to be shipped through Barquisimeto, the route passing by the small town of Cabudare. A similar road connects Barquisimeto with Tocuyo rather more than forty miles to the south-west.

Though the population of Tocuyo to-day is scarcely two-thirds that of Barquisimeto, it is the older town of the two, being founded by Carvajal in 1545. Its substantial, well-built houses bear witness to its former importance, and even now there is a continual stream of carts passing along the road to the capital, bearing not only coffee, sugar, and cocoa, which grow in the plantations of the valley near the town, but also wheat and temperate fruits from the hills. There are extensive potreros in the district, too, for raising sheep as well as cattle. The club building is a fine old mansion, comparable to any in Carácas, with a large patio and broad veranda.

The "road" to Barquisimeto is merely a casual track over the sand and gravel plains, but it serves its purpose, and one may make the journey in a strange vehicle, rather like a stage-coach in shape when seen from a distance, though without any outside seats, for the very good and sufficient reason that the apparently solid sides and top are of oilcloth and can be rolled up if desired. In leaving Tocuyo, *el Señor cochero* tells us we must be ready to start at 4 a.m., reserving to himself the right to turn up at two or five as may suit him best. This brings us to Quíbor, a little town, whose chief trade is in the temperate fruits (quinces, &c.) of the Sanare Hills, at about eight, and we leave again after midday, arriving dusty and sore at Barquisimeto by 5.30.

There are reported *minas* of metal and coal round about Tocuyo, and the latter certainly exists, though, like the less authentic minerals, it has never been worked.

If, in place of travelling to the capital of the State, we followed down the river from which Tocuyo takes its name, we should shortly find the cactus-covered hills replaced on the left bank by grass plains, the llanos of Carora, in the middle of which the town of the same name was founded in 1572. Like most of these more ancient towns of Venezuela, it contains many substantial buildings, and it is the market centre for the grazing lands surrounding it, where sheep as well as cattle are raised. From more remote districts come goats on the one hand, coffee and cane on the other, these last from the fertile valleys to the west. There are said to be outcrops of coal near by, a by no means improbable occurrence.

A whim of ex-President Castro's led to the expenditure of a considerable sum on the surveying and construction of a cart-road over the Sierra Empalada to San Timoteo, on the Lake of Maracaibo. It was manifestly impossible that such a scheme could succeed, involving, as it did, the use of a hundred miles of road over a range of hills instead of some sixty miles across the level to the Bolivar Railway terminus at Barquisimeto; at the present time much of the road has fallen into disuse, the remainder forming a standing monument to misplaced energy.

In addition to the level road to Barquisimeto there is another which in some fifty miles brings us to Siquisique, the head of possible steam navigation on the Tocuyo River. Up to this point steamers were run for a short time, but the undeveloped country on either bank was not brought under cultivation as a result, and the produce of the rest failed to make the venture pay. Once again, want of population and of incentives to labour have proved the main drawbacks in a feasible project. The hills both north and south of the lower river produce, and are capable of producing more, wheat, coffee, and cocoa; downstream there are virgin forests of valuable timber, and on the north bank indications of petroleum over a wide area almost uninhabited and unexplored.

From Siquisique several roads cross the hills on the borders of Lara and Falcón to the towns of the latter. Only one town of any importance (San Luis) is situated in the hills, but about half the area of the State is accounted for by grass-clad hills and fertile valleys, the remainder being the better known coastal plain, with its dry climate and cactus vegetation, a repetition of the Barquisimeto plateau.

Coro, now only the capital of a State, but once the capital of the whole province, is situated on the plains at the base of the peculiarly shaped peninsula of Paraguana. Next to Cumaná it is the oldest town in South America, and has frequently been the landing-place for troops both in the revolution against Spain and in the course of domestic quarrels. The old church, known as the *Iglesia Matriz*, is interesting as the first cathedral of the New World, but, like the rest of the town, it has fallen upon evil days.

The flesh and hides of goats are the chief articles of commerce in Coro. Bred at little cost on the cactus plains, they give returns said to be enormous. I heard of one owner of a ranch along the coast who, in the course of two or three years' breeding of and trading in goats, accumulates sufficient wealth to travel extensively in Europe, returning when his money is gone to repeat the process. The coalmines and salinas of the region count for little in comparison with this simple form of stock-farming, but there are extensive coal deposits in the foothills of the Cordillera de San Luis, whose valleys produce maize, coffee, cocoa, and arrowroot, chiefly for local consumption. The greater part of the foothills is forest-covered, and the timber and vegetable products of these will continually add to the revenues of the State in the future. Last, but not least, the coastal plain near Coro is admirably situated for the cultivation of cocuiza and other aloes, and attempts are now being made to manufacture fibre equal in quality to that of Mexico. Already Coro makes sacks and hammocks from cocuiza, in addition to soap and cigarettes, the only other industries of the place. All the produce exported passes along the seven-mile railway to the harbour of La Vela, not to be confused with the cape of the same name far to the west in Colombia.

Capatárida, a small town on the coast some thirty miles west of Coro, is chiefly famed for the excellent quality of the tobacco grown in the valley south of the town. The plains of Falcón and the peninsula of Paraguana are, however, chiefly devoted to goat-farming, the character of the country being almost identical with that of Curaçao, and most of the other coastal islands.

WILLEMSTAD: CURAÇAO.

THE HARBOUR: WILLEMSTAD.

Curaçao is, of course, Dutch territory, but the relations of the island with Venezuela are very close—too close, in fact, from the point of view of the Government. The legitimate and registered trade between the two is small, but an enormous amount of smuggling is carried on, while Willemstad has more than once proved a convenient base for intending revolutionaries.

The town is a strange mixture both in people and language, and in character a strong contrast to those of the Venezuelan coast. If one is up betimes on board, watching for the entrance to the harbour, one wonders if it is not really a confused dream of Flushing and a desert island, so much does the port resemble a homely Dutch town transported bodily into the heat of the West Indies, and set down on a barren rock. When the steamer has entered the harbour, and the pontoon bridge has swung back behind her, one can hardly believe that the land of mañana and *dolce far niente* is only a few miles away across the sea.

Harbour police, in plain but good blue uniforms and helmets, in place of dirty white ducks adorned with much gold braid, pronounce us, after some conversation in very guttural Spanish, fit and proper persons to enter her Majesty's colony of Curaçao, and we go on shore to examine this fragment of Holland.

The very cleanliness of the town seems the cause of the only discomfort experienced as one lands, for the dry soil will not support avenues of trees, and the glare from the white stone pavements and walls is almost painful. The names over the shops are sometimes Dutch, sometimes Portuguese and Spanish, often combinations of these, while the people who fill the streets are largely negroes of a strong, healthy type, talking a language which sounds like Dutch as far as accent is concerned, but on fuller acquaintance develops a likeness to Spanish. Those who know it say that all languages contribute to genuine Curaçao, and I am almost certain that I heard a Russian word used by one dusky Dutch subject. The notice on the end of the bridge tells us alternately to "*Langzaam rijden*" and "*Kore poko poko*," the latter being the genuine Curaçao "as she is wrote," practically Spanish spelt phonetically.

On the east side of the harbour are the Government buildings, Post Office, &c., together with the large business houses and the Dutch Reformed Church. As it was August when I visited the island, most of the comfortable-looking mansions were empty, the owners being away on home visits.

The prosperity of Willemstad, it is evident, does not depend upon natural products, of which there are none; even the oranges with which the famous liqueur was made are not grown in Curaçao now, but the building of small sloops and supplies for these, with the custom of visitors who come to buy in a free-trade market and avoid the all but prohibitive prices behind Venezuela's tariff wall, provide work for the numerous warehouses, not to mention the illicit trade with the mainland. The official returns show straw hats as the most considerable export, although formerly a fair amount of guano and phosphate of lime was shipped away. With a water supply dependent upon casual rains and a few shallow wells, there can be no drainage system, but the dryness of the climate and the stringent sanitary regulations combine to give Curaçao absolute freedom from epidemics and a deserved reputation as a health resort.

The smaller islands of the Las Aves, Los Roques, and other groups used, like Curaçao, to export a considerable quantity of guano, and phosphate produced by atmospheric action from coral limestones under the guano. Now, however, the few small settlements are mere fishing villages, whose catch is sold on the mainland.

CHAPTER XII
IN THE "ORIENTE"

Restricted use of term "Oriente"—Margarita—Asunción—Porlamar and Pampatar—Macanao—A primitive population—The priests, the comet, and the people—Cubagua—Pearl fisheries—Coche—Cumaná—Las Casas—A diving feat—Petroleum and salt—Fruit—The Manzanares—Cumanacoa—In the hills—San Antonio and its church—The Guacharo cave—Humboldt—Virgin territory—Punceres—Oil-springs—The Bermudez asphalt lake—Carúpano—"*Ron blanco*"—Sulphur and gold—Rio Caribe—Peninsula of Paria—Cristobal Colón—An ambitious project—The Delta—the *Golfo Triste*—Pedernales—Asphalt and outlaws—In the *caños*—Tucupita—Barrancas—Imataca iron-mines—Canadian capital for Venezuela—Guayana Vieja.

As the term "Oriente" is used to-day in Venezuela, it includes the cities of Barcelona, Maturín and Ciudad Bolivar, with their surrounding districts, but since these are more fitly considered in succeeding chapters, the use of the word is restricted here to the eastern part of the Caribbean Hills, the Island of Margarita, and the Delta of the Orinoco.

The "Oriente" thus includes those parts, not only of Venezuela but of the New Continent, which were first visited by Europeans. The names of the Boca del Draco (between the peninsula of Paria and Trinidad) and of Margarita were given by Columbus; Cubagua supported the first settlement of adventurers, and the shores westward of Cumaná were visited by Alonso de Ojeda on his first voyage.

Margarita lies some twenty miles north of the mainland, with the islands of Cubagua and Coche between. It is practically two islands joined by a sandspit, the two halves being equally rugged and mountainous; the western is known as Macanao, and contains but few inhabitants, the towns being all in the eastern half or Margarita proper.

With the surrounding smaller islands it constitutes the State of Nueva Esparta. The capital, Asunción, founded in 1524, is in a sheltered valley at the eastern end of the island. A ruined fort above the town, ruins of substantial houses, grass-grown streets and a general atmosphere of decay make the town somewhat depressing. To the south-east are the ports of Pampatar and Porlamar, the former most important, since to this come European liners, but Porlamar has the larger population. The bay of Porlamar is generally full of small fishing-smacks and pearling vessels, which carry on two of the chief industries of the island, though from Pampatar, with the pearls, they export also tiles, hats of straw and of a kind of velvet known as *pelo guamo*, hammocks, and embroidery.

The western half of Margarita is dry and barren for the most part, with small, scrubby vegetation, but here and there one finds grass-covered glades and more fertile soil; the inhabitants are chiefly fishermen, living in great poverty, with poor diet, yet contented and at the same time amazingly ignorant of the outside world. Who may be president in Carácas matters little to them, and European countries and cities are unknown. Probably fibre could be grown here with advantage, but the only land industry appears to be the farming of goats or cattle. Some of the outlying homesteads are conducted on patriarchal lines, and the families of the owners are occasionally enormous. Many of the people seem to be direct descendants of the ancient Guaiquerias, of strangely Mongolian appearance.

In Porlamar one may arrange for a passage in one of the little sloops or schooners to any of the other islands of the State, and it is as well to be prepared for a drenching if it is necessary to sail against the wind. Porlamar is a *triste* little town with about 3,500 inhabitants. We had the good (or ill) fortune to be there on the night when this planet passed through the tail of Halley's comet, which for some time previous had been a magnificent sight in the early morning. The priest had given out that the earth was to be destroyed by the comet at 2 a.m. prompt unless perhaps repentance, signified by devotion to mother-Church, was sufficiently general to avert disaster. As a result all the evening the churches, brilliantly lighted by myriads of candles, were crammed with devotees who professed and doubtless felt penitence for past misdeeds, if thereby they might prevent the threatened destruction or secure safety for themselves. Two o'clock came and passed, but, the night being cloudy, there was no sign of the comet, and the crowd flocked to the club and the *botiquins* to make up for lost time. It was in vain for the priests to tell them that the comet would come back if they persisted in their evil ways: the churches have remained as empty as they were before the months of the comet.

After this digression we may glance at Cubagua, the once famous pearl island, now perhaps on the eve of obtaining a new importance as a source of petroleum. There are springs of mineral oil along the northern shore, a tiny fishing village at the south-west corner, one small patch of cultivation with a single hut near the centre of the island, and a small cattle-ranch at the eastern end, and that is all—not a visible trace on all its barren surface of the once great city of New Cadiz. The eastern end is the most pleasant to-day, supporting more vegetation than the rest, and it is here, I was told, that diligent search and delving will reveal relics of the fifteenth-century settlement. Nothing seems to have been done in the way of archæological exploration, and even the old coat-of-arms graven in stone was picked up by chance on the shore to be lost again (apparently) in Carácas. It was displayed at the Bolivar Centenary Exhibition in 1883, and lay neglected in the patio of the building in 1891.

The west end of the island has a fine bay, with deep water, sheltered from the constant east wind, so that it is hard to see for what reason the city was founded at the other extremity; harder still, perhaps, to understand why it was founded at all on a barren island where practically every drop of water had to be brought from Margarita or from the Rio Manzanares at Cumaná. Its end came after its partial destruction by earthquake and hurricane in 1543, with the subsequent decrease in the output of the pearl fisheries, already spoilt by the extravagant and careless exploitation of the Spaniards, who soon paid more attention to those of the neighbouring island of Coche. It was infamous during its existence for the cruelties of its slave market, where the captive Indians of the mainland were branded with the initial letter of the city, and even after its final abandonment the memory of that fatal "C" rankled in the minds of the unfortunate Caribs and Chaymas.

Now, however, barring the heat in the valleys and to leeward of the cliffs of its treeless surface, the island is pleasant enough, and the clear shallows with their safe bathing-places are a compensation for the midday heat, while in the rock-pools the squids, water-snakes, and many-coloured shells of the tropical seas are a continual source of delight (to the eye); often, too, one may see the giant rays splashing in the strait between the island and Margarita, like huge pieces of armour-plate leaping from the water.

Coche still possesses a town in San Pedro de Coche, whose population live partly by their fisheries, but chiefly by the exploitation of the white salt of their *salinas*, almost the finest in Venezuela.

Separated from Cubagua and Coche by only a few miles of shallow water is the peninsula of Araya, behind which lies the Gulf of Cariaco, a long east and west arm of the sea. At the entrance on the south side is Cumaná, capital of the State, which, since the chief city was the birthplace of José de Sucre, of revolutionary fame, is now called after him, while the actual port of Cumaná is known as Puerto Sucre. The town was founded in 1520, and has a special interest in that it owed much in its early years to the labours of Bartolomé de las Casas. It has more than once suffered severely from earthquakes, and these earth tremors have, at times, played a considerable part in its history.

The town is connected with the port by about half a mile of dusty road across the sand-flats, and alongside runs a tramway, the motive power for which is supplied by mules; projects for utilising steam-engines have been formed but have never materialised, though an efficient service ought to pay. To the east the Gulf of Cariaco stretches away for about fifty miles, with a mean width of six or seven. At the eastern end its waters are covered with wild fowl of all kinds, and the local peasants catch them for their plumage by diving under the birds and drowning them, a feat necessitating a considerable development of fish-like qualities.

At the western end of the peninsula of Araya is the site of the old castle of Araya, built at the suggestion of Las Casas for the preservation of peace between the Cubaguans and the Caribs; here, too, are the extensive salinas, and on the south side there are oil-springs, indicating deposits whose value and extent have still to be investigated. The product of the salt-pans is, both in quality and quantity, second only to that of Coche, and amounts to some 6,000 tons in the year.

The neighbourhood of Cumaná, along the banks of its river, the Manzanares, is famous for fruits of all kinds, principally pineapples, grapes, and mangoes; the less fertile hills look like cotton country, but none is grown, or very little. The chief exports of Puerto Sucre are coffee, tobacco, sugar, beans, and hides, brought from the interior.

This produce is carried on mule-back along the mountain roads of Sucre. The main route from the interior follows the Manzanares for most of its course, but the last few leagues lie over a steep ridge, a shorter but more troublesome route than that along the river, were the latter properly looked after. The upper valley of the Manzanares has some beautiful pieces of scenery as the gorge is followed through the limestone hills; until Cumanacoa is reached, however, fifty miles from Cumaná, there is no cultivation in the valley, and little possibility of it, and the coastal region generally seems only fit for cotton or fibre cultivation.

Round Cumanacoa there are fertile hillsides and rich alluvial flats, chiefly devoted to coffee and sugar or beans. When the town was founded by Domingo Arias in 1717, he named it San Baltazar de las Arias, but as in the case of Cumaná, the old Italian name of the district has ousted the later Spanish one. Above Cumanacoa the valley narrows down into a gorge running up into the mountain-mass on the borders of Sucre and Monágas, the watershed forming the boundary between the two States. On the high, open grass-lands there is pasturage for many more sheep and cattle than one sees at present, and the change in climate from the hot, damp valleys is very pleasant, though somewhat sudden.

Some twenty-five miles southward of Cumanacoa is the town of San Antonio, in Humboldt's time a flourishing mission with a massive stone church built entirely by the Indians; the church, with its beautifully bright frescoes, is still standing, but sadly in want of repair, and one of the towers is cracked and overgrown at the base. Four or five miles to the south-east lies the Caripe valley, famous for its tobacco, and for the Guacharo cavern so well described by Humboldt.

From his account a good idea may be gained of the beauty of the approach and the impressiveness of this hole in the limestone. He describes how, as he and Bonpland, with their friends and guides from the Mission Caripe, travelled up the valley, they were unable to see the mouth of the cave even at 400 paces distant, their way lying under an overhanging cliff, with the stream almost in a crevasse below them; then, turning a corner, they were suddenly in full view of the opening, 80 feet wide and 72 feet high, with stalactites and stalagmites within and huge trees above, while the aspect was different from anything of the kind in Europe on account of the luxuriant tropical vegetation all about. As they walked through the cave it was often necessary to step into the stream, which was only 2 feet deep, while overhead the Guacharos,[6] from which the cave has its name, were uttering their raucous cries. In the broader part of the cave the Indians were accustomed to venture at one season of the year to catch the young birds for their fat, which they used in cooking in the mission, but beyond they would hardly go, believing the spirits of their departed ancestors to be there. At the limit of Humboldt's exploration in this narrower part he found an underground waterfall, which marks the visible source of the Rio Caripe.

Thirty miles from San Antonio, at Aragua de Maturín, the edge of the hills is reached and the Llanos begin, but to the north-east there lies a stretch of little-known territory, chiefly forest-clad hills, capable of supporting millions of cacao-trees when a growing population shall settle there. Near Punceres there are oil-springs, and at other points in the region indications of petroleum are known, which may one day lead to the development of this rich and well-situated stretch of country, for at the east end is the old Puerto San Juan of colonial days, with a depth of water in the *caño* of the same name sufficient for steam or sailing craft of considerable size. At present most of the produce of all the northern part of Monágas, as well as of Sucre, passes out over the hills to the Caribbean.

An exception to the above must be made in the case of the asphalt from the Bermudez Lake, which is shipped across to Trinidad. This has been worked for many years by an American company, and is almost as well known as the famous Pitch Lake of Trinidad. It was once thought that the quantity of asphalt visible was much greater here, but fuller investigation showed that though a larger area was covered the thickness of the deposit was very much less than in Trinidad. Over 32,000 tons were exported in the fiscal year 1909-10.

The principal port of the Oriente is Carúpano, on the north coast, midway between the two peninsulas of Paria and Araya. The town, seen from a steamer, seems to be as much huddled up at the foot of the mountains as La Guaira, but in a similar way it extends up the valleys of two streams which here reach the sea. Its position thus makes it hot, though it is sufficiently open to the sea breezes to be healthy. A white zigzag line up the slope behind the town represents the road, down which comes the cocoa of the hills and valleys of Sucre, for which Carúpano is famous, as well as cotton, sugar, timber, and alcohol. This last is a spirit of exceptional purity, and the "white rum" of Carúpano is famed throughout the country. The hills about the town also support aloes, of the fibre of which ropes are manufactured in the town, and near by there are potteries. It is an important place, then, with its population of some 11,000, in spite of the fact that the steamers which visit it have to lie in an open roadstead sheltered only by a promontory to the east from the prevalent winds. Sulphur is found near by, and, it is said, auriferous quartz of high quality, but the minerals have never been systematically worked.

PUERTO CRISTOBAL COLÓN.

A few miles east of Carúpano is the small port of Rio Caribe, where the roadstead is not sufficiently sheltered to allow steamers to lie; small sailing craft carry away the local produce, which consists principally of cacao. Beyond Rio Caribe is the peninsula of Paria, a beautifully wooded mountain mass rising sheer from the water's edge and separated only by a narrow strait, with numerous islands, from Trinidad. The northern side of the peninsula is practically uninhabited, but the coast facing the Gulf of Paria has several settlements, chiefly occupied in cultivating cacao or cutting timber; their produce is shipped across to Trinidad.

Cristobal Colón is the most easterly port of Venezuela, and its position at the eastern end of the peninsula of Paria, opposite to the Delta of the Orinoco, led Castro to suppose that a small expenditure of public money would lead to a diversion of all the freight now passing via Port-of-Spain to Ciudad Bolivar, from Trinidad to Venezuela—an ill-founded hope, however, as events proved, for the roadstead is very poor, open to a continual heavy swell coming in through the Bocas, which could only be overcome by extensive harbour-works, the cost of which is entirely unwarranted by the circumstances of the case. The wharves and warehouses erected represent, therefore, a sacrifice of public zeal to a private whim as reprehensible as the construction of the Carora and San Timoteo road.

The trade with Southern Venezuela is normally carried on through Port-of-Spain, goods being there transferred to the Orinoco steamer *Delta*, which crosses the Gulf of Paria to the Caño Macareo, up which lies the normal route to Ciudad Bolivar. Columbus named the Gulf of Paria "Golfo Triste," and when one has left the beautiful hills and islands on the north side behind it certainly wears a very gloomy aspect, particularly on a cloudy day.

Near the mouths of the Orinoco the water becomes muddy and musky, full of floating masses of water-hyacinth or dead timber, while away on the horizon one can see a dark band of mangroves marking the beginning of the swampy Delta territory.

Pedernales is the only settlement on the coast of the Delta proper—a gloomy, unhealthy-looking spot, though the islands on which the houses are built are more solid than the surrounding swamps. For the new town one lands at a stone causeway leading across the black mud to a single row of houses, one of which has a flagstaff indicating it as the seat of authority. Crabs crawl on the slime and mud all around, and the black patches of natural asphalt along the main street and foreshore offer no contrast to the dirty pools which necessitate a wary eye and foot in walking. The ruins of the German asphalt and oil refinery a mile or so away add to the desolate effect, and the greeting from outlaws from Trinidad, broken-down whites, and villainous-looking negroes make one even more ready to leave this fever-stricken spot, where the floors of the houses are flooded by frequent downpours in the rainy season. The inhabitants exist chiefly by cutting and exporting mangrove-stems for dyeing and tanning purposes; the asphalt industry seems to be quiescent.

Up the caño the scene is one of great beauty, in the varying foliage of the high green banks, whose inundated forest is hidden by the mass of creepers, bamboos, &c., which come down to the water's edge; beyond only the tops of the high trees can be seen, though sometimes behind a bank of reeds or water-hyacinths, looking in the distance like well-kept turf, the forest itself can be seen. The masses of floating hyacinth, as they float down the stream, the muddy water, and the alligators on the banks here and there, with the macaws, flamingoes, and parrots above and around us, complete the picture. Here and there through the creepers there is a narrow archway cut by the Guaraunos, who live behind in huts raised above the swampy ground, and eat, drink, and clothe themselves with the products of the Moriche palm, besides making their roofs of its fronds.

Higher up there is unflooded forest and open country, where the savannahs bear rich grass for thousands of herds of cattle, and on the banks scattered groups of a few houses mark partly civilised settlements. A fine cacao ranch is passed on the right bank not far below Tucupita, the capital of the Delta-Amacuro Territory, a dismal, unhealthy-looking place, though with some signs of commercial life in the number of goletas in front, not to mention steam craft.

Soon after Tucupita the mountains of Guayana come in sight far to the south, and an hour or so brings us to Barrancas, the lowest port on the Orinoco proper, whose grass-grown streets and broad laguna behind the settlement do not suggest health. Here the character of the navigation changes, and one begins that journey, so finely described by Humboldt, up the thousands of miles of waterways, which will conduct the traveller, if he wishes it, through to the Amazon, and even by devious routes to the Plate.

The Delta territory southward of the main stream consists, in part at least, of hilly country, and here on the flanks of the Sierra Imataca there are rich deposits of iron ore, soon to be worked by a Canadian company by whom the rights have recently been acquired. To aid in the work the company has the right to establish a port (Nueva Angostura) with a custom-house on the Caño Corosimo, in order to avoid the long journey up to Ciudad Bolivar and back.

A few miles above Barrancas, on the south bank of the river, is the castle of San Thomé, now known as Guayana Vieja or Los Castillos, where Raleigh had several encounters with the Spaniards on his last fatal expedition. There are only a few houses round the citadel to-day, and the place possesses no importance.

CHAPTER XIII
THE LLANOS
Monágas, Anzoátegui, Guárico, Cojedes, Portuguesa, Zamora, and Apure

The great plains—An ocean without water—*Bancos* and *mesas*—Drought and flood—A living floor—Streams which flow upwards—Heat—Cattle and horses—Imported butter—Methods of milking—Civil wars—Future prospects—A mean annual temperature of 91° F.—Barcelona—History—The massacre of the Casa Fuerte—Survivors—Guanta—Coal of Naricual—Aragua de Barcelona—Maturín—Low death-rate—Caño Colorado—Bongos—Athletic boatmen—*Casitas*—Travelling on the Llanos—an *hato*—Areo—An ancient cotton-press—The men of Urica—Churches and wayside shrines—A gruesome monument—Calabozo—Barbacoas—Ortiz—Zaraza and Camaguan—San Carlos—Barinas—Guanare—Past prosperity and future prospects.

The llanos of northern South America form one of the remarkable great plains of the world. They stretch from the Orinoco Delta in the east right to the Cordillera of the Andes in the west.

The foothills and highlands on the south side of the coastal range limit them in the north, and where the continuity of the mountain chain is broken, near Barcelona, they reach the coast itself.

The Orinoco constitutes their southern boundary as far west as its junction with the Apure. Beyond this point the course of the Orinoco is from south to north instead of from west to east, and out west of this the great plains stretch away to the south far beyond the southern boundary of Venezuela. In fact, formerly the settlers in the Venezuelan llanos, who knew of the Argentine pampas and their cattle industry away somewhere to the south of them, but had vague notions of geography and no knowledge of the high country in central South America, believed that the llanos went right away south to Patagonia.

The stretches of plain from the south of Cumaná, Barcelona, and Carácas down to the Orinoco are called the llanos of Cumaná, Barcelona, and Carácas respectively, while the extreme west corner is known as the llanos of Barinas.

Near the northern and western limits of this great plain there is a gradual passage from the foothills and the adjoining broken country to the plain, but once away in the interior the flatness of the llanos is remarkable. There are neither the undulations of rolling prairie-lands nor the sandhills and ridges of the desert. The mountains can, of course, be seen for a considerable distance, and to fully realise the curious effect of the llanos it is necessary to be out of sight of them.

In some places nothing, not even a tree, can be seen in any direction but the flat plain, covered with short grass; the traveller has the illusion of being on the ocean stretching in every direction to the horizon, and it is very easy to get lost if he leaves a beaten track.

The llanos are not, however, absolutely level; there are flat banks of slight elevation (a few feet) called *bancos*, only to be observed at their edges, and extending for miles, and also *mesas*, convexities gently, almost imperceptibly, rising to a very moderate height, and yet sufficiently important to form water divides.

A glance at the map shows that in the llanos south of Carácas the streams flow right across Venezuela, from the hills to the Orinoco or its tributaries, and, in fact, the whole of the western llanos are very gently inclined to the south-east, but in the eastern part of the llanos south of Cumaná we see a water divide, the Rivers Tigre and Guanipa flowing eastwards to the Delta, and farther west a number of rivers flowing into the Orinoco, while north of the divide various streams, the Aragua, the Unare, and others, empty themselves into the sea west of Barcelona, this being due, not to a range of hills but to the convexity of the plains, the mesas of Tigre, Guanipa, &c.

It is hard to understand that lack of water is one of the difficulties besetting the traveller on the llanos when one sees the network of streams indicated on the maps. In the wet season there is of course plenty of water, but in the dry season most of these tributary streams cease to flow. Those which take their rise in the hilly country have, indeed, some water in their upper courses all the time, while in their lower part water from the main streams, the Orinoco, the Apure, the Portuguesa, and others, is able to back a good way up, on account of their very gentle fall, but their middle courses run quite dry, pools remaining here and there in the hollows. The water in these gets somewhat foul, but by digging in the sand in their neighbourhood sweeter water may be obtained. The River Guárico, which partly dries up in this way, is said formerly to have flowed all the year round. It takes its rise near Lake Tacarigua (Lake of Valencia), and perhaps the diminution of its water supply is due to the same cause as the shrinking of that lake, the cutting down of forest and the cultivation of land near its source. In the wet season many of the streams overflow and flood wide areas, the cattle having to take refuge on slightly higher tracts. When the waters again retire many alligators and water-snakes bury themselves in the mud, and one hears of people being startled by sudden upheavals of the ground, followed by the emergence of some disturbed monster. In one case a traveller settled for a night in a hut which had been flooded the previous season, and the barking of the dogs awoke a huge alligator, who heaved up the floor, made a dash at the dogs, and then fled into the open.

Referring once again to the fact of the water in the main streams backing up the tributaries, so very slight is the inclination of the western plains, and so small the fall of its streams, that swelling of the Orinoco, or wind pressure, will force the water to flow up the tributaries, whirlpools forming where the opposing currents meet.

Humboldt states that under these conditions many natives firmly believed that in travelling up these streams in their canoes they were really descending for a considerable distance.

Apart from the change of season from wet to dry, the great factor in the climate of the llanos is the trade wind, which blows across from the east to the west. The sandy ground, thinly covered with grass, becomes very hot in the daytime and heats the air near it. In the east the trade wind, arriving fresh from the sea, lessens this effect, and makes the air pleasant, but as it sweeps across the hundreds of miles of burning soil it becomes itself heated, and as it gets farther west adds to the discomfort, instead of correcting it.

In fact, the western llanos are very hot, and although there is a twelve-hours night in which to cool, there is so much heat to be radiated off from the earth that when dawn, the coolest moment, arrives very little diminution of temperature has been attained, and the heating process begins again.

The llanos, then, are neither prairie nor desert, but hold rather an intermediate position, varying towards one or the other according to the season. Various grasses suitable for feeding live stock grow here, and there are some trees, notably varieties of mimosas, one with sensitive leaves (*dormideras*) very good for cattle. There are also palms, notably the Corypa palms, or *palmas de Cobija*, with hard wood, which are good for building huts, their leaves being used for the roof, and the Moriche palm (*Mauritia flexuosa*), which, as already noticed, furnishes nearly all the necessities of life to the Guarauno Indians of the Delta.

The llanos originally contained deer, the river swine or capybara (*chiguire*), and the jaguar, also wild ducks and geese. In 1548 Cristobal Rodriguez started sending cattle into the plains to multiply. In Humboldt's time the live stock were estimated at 1,200,000 oxen, 180,000 horses, and 90,000 mules. Wars and diseases have at different times interrupted their increase. Horses, asses, and mules were abundant and cheap up to 1843, when a pestilence destroyed nearly all the wild ones, the loss being estimated at between six and seven million beasts.

The cattle are believed to have decreased between the years 1863-73 from 5,000,000 to 1,400,000, but by 1888 were estimated at 8,500,000 again.

Cattle-breeding should be a great and important industry for Venezuela, and it is to be hoped that it will be put on a better footing before long. An up-to-date factory for killing and chilling meat has been established at Puerto Cabello, and the first shipment took place in 1910.

One of the chief difficulties this industry has to contend with is the loss of condition the cattle sustain on their journeys to the port from distant ranches. There are, however, plenty of outlets from the llanos, for the southern part, the Orinoco, and for the west, central, and eastern parts, Puerto Cabello, Barcelona, and Caño Colorado, the port of Maturín.

Most of the cattle in the llanos are in a half-wild state. It is rather melancholy to find that in country towns surrounded by vast areas of pasture-land milk and butter are often difficult to procure; in fact, a lot of imported butter is used. The calves generally get all the milk, and the cows are so unused to being milked for the benefit of mankind that it is necessary to bring the calf and tie it to the mother's leg and allow it to begin the operation before the milkmen can do anything, the cow apparently being deluded into the idea that she is feeding the calf all the time. The farmers and llaneros in most parts seem surprised to hear that milking can be done in any other way.

This pastoral industry, like the others, has suffered from many causes, but the chief has been political unrest and internal wars. There is little doubt that if the country once settles down, as it now bids fair to do, and a feeling of security is established, the farmers will show more energy and increase their knowledge of their art, and in time the physical conditions of the vast plains may, nay, will, be gradually improved. Irrigation and the planting of trees, protecting them when young from the cattle, will bring this about. One would think that this process should be begun in the east and gradually worked westward. In the east the climate is pleasanter, and the prevailing east wind cool (not having passed over a hot, arid land surface), and as each strip of country is improved it would render easier the amelioration of the area immediately to the west of it. But all this requires capital, work, and patience, and men will not be found to undertake it as long as they have reason to fear that civil wars will prevent them enjoying the fruits of their labour.

RUINED CHURCH: BARCELONA.

CASA FUERTE: BARCELONA.

The general physical description of the llanos applies to all the States named in the heading to this chapter. A glance at the map shows that the first six, Monágas to Zamora, actually constitute the east to west extension of the great plain, whilst Apure forms the beginning of the southerly extension, which, as already pointed out, stretches far beyond the boundaries of Venezuela.

The chief towns of the eastern llanos are Maturín, in Monágas, Barcelona and Aragua de Barcelona, in Anzoátegui. The northern part of these two States includes some of the highlands south of the Cumaná range, pleasant pastoral country with a good climate. The central part of the llanos is very hot, and arid in the dry season. Calabozo, in Guárico, and San Fernando de

Apure are the two hottest places in the country, the latter having a mean annual temperature of 91°.

In the extreme west, as the Cordillera is approached, the heat diminishes, and the typical llano is often replaced by well-wooded country. The chief towns here are San Carlos, in Cojedes, Guanare, in Portuguesa, and Barinas, in Zamora, the last-named town not being much hotter than Maturín.

The town of Nueva Barcelona was founded in 1637 by Juan Urpin, at a spot some two leagues distant from its present site.

In 1671, in order to terminate the frequent quarrels between its inhabitants and those of a neighbouring settlement, Cumanagoto, the Governor, Angelo, united the two populations at the spot where Barcelona now stands. This shifting of towns and villages at the order of a Governor, or even a priest, was not uncommon in the colony in the early days.

Towards the end of the eighteenth century Barcelona grew considerably in importance. There was a large and growing demand in the Antilles, especially in Cuba, for meat to feed the slaves on the plantations and for horses and mules. The journey from the River Plate in sailing-ships was a very long one, and the Cuba merchants preferred to get their goods from the north coast. Barcelona's position at the point where the llanos extend right to the coast, and where consequently there are no mountains to cross, gave her a big advantage over Cumaná and other seaports, and her trade and population grew rapidly. From 1790 to 1800 her population grew from 10,000 to 16,000. But it was in adversity that Barcelona was to become famous, and in 1817 she gained a crown of martyrdom, becoming the scene of one of the most tragic events in the history of South American independence.

Bolivar, after several encounters with the royalists in February, had left Barcelona to beat up recruits. The Captain-General, Juan de Aldama, having failed to intercept him, turned eastward to the doomed city, where he was joined by some troops from Cumaná and by some vessels of the fleet, which provided him with guns. A devoted band, consisting chiefly of Venezuelans, with some Colombians and a few foreigners, in all 600-700 fighting men, and some 300 civilians, women, and children, determined to resist to the last, and prepared to defend the convent of San Francisco, better known to history as the Casa Fuerte, which stands in an open space in the town.

Aldama's sharpshooters having cleared the town, he invested the convent, placing ordnance on two sides of it and stationing troops on the far sides to prevent the escape of the garrison. He then invited the patriots to capitulate, promising to spare their lives, but they refused, and at dawn of April 10th he began the bombardment.

The Casa Fuerte was not strong enough to withstand his artillery, and at two in the afternoon a large breach had been effected. The royalists charged from cover across the open space round the convent, and a desperate fight ensued, the Venezuelans selling their lives very dearly. The walls of the room in which the last of the patriots died are still standing, and the stones are deeply scored all over from the blows of the weapons of men fighting in a confined space.

Aldama states in his official report to the King that he invited the garrison to capitulate before the bombardment, with a view to avoiding any unnecessary bloodshed and to demonstrate his Majesty's clemency, but any humane intentions seem to have deserted the royalists during the day, for, not content with annihilating the combatants, who disdained to ask for quarter, nearly all the women and children were outraged and murdered. It is even said that Aldama gave orders to have the sick in the hospital butchered, but the officer to whom this task was deputed would not carry out his instructions. A few individuals escaped, fighting as they went.

The military and civil Governors of Barcelona, General Pedro Maria Freites and Colonel Francisco Esteban Rivas, were taken wounded and prisoners to Carácas, and there shot on April 17th.

In connection with the centenary celebrations this year, 1911, an interesting little booklet has been written by the historian M. L. Rosales, and officially published by the President of Anzoátegui, General A. Rolando, giving the accounts of the affair by Aldama on the one hand and by General D. F. O'Leary on the other.

Most of the victims' names are lost, but the historian has collected some seventy-seven, six of whom were priests and eighteen women. Among them we may note one Carlos Chamberlain, of Jamaica, a colonel in the Republican Army, and his mother, Doña Eulalia. Another lady, Doña Juana de Jesus Rojas, died of seven bayonet wounds, while the last on the list is a little girl, Dolores Rodriguez, only four months old, who had a hand cut off, but survived and died in Carácas as lately as 1898.

Barcelona is a town of good appearance, with fairly well paved streets, and many houses of more than one storey, which show that there is not the same dread of earthquakes as at Cumaná. There are three fine churches and a well-equipped theatre. The sea near the town is shallow and has many shoals of sand, and is therefore unsuited to vessels of any size. Guanta, some 19 kilometres to the east, has an excellent natural harbour, and is now the port of Barcelona, connected with the city by a railway, which runs also to the coalmines at Naricual and Capiricual, another 19 kilometres distant. These furnish a useful bright burning coal of a later geological period than the British coal which is used on the railway and supplied to the Venezuelan steamers which ply from the Orinoco to the ports on the north coast.

Briquettes are also manufactured with the coal and pitch brought from the north-east coast and Trinidad. The Barcelonians conduct the railway, the coalmine, and the briquette factory themselves, and are rather proud of their "home industries," since in Venezuela most modern enterprises are conducted by foreigners.

The imports are mixed goods, chiefly from the United States and Holland, while the exports are mainly beasts, hides, horns, and coffee.

Aragua de Barcelona is better placed than Barcelona itself as a trade centre, and is growing in importance, becoming a serious rival to the older town. It is chiefly concerned with the cattle industry, but the inhabitants also make hammocks and various textile goods.

Maturín, the capital of Monágas, stands in the N.E. corner of the llanos, on the River Guarapiche, and from its situation it is likely, to grow considerably, in importance as the country develops. At first sight it does not produce a particularly favourable impression. The streets are not paved, but in front of the houses run narrow raised sidewalks often two feet or more above the roadway. It improves, however, on further acquaintance. There is not the air of decay and diminished importance which is badly evident in some parts of the country; the inhabitants are cheerful and sociable, and inclined to progress, and a fair amount of business appears to pass through the town.

There is probably no part of the llanos pleasanter than the country round Maturín. The grassy plain is well supplied with streams, which have generally cut their channels fairly deep, and are well wooded along their banks, and the climate is pleasant even for Europeans.

The death-rate, although there is no sanitation, is very low, under 12 per 1,000, or less than half the average rate for the republic, and lower than that of London.

Most of the trade of this part of the country is carried by schooners, which come from the sea up the Caño San Juan, to the point where the Rivers San Juan and Guarapiche join. Here there is an old guardship, where some Customs officials are stationed. The San Juan leads to Guanoco, where the Bermudez Asphalt Company carry on their business. A few miles up the Guarapiche stands the village of Caño Colorado, the headquarters of the Customs. The jungle is dense on both banks of the river, but on one side a narrow clearing has been made, just sufficient for a row of small houses, with a little back garden to each. Maturín is about thirty miles from here across country, but much farther by river. From the point at which the schooners stop the trade with Maturín is carried in bongos, which are propelled, like punts, by long poles. Planks are fixed on the two sides of the boats, and the crews, standing on these, plant their poles firmly, and then walk towards the stern. When they can go no farther, they pull out the poles and run towards the bows. The river is narrow and very swift, so that coming down stream is very easy, but going up so much way is lost between the strokes, that the men, when they pull up their poles, have to rush forward again as fast as they can. It takes three days to get from Caño Colorado up to Maturín like this, and the men are able to work almost continually during the day. Once out of sight of the houses, they generally strip completely, only throwing on some light covering on reaching one of the few settlements on the river. The exercise develops every muscle of the body and limbs, and the men engaged in it are as fine a set of athletes as any artist or anatomist could wish to see. Although the river is so wild, and human habitations so few and far apart, this scene is quite lively at intervals as groups of these bongos come along, and "man overboard," a frequent event, is always the cause of much merriment.

The country round Maturín is dotted here and there with villages, as well as with isolated cottages. The larger cattle-owners often live in the towns but have here and there small houses for their employees. A typical *casita* is simplicity itself. Upright posts, tree-trunks with their branches trimmed off, are planted firmly in the ground, six feet or more apart, and cross-pieces are tied to them, at a height of about eight feet. The rafters of the roof, lighter poles, are also tied on, and palm-leaves form a most efficient thatch, throwing off the heaviest rain, and lasting for years. At one end of this roofed enclosure a small space is rendered more private, to serve as the retiring-room of the inhabitants. A few light trunks or branches are tied horizontally across the uprights, about a foot apart, and either palm-leaves are tied to these, the bedroom walls, in fact, being thatched like the roof, or a more solid mud wall is constructed on the wooden framework. The soil itself is the floor. The traveller seeking a night's shelter slings his hammock to some of the uprights in the outer room, having no walls around him, but a roof over his head. A small fire is kept going in a corner of the outer room for cooking purposes. In the simpler cases very little furniture is required: a log or two to sit on; a few bowls of different sizes made of gourds cut in half, serving as cups or plates; an iron pot on the fire; an upright log, stuck in the ground with a bowl-shaped hollow at the top serves as a sort of mortar, in which maize, &c., may be ground; and another somewhat similar device, with a wooden lever for crushing sugar-cane, the juice running out below into the gourd placed to receive it.

It is easy to set up a home of this sort; the site once selected, the materials for house and furniture are always at hand, and the whole thing can be done in a few days.

The traveller, of course, always carries his own hammock, rolled up tight in a sausage-shaped bag carried across the saddle, either before or behind the rider. On arrival at one of these homesteads he can almost invariably count on a civil reception, and without further preliminaries slings his hammock, which then serves him as chair as well as bed. Sometimes he may chance on a spot where food is scarce at the moment, but generally the good people will find something for him. A sancoche made of a fowl stewed in its own juices, cassava in thin cakes, sprinkled with a few drops of water to soften it, some beans, and some roast plantains (cooking bananas) form a menu which, even if it does not appeal to an epicure, proves both tasty and satisfying after a long day in the saddle. Houses of this type are generally inhabited by one family only, who are looking after the flocks and herds of some wealthy owner or are in a very small way of business themselves.

A more animated scene is presented by the *hato* of a regular farmer, a proprietor living on the premises, employing several hands and working with them. Here we may expect to see a solid house of several rooms, with mud walls and an earth floor. If the farmer is a person of substance and taste, his bedroom may be furnished with an up-to-date bedstead, and a wardrobe or chest of drawers, and a few chairs, while the chief living-room probably has a rough table and a few chairs also. In the living-rooms the mud or clay of the walls is broken here and there about six feet above the ground, giving glimpses of the wooden framework inside the wall. This is, however, not due to accidental damage or neglect, for at night strangers, or some of the farm hands, sleep in these living-rooms, and passing their hammock-ropes through these holes, attach them to the wooden posts inside.

Round about the house, or near it, is an enclosed stockyard, built, like the houses, of upright posts, with horizontal poles attached to them. In the middle of this yard is an upright post, to which the beasts requiring any sort of operation are secured one at a time. There are, perhaps, other similar enclosures, some covered with palm thatch, in which any part of the stock may be kept separate if desired. These yards are also used at times for the accommodation of travelling herds, especially if the farm be on or near the recognised route to some market town or port. The drovers pay the farmer a small rental, generally based on the number of cattle they have, and secure them for the night, thus preventing them from straying about the plains and ensuring an early start in the morning.

Near the house, in a roofed shed, is the bakery; there we may find a small fireplace with clay walls, the top of which is formed by a circular iron plate about three feet in diameter, the whole being about the height of an ordinary table. On this the cassava-bread is baked. The flour, duly prepared and freed from superfluous water, is thinly spread on the iron and rapidly baked, the finished loaf being a large circular disc very hard and brittle, and thinner than our ordinary milk biscuits.

The cattle may be seen dotted about the plain, and near to the homesteads a few horses are grazing, tethered so that they may be at hand when wanted. There is none of the continuous work, laborious cultivation of the soil, constant attention to the live stock, &c., which we are accustomed to connect with farming at home. The farm hands spend a good deal of their time loafing about, chatting, smoking, and playing their guitars and maracas. At other times there is plenty of bustle and activity; they rush for their horses and gallop off to collect the cattle, or such of them as may be required, and drive them into the enclosure, where they are lassooed one at a time, and milked, or fastened to the post in the middle to be branded, or have hurts attended to, as the case may be. The amount of comfort to be found in these farms, and the amount of skill and energy displayed in their exploitation varies a good deal from place to place, depending mainly, after all, on the tastes and character of the owner, but partly on circumstances. In many cases absolute slackness and indifference prevail, the cattle are almost entirely left to shift for themselves, and the human beings are content to exist miserably rather than bestir themselves. There are some estates, again, where the owner is a wealthy, educated, and perhaps a travelled man, which are managed on far better lines than the average.

Maturín has a creditable record from the War of Independence, a Spanish army having been twice repulsed, and finally almost completely destroyed there. At Areo, a day and a half west of Maturín, there is in the open space by the church a huge wooden screw press, like a giant letterpress, which the inhabitants say was used by the Spaniards to press cotton. At Urica, farther west, the inhabitants are somewhat interesting. They have the reputation of having been of a brave and warlike disposition from the earliest times, and fought desperately in the War of Independence. There is something in their appearance, and a general suggestion of freedom and independence in their manner, in their very gait, which can scarcely fail to strike the traveller, even if he be unacquainted with their history.

At the little village of Curataquiche, near Barcelona, are the ruins of the Mission of St. Joseph; the walls of one end of the church, and a bit of the adjoining enclosure, very solidly built in stone, are all that remain of a once important mission. The church bells have been preserved, and are hung to a large wooden trestle on the village green.

Most of these towns and villages possess churches, but resident priests are rarely to be found. The inhabitants generally meet on Sundays and hold some sort of service among themselves, but can only hear Mass when a travelling priest comes their way. At either end of a village, at the side of the track, a plain wooden cross is generally erected, and often in its neighbourhood will be found a small shrine about which are hung various little objects placed there by pious hands as thankofferings for answers to prayers. These shrines generally contain a cross with the instruments of crucifixion, the ladder, nails, hammer, crown of thorns, spear shaft with sponge, dice, &c., but without the figure of Christ. They are often illuminated with a little flickering light at night. To the west of Barcelona there is one on the spot where a man was killed. It contains his skull, which is lit up from inside at night, producing a somewhat weird effect.

MESA OF ESNOJAQUE: TRUJILLO.

MÉRIDA: LOOKING SOUTH FROM UNIVERSITY.

Calabozo, the chief town in the State of Guárico, and the seat of a bishopric, founded in 1730 by the Guipuzcoana Company, is a town of some importance to-day. There is a good grazing country round it, and it has a trade in cattle, mules, hides, cheese, and other things. It is a hot place, but has not the reputation of being unhealthy. Its communications are liable to be cut off by floods in the wet season. It has always been specially noted in the records of travellers for the electric eels which abound in its neighbourhood. Humboldt, when visiting Calabozo, offered a fair price for a number of these creatures. Horses were cheap at that time, and some of the inhabitants obtained the desired specimens by driving a number of horses into a pond infested with them, and prevented their escape by surrounding the pond armed with sticks. When the gymnoti had exhausted their energies on the unfortunate horses, they were able to secure them without risk. Several of the horses died, either directly from the attacks of the eels or, more probably, from drowning during the temporary paralysis caused by the electric shocks.

Among the other principal towns in Guárico is Barbacoas, pleasantly situated in a raised plain east of the Guárico, with woods to the north of it and a fertile plain to the south.

At Ortiz, founded by the cacique of that name, Bolivar was nearly killed on April 16, 1818. This town and Guayabal, which was founded by the Capuchins in 1758, were both burnt by the Spaniards during the war.

Zaraza, on the River Unare, and Camaguan, on the Portuguesa, are also of some importance; the latter was built by the Capuchins in the seventeenth century. Inundations from the Portuguesa, the Apure, and the Apurito have formed a considerable lake near Camaguan, which appears to be permanent; the Rivers Unare and Apurito are navigable to the neighbourhood of these towns in the wet season.

In the State of Cojedes, the town of San Carlos was formerly a flourishing place, but has now a very reduced population, and many formerly fine buildings are going into decay. The same sad state of things obtains at Barinas, on the River San Domingo, in the State of Zamora; its neighbourhood was formerly a famous tobacco district. Barinas is at the extremity in this direction of the telegraph service of Venezuela. Near it, at Pedraza, are some ruins, traces of an earlier Indian civilisation.

In the State of Portuguesa the chief town is Guanare, founded in 1593 by Francisco de Leon. Besides the usual cattle and live-stock industries, coffee and cocoa are grown in the neighbourhood.

The western part of the country was settled by the Spaniards earlier than the east, but about the towns of the western llanos there appears to be a melancholy air of past prosperity and of arrested development. They have suffered much from wars and political troubles, also from cattle plagues. Their inhabitants now depend chiefly on their cattle, mules, hides, &c.; in some places coffee, cocoa, and tobacco are grown, and there are a few simple manufactures, hammocks, straw hats, earthenware goods, sugar, cheese, &c., being the chief.

Nevertheless, the western llanos undoubtedly possess great resources and convenient outlets. To the north they can communicate with Barquisimeto, Puerto Cabello, and other towns, whilst the streams on which they are situated are all tributaries of the Orinoco, or of its main feeders, thus putting them into communication with Ciudad Bolivar. If good government continues, and capital is attracted, there must come to this great territory a degree of prosperity far greater than it has enjoyed in the past, or than its present inhabitants probably even dream of.

CHAPTER XIV
THE CITY AND STATE OF BOLIVAR

An enormous area—How to reach it—Ciudad Bolivar—Climate—San Felix—Falls of the Caroni—Trade of San Felix—Quality of "roads"—Upata—Guasipati—Balatá industry—Extravagant exploitation—Former importance—The goldfields—El Callao—The discovery—Callao Bis—Big dividends—The common pursuit—Venamo Valley—High freights—Poor quality of labour—Unsystematic working—Goldfields of Venezuela, Ltd.—Savannahs—Stock-farming—Sugar—Old settlements—An ancient bridge—Tumeremo and the balatá forests—Killing the goose that lays the golden eggs—The Caroni—An opportunity for a pioneer—Up the Orinoco—The "Gates of Hell"—The Caura—Rice and tonka-beans—*Lajas*—Rubber of the Nichare—Falls of Pará—André's journeys—Mountains of the upper Caura—The Waiomgomos—Reticence regarding names—Ticks—Caicara—The Cuchivero—Savannahs and *sarrapiales*—Sarsaparilla—Climate of the Orinoco Valley.

Less than two miles up-stream from the ancient citadel of Guayana Vieja, the boundary of the Delta territory crosses the Orinoco, and the right bank of the river becomes the northern limit of the State of Bolivar under the Constitution of 1909. This State includes a vast unexplored region, in addition to the gold-producing district bordering on British Guiana, and occupies in all 238,000 square kilometres, or 90,440 square miles, mainly covered with virgin forest.

The capital of this huge State is the city of Angostura, named in 1846 Ciudad Bolivar, in honour of the Libertador. Its intercourse with the outside world is carried on solely through Port-of-Spain, in Trinidad, from which shallow-draught river steamers run over in about two days, once a week in the busy season, when the rubber, balatá, and other forest products from the interior are being exported in largest quantities, and once every ten days at other times; from the city smaller steamers ply up the Orinoco and the Apure to the borders of Colombia.

Founded in 1764 by the then Governor of the Orinoco province, Don Joaquin Moreno de Mendoza, on the slope of a granite hill overlooking the river, the new city received the name of San Thomé de la Nueva Guayana, as opposed to Guayana Vieja down the river. Later the name changed, naturally, to Angostura, from the fact that the river at this point narrows down to 800 metres, a physical feature which accentuates the rise of the Orinoco to such an extent that in the rains the water-level rises some 40 feet, flooding the lower parts of the city. There is a gradual descent from the fort and cathedral behind the town, with the cemetery again behind them, to the waterside, where there is a good road along the river-front, having the principal private houses and the large stores, many of which are owned by German firms; elsewhere there are scattered mansions dating back to colonial times, with massive walls as protection from the heat. The granite on which the city is built seems to absorb the heat throughout the day, and the radiation after sunset renders the atmosphere unusually oppressive for a town in so fine a position. The mean annual temperature is 86·6° F.

Ciudad Bolivar is the official port of entry, not only for the hinterland of Guayana but also for the eastern gold-mining region, the port of which is in reality passed on the way up the river, and is known as San Felix or Puerto Tablas, a few miles eastward of the mouth and falls of the Caroni. A special permit is occasionally granted for passengers to land at this point without first visiting Bolivar, but normally all passengers and goods perform the eight-hours journey between San Felix and Bolivar twice over, in order to pass through the custom-house at the latter.

The falls of Caroni, near Las Tablas, have been made famous by many travellers since the days of Raleigh, who was struck with the magnificent spectacle of their huge body of water descending a sheer 60 feet over black polished granite to join the greater river of which it is a tributary, after its hundreds of miles of comparatively quiet travel from the slopes of the Sierra Pacaraima, on the borders of Brazil. East of Caroni lie the two most populous districts of Bolivar, those of Piar and Roscio, containing numerous towns and fairly well provided with roads. The district of Heres has in the aggregate a larger population than either of the more easterly divisions, but over two-thirds of the whole of this is accounted for by the congregation of souls in the capital, so that from a general point of view the goldfield area is the most densely populated of all, and included 22,392 of the total of 55,744 in the State at the census of 1891.

San Felix receives its second name of Las Tablas from the elevated plateau behind the town, over which the road climbs to the interior. It is a busy little town, though small, with an hotel, a few stores, telegraph office, and custom-house; the last is rather a coastguard-station, as we have seen that all duties are collected in Bolivar. There is a British consular agent in the port. With the enormous possibilities of the water-power present in the Caroni falls, it seems strange that the place has not developed ere this into a flourishing and important city, instead of the small terminus town that it remains. As it is, the size of the place is no criterion of its commercial standing, for all the imports and exports of the two eastern districts pass through San Felix, and the freight paid there amounts alone to £200,000 annually. Merchandise proceeds southwards on ox-wagons and mule-carts, which carry in cotton goods and hardware and bring back balatá and hides, with the small amount of gold at present produced. The 215 kilometres to Guasipati may take any time from ten days to two months for the wheel traffic, according to the kind used and the season of the year, for the "road" is exceedingly primitive. Bridges are rare, and the route is a mere track cut through the forest or winding over sandy plains, without any attempts at surveying, metalling, or draining, so that deep mud-holes are frequently formed, wherein the wagons may stick for two or three days before they are hauled out with block and tackle. In these circumstances it is not surprising that the ordinary traveller hires a mule for the journey from San Felix, and so covers the distance to Guasipati in about twenty-five hours' actual riding.

The road to Guasipati passes through Upata, the capital of the Piar district, which is about ten and a half hours distant from Las Tablas. After one and a half hours across sandy, open ground, with stunted trees, the edge of the forest is reached, and the road continues through this for some seven hours more, beyond which two hours' riding across open savannah is required to reach Upata. This is a small agricultural town with a population of less than 3,000, forming a market for the neighbouring villages and haciendas, and possessing a hotel, telegraph office, and a few shops.

After Upata the main road to Guasipati crosses the Orinoco-Cuyuni watershed, and winding all the way across open savannahs on which are grazing large herds of cattle, with villages here and there, finally enters the capital of the Roscio district, about fifteen hours' continuous riding from Upata. Needless to say, the journey from San Felix is not necessarily one of two long stages, and those who do not mind putting up with the discomforts of small posadas may take four or five days over the journey.

In 1891 Guasipati had a population of over 3,000, and was then and subsequently the centre of the balatá industry, large quantities of the gum being obtained from the neighbouring forests. Unfortunately, the local operators adopted the extravagant and lazy habit of cutting down the trees in place of tapping them, and the source of supply has consequently retreated into the forests away from the town. For this and other reasons, notably the decreased activity in the goldfields, Guasipati has of late years decreased in size, but it is still the district capital, with the chief courts and registry offices, and possesses a fine plaza and church, hotel, telegraph office, and numerous stores.

While the botanical and zoological resources of the region have proved, as is usual, more satisfactory in the long run than mineral wealth, the principal attraction and chief source of revenue was originally, and to some extent still is, the gold of the El Callao region to the south of Guasipati. The town of that name lies some twenty-five kilometres, or three hours' ride, from Guasipati, on the right bank of the River Yuruari. The town is built on and around the site of the famous mine of the same name, which is said to have been worked by Indians in very early times. The hills above the town are covered with dense tropical vegetation, the second growth which has replaced the former forests, whose trees supplied the fuel used in working the mines. The commencement of recent work and the discovery of the various alluvial and reef deposits is attributed to more than one source, but the most probable story is that which follows:—

The Spanish monks had a station at Tupuquen, on the left bank of the river some four miles above El Callao, and prospectors from this settlement followed up the rich alluvial valley of a small tributary known as the Mocupia, founding there the settlement of Caratal, where there are still many prospecting shafts working free gold from a depth of about 20 feet, with the ruins of various mills erected at a later date, during the boom of the early eighties, including that of the notorious Callao Bis. From Caratal the prospectors spread over the surrounding country and found numerous rich deposits, the chief being El Callao, about two miles from Caratal. In 1842 a Brazilian named Pedro Ayares visited Tupuquen, and recorded the existence of auriferous sands in the river, but primitive washings were not established there till 1849, when good returns were obtained. After many years of prospecting and handwork the El Callao company was formed, and a mill was erected, yielding the following results:—

Year.	Tons crushed.	Gold produced.	Average per Ton.
		Oz.	Oz.
1871	315	3,219·60	6·25
1874	3,963	17,187·68	4·33
1876	12,419	42,542·05	3·42
1878	9,673	49,638·88	5·13
1881	24,978	72,254·62	2·89
1884	30,936	177,055·16	5·72
1886	73,708	118,040·20	2·45
1889	57,301	52,971·35	0·91
1892	52,910	31,945·27	0·60

paying in dividends, from 1871 to 1892, 48,332,200 francs, or £1,933,288. Since that time little of importance has been done, and at the present time the mine is practically shut down, after having been involved in endless lawsuits.

That there is good reason to suppose that the region contains vast mineral wealth can hardly be denied, in view of the widespread indications of gold, so general that it is almost a daily occurrence to see men, women, and boys setting out with pan, pick, and shovel, carried on a donkey's back, to try their fortune at some fresh alluvial discovery. A big rush of men took place to the Venamo Valley, on the borders of Guiana, in December of last year, and the field there is now being opened up, some sixty or seventy miles southward of Callao, and accessible by water only. One of the chief drawbacks to development of any part of the district is the high cost of transport—the freight from San Felix by ox-cart is 9 cents per lb., or over £30 per ton—and this is followed by a scarcity of labour, which is almost entirely derived from West Indian coloured settlers and immigrants, often of a very low type, so that it is necessary to pay B6.00 per day for the lowest class of unintelligent manual labour, and up to B16.00 for skilled (*i.e.*, indifferent fitters') work. These difficulties may, and doubtless will, be overcome in time; but the country moves forward slowly, if at all, and the early attempts at working the mines appear to have been too careless and unsystematic to offer much encouragement to immigration of a good class of settler. Mills were put up on any rich strike, and when that was worked out the company died, without any attempt to find any other sources of ore. Among many companies that have been thus floated from time to time may be mentioned the Nacupai, Chili, Potosi, Union, Victory, and Choco. Practically the only mine now worked regularly is the Goldfields of Venezuela, which has absorbed many of the old companies and employs modern methods under the direction of a superintendent of many years' experience of the peculiarities of the country.

Outside the forest-clad hills of the auriferous territory there are immense stretches of savannah, which are divided up into ranches, and have been found excellent for cattle-breeding, though as yet the horses raised there are of very indifferent quality; the stocks are small, however, and much extension is possible in the industry, which is hardly so important at the present time as the cultivation of sugar. Many plantations and mills are to be found in the eastern districts of Bolivar, and the large quantities of rum and *papelon* (raw sugar) produced give a good return, the local demand for these commodities being considerable.

There are still some ruins, and in some cases modern villages, to mark the sites of the old Spanish settlements, among which may be mentioned Tupuquen, Carapo, Sicapra, and Cura; the last named must once have been a place of considerable importance, as near by are traces of a bridge over the

Yuruari, the only one on record, and of a brick and tile factory. It is said to have been the port for small trading boats coming up the Essequibo and the Cuyuni from Dutch Guiana; the old Dutch bells found near by are adduced as evidence in support of this statement. The place is now entirely abandoned and in ruins.

Some six hours' ride south of El Callao is the town of Tumeremo, which is rapidly coming to the fore as the centre of the balatá industry. At present it is near the forests, which are of enormous extent; but the system of wholesale destruction of the trees still prevails, and it is to be feared that the history of Guasipati will be repeated here, and that the industry will perish by a suicide's death at no very distant date.

CARRYING THE TILES ON OX-BACK; NEAR TOVAR.

Famous as are the falls of the Caroni, the upper course and tributaries of this great river are practically unknown. For some fifty miles from its mouth, until the savannahs finally give place to forest, villages may be found on the sites of the old Capuchin Missions. The chief tributary is the Paragua, but this and the minor affluents are alike known chiefly from the casual information of the Indians who inhabit the forests along the banks. Yet there may be extensive savannahs in the uplands, and the geology of Guayana would lead one to expect to find gold, while the forests undoubtedly contain great wealth of timber and vegetable products, all waiting to reward the industry of the pioneer bold enough to take his lot in these remote regions.

Above Bolivar the Orinoco has a tranquil course for some distance between llanos on the north and granite hills and savannahs on the south. Above Moitaco, however, there is a sharp S bend, with many islands, where the current gradually increases in strength as one approaches the Puerto or Boca del Infierno (Gates of Hell), where the whole stream rushes through a narrow gorge with such force as to occasionally drive back the river steamers. Beyond this to the mouth of the Caura the main river, though full of rocks, is wide and the current less rapid.

Like most of the Guayana tributaries of the Lower Orinoco, for the last forty or fifty miles before it joins the main river the Caura flows through wide savannahs, broken here and there by wooded hills, and by the belts of trees along the river banks. In these more fertile belts clearings have been made at a few spots, with one or two miserable huts, whose occupants cultivate the sugar, rice, bananas, manioc, sweet potatoes, and yams of these tiny plantations.

Higher up the forests begin, and, as far as is known, the upper valley of the Caura is all forest, with very few savannahs. In these forests the tonka-bean (*sarrapia*) grows to perfection, and the collecting of these, and of a certain amount of copaiba-balsam and cedar-wood, constitutes the chief industry of the Caura settlements. Of late years the tonka-bean has gone down in value, and the inhabitants have turned their attention more to rice-farming, for which the Caura lowlands are well fitted. Most of the produce is used locally, but a small surplus is shipped to Ciudad Bolivar.

The dense forests are not absolutely unbroken, however, for here and there are bare open spaces of flat granite rock, known as *lajas*; it is to these that the foresters come often to crush and dry the tonka-beans. Up the Nichare, a western tributary of the Caura above the Raudales of Mura, there is said to be much rubber of good quality, but it remains practically untouched for want of population in the region.

Some 130 miles up the Caura from its mouth are the falls or rapids of Pará, with a total descent of apparently about 200 feet, according to André, the author of the only reliable account of the Upper Caura. Some day, as he suggests, the falls may provide power for saw-mills and a town whose prosperity is founded upon the natural wealth of the surrounding forest; at present all is wild, and almost unknown. There is a portage over the falls, by way of an island in the middle, and then begins the Merevari, as the Caura above Pará is called.

The two chief tributaries on the west bank are the Nichare, already mentioned, and the Erewato, above Pará, once colonised by the early missionaries and afterwards the line of a short cut to the Upper Orinoco; now the valley is unknown to Europeans.

Two days' journey in canoes above the big rapids is the gorge of Ayaima, where the great stream is forced to rush through a channel 30 feet wide, between walls of granite. Above this the flat-topped, steep-sided peak of

Achaba, and beyond it those of Arichi to the west and Améha to the east, may be seen. On his adventurous journey André reached the last of these, where he experienced one of the severe thunderstorms of the region, interpreted by the Waiomgomos as the angry voice of the spirits of the mountain.

These Waiomgomos are found in their original haunts round the head-waters of the Caura, and there they are said to go about with faces and bodies painted bright red, wearing only the *guayuco* or *buja*. It is strange that they are very reluctant to give their Indian names to outsiders, and always on approaching the bounds of civilisation adopt a Spanish name.

The forests and savannahs of the Lower Caura, like most of the districts near the Orinoco, are frightfully infested with bush-ticks, mosquitoes, and sandflies; higher in the hills these pests decrease, but they effectually prevent absolute enjoyment of an exploring trip where they are found.

Beyond the Caura's mouth the main river is devoid of special interest to Caicara, where it comes sweeping round a hill, leaving a fine backwater behind as a safe anchorage for boats—the reason of the former importance of the town, now, alas! only a village of mud and wattle huts. Its commerce is confined to rice, tonka-beans, and hides, the latter from the savannahs which stretch away southwards in all directions to the hills.

The Cuchivero, which enters the Orinoco fifteen miles east of Caicara, is, in part at least, far better known than the Caura, and, though smaller, is a more important river at the present time, since the savannahs of the Cuchivaro support many cattle, and there are *hatos* here and there as far as the Raudal Seriapo. These savannahs are of guinea-grass, broken here and there by *chaparral*, moriche-palms, or *morros*—*i.e.*, small rocky hills covered with trees, amongst which the *Dipteryx odorata* is common, giving to the wooded mounds the name of *sarrapiales*.

The waters of the Guaniamo, a tributary of the Cuchivero, are said to be noticeably affected by the quantity of sarsaparilla on the river's banks, and the whole upper valley of the Cuchivero is rich in rubber, copaiba, quinine, mahogany, "cedar," and other valuable forest products. According to Major Paterson, traces of gold, cinnabar, and silver are found in the hills. In the distant south are the typical mushroom peaks of Guayana, showing that here also the geology is similar to that of the goldfield area, and the minerals may therefore also be alike.

It is not pleasant travelling in the Cuchivero forests, Major Paterson tells us. The trees grow over loose rock, and the crevices under the tangled roots may often cause nasty falls; and there are the ubiquitous mosquitoes and sandflies, to make matters worse. But higher up the insects become fewer, and from the occasional savannahs or *lajas* splendid views may be obtained of the hill ranges to the south, between the Caura and the Ventuari. The Indians of these forests are presumably the Piaroas, said to be a peaceable, mild race.

The climate of all the lower Orinoco Valley is far from pleasant in the rains, but in the dry season, which lasts from October to March, an easterly breeze blows both morning and afternoon, the sweltering interval during the lull at midday serving only to accentuate the pleasant comparative coolness of the rest. The nights then are often chilly, owing to the heavy dews.

CHAPTER XV
THE AMAZONAS TERRITORY

Area—General character—San Fernando de Atabapo—The upper Orinoco—Communication with outside world—Atures and Maipures rapids—Humboldt's description—The Compañía Anónima de Navegacion Fluvial y Costanera—General Chalbaud—Railway projects—The Piaroas—*Curare*—Savannahs—Rubber—Brazil-nuts—Wild cocoa—Mineral wealth—Water-power—Rubber prospectors—Method of working—Esmeralda—The place of flies—Mt. Duida—Gold possibilities—The Raudal de los Guaharibos—The limit of exploration—The Ventuari—An old Spanish road—A midnight massacre—Stock-raising lands—The Maquiritare—Trading with gold-dust—The Casiquiare bifurcation—Life of the natives—Eau de Cologne in the wilds—The Guainia and Rio Negro—Maroa—Cucuhy—The Atabapo—Lack of population—Education—Colonisation—General prospects.

On the right bank of the Orinoco above the confluence of the Meta and below that of the Atabapo, and south-eastward of this on both banks of the main river, lies the great but little known Territorio Amazonas, extending over the ill-defined watershed into the Rio Negro, and, therefore, the Amazon, basin. The area included in the territory amounts to some 281,700 square kilometres or 101,400 square miles, and of this vast region practically nothing is known, save the character of the banks of the larger rivers and of such parts of the hills and forests as may have been traversed by the few explorers who have entered the hinterland of the Guayanas.

On the northern and eastern borders the general character of the region is like that of the greater part of the State of Bolivar, the boundary to the north being more or less arbitrary, in part at least. The Brazilian frontier follows the watershed of the Sierra Parima in its northern part, but near the Rio Negro this line also ceases to be determined by any clearly marked natural features.

The capital of this huge and almost unknown area is San Fernando de Atabapo, little more than a village from the point of view of population, which amounted to only 388 in 1891, but still the largest centre in the region. It is situated at the junction of the Atabapo and Orinoco, the land on which it stands being practically an island on account of the channel connecting the two rivers behind the settlement; the Inirida and Guaviare enter the Atabapo opposite the town, the contrast between the white waters of the Guaviare, the black, clear stream of the Atabapo, and the muddy Orinoco being very noticeable. The capital is the seat of the Governor and a Judge of First

Instance and minor officials, who constitute an appreciable fraction of the population.

The upper Orinoco basin includes some of the best known, as well as some of the least explored districts in the whole territory. The old mission station of Esmeralda (longitude 65° 40′ W., latitude 3° 11′ N.) marks the limit of any attempt at civilisation on the upper Orinoco, and beyond this point our knowledge of the country is very scant indeed. Below this point the river and forests and savannahs near its bank are comparatively well known, from the number of travellers and small rubber prospectors, as far as San Fernando, and below this again little exploration has been carried out away from the river, which, nevertheless, is the main line of communication with Pericos, below the Atures Rapids, whence steamers run down the lower Orinoco to Ciudad Bolivar, and so afford communication with the outside world.

The Atures Rapids, the biggest on the Orinoco, form at present an effectual barrier to through communication by steamer, between the upper and lower river, a difficulty formerly obviated by the construction of a now disused cart-road from Pericos to Salvajitos, above the rapids, a distance of 14 kilometres. But though the rapids have thus barred the advance of civilisation, their great beauty and the possibility that one day they may afford the power for an electric railway along the line of the old cart-road beyond compensate for any such disadvantage.

Humboldt thus describes the Maipures and Atures Rapids in his "Ansichten der Natur." They are, he says, "to be regarded as a countless number of small cascades succeeding each other like steps. The *Raudal* (as the Spanish term this kind of cataract) is formed by an archipelago of islands and rocks, which so contract the bed of the river that its natural width of more than 8,500 feet is often reduced to a channel scarcely navigable to the extent of 20 feet. At the present day the eastern side is far less accessible and far more dangerous than the western.

"... It was with surprise I found, by barometrical measurements, that the entire fall of the Raudal (of Maipures) scarcely amounted to more than 30 or 32 feet.... I say with surprise, for I hence discovered that the tremendous roar and wild dashing of the stream arose from the contraction of its bed by numerous rocks and islands, and the counter-currents produced by the form and position of the masses of rock.

"... The beholder enjoys a most striking and wonderful prospect. A foaming surface, several miles in length, intersected with iron-black masses of rock projecting like battlemented ruins from the waters, is seen at one view. Every islet and every rock is adorned with luxuriant forest trees. A perpetual mist hovers over the watery mirror, and the summits of the lofty palms pierce through the crowd of vapoury spray. When the rays of the glowing evening sun are refracted in the humid atmosphere, an exquisite optical illusion is produced. Coloured bows appear, vanish, and reappear, while the ethereal picture dances, like an *ignis fatuus*, with every motion of the sportive breeze.

"... A canal might be opened between the Cameji and the Toparo ... which would become a navigable arm of the Orinoco, and supersede the old and dangerous bed of the river.

"The Raudal of Atures is exactly similar to that of Maipures, like which, it consists of a cluster of islands between which the river forces itself a passage extending from 18,000 to 24,000 feet.

"... rocks, like dykes, connected one island with another. At one time the water shoots over these dykes, at another it falls into their cavities with a deafening hollow sound. In some places considerable portions of the bed of the river are perfectly dry, in consequence of the stream having opened for itself a subterranean passage. In this solitude the golden-coloured rock manakin builds its nest."

The contract recently entered into with General R. D. Chalbaud, the President of the Compañía Anónima de Navegacion Fluvial y Costanera de Venezuela, stipulates for a railway worked by steam or electricity to provide a land connection between a service of upper Orinoco steamers above the Maipures Rapids and the lower Orinoco steamers already plying below those of Atures; the time may not be far distant, therefore, when these beautiful falls will also add to the sum of the world's happiness by assisting in opening up a vast extent of territory rich in agricultural and mineral products, which hitherto they themselves have been largely instrumental in closing.

From the right bank of the Orinoco in the region of the rapids along the Sipapo and Cataniapo tributaries to the hills forming the watershed between that river and the Ventuari, and beyond these, is the unknown territory of the Piaroa Indians, whose sacred mountain of Sipapo is visible from the Orinoco banks. The name Piaroa appears to be a general term including those branches of families of the Maipures, Atures, &c., which were formerly considered to be separate tribes. Tavera-Acosta describes them as a timid people, devoted to agriculture, and they are said to be very light in colour. They frequently come down to the town of Atures to exchange their curare, cotton, cassava, plantains, and game for general merchandise and tools; and their curare is held in high esteem for its purity and high quality by the other tribes.

Of an unexplored country such as that of the Piaroas little or nothing can be said definitely with regard to the products, but the observations of travellers as to the country along the river banks and the circumstantial accounts of the remainder derived from some of the inhabitants point to this region as one rich in all manner of resources.

Near the Orinoco and at intervals throughout the region there are grass plains, or savannahs, which may some day, like those elsewhere in Guayana, support many thousand head of cattle. In the forests which surround these savannahs there are quantities of untouched rubber-trees (*Hevea guianensis* and *H. Brasilensis*). Though near the rivers, the wild rubber has been exploited to some small extent, not always wisely, the output of the district is very far below what it might be, apart from the possibility of plantation rubber, the lack of development being due, as throughout the Orinoco region, to lack of population. Practically all the available hands work at the collection of rubber, but a few trees of *Bertholettia excelsa*, the Brazil-nut, have been planted near San Fernando, and the enormous quantities of wild nuts which at present lie on the ground and rot will doubtless one day be systematically collected and exported; to mention only one other of the many forest products, there are, along the Orinoco below San Fernando, many natural cacao patches (*Theobroma cacao*), as yet untouched and undeveloped. It is hardly necessary to speak of the valuable timber-trees of which the forests are largely composed, and the quantity of natural vegetable products of the region is as yet only to be surmised from the casual specimens brought in by natives or travellers.

Nor is there lack of mineral resources; the *lajas* which so often occur both in the savannahs and as bare patches in the midst of the forest frequently show indications of metallic ores, and below Pericos, on the Orinoca, copper is said to be visible in the river banks. The Indians frequently show specimens of ores, iron, manganese, copper, and even gold, the localities of which they are not unnaturally unwilling to reveal until there is some prospect of development of the "mine."

Finally, the big falls on the Cataniapo and Sipapo and other tributaries of the Orinoco, with the rapids of the main river, promise a supply of power in the Piaroa territory sufficient for all probable demands for many years to come.

The 75 kilometres of open water between the Atures and Maipures Rapids is navigable for steamers during the greater part of the year, but the upper of the two great "raudales" proves a bar again to through communication with the upper Orinoco and its tributaries. Above Maipures, however, there is no serious hindrance to navigation, even through to the Amazon basin by way of the Casiquiare bifurcation.

CROSSING THE TORBES IN FLOOD.

Some twenty miles above Maipures the Orinoco receives the large volume of water drained by the River Vichada from the llanos of the San Martin territory of Colombia, and a little over one hundred miles from Maipures the Guaviare and Atabapo discharge their waters side by side into the main stream.

From the mouth of the Guaviare up to Esmeralda is probably the best known portion of the upper valley, since it is here that the majority of small rubber prospectors have obtained small fortunes after a short period of hard and rough labour in the insect-infested forests. The same causes as those referred to above in the lower parts of the Orinoco have here also prevented more systematic and continuous exploitation; those who have ventured to brave the discomforts and dangers of the forest have almost invariably retired with their gains to taste such pleasures of civilisation as the towns of the Lower Orinoco and neighbouring regions afford; thus the scanty population remains stationary, and previously, from want either of sufficient interest or opportunity, capital has never attempted to introduce colonists or to develop the resources of the region with such labour as can be had.

The *picadores de goma* have thus only seen the forests along the river for a few kilometres on either bank, and the remoter parts of the region are as little known as any other part of the territory of the Amazons. The rubber collectors enter the forest in the month of October, the season lasting from then to February or March, and parcel out the forest among themselves, each man taking an area including some five hundred trees or more. He then proceeds to cut an *estrada* through the forest along a tortuous course, so arranged that about half the rubber-trees lie on either side. He will begin to traverse this path at sunrise and tap the trees of either group on alternate days, the latex being carried back to the river late in the day and put to smoke in huts by the river. Each day he may collect eight or ten gallons of sap, and so twelve or fifteen hundredweight in the season, in addition to inferior gums derived from the creepers which hang everywhere from the large forest trees.

The rubber and other valuable trees, including the wild cacao and brazil-nuts, seem to become less scattered above Maipures, and this is doubtless an additional reason for the greater extent of exploitation in this more remote district, while it should also be remembered that the Casiquiare affords a highway for the bold and industrious Banibas and other Indians of the Rio Negro basin to the rubber-producing forests, which afford better returns than those in their immediate neighbourhood.

About forty miles above the mouth of the Guaviare, where the Orinoco again changes the direction of its course from parallel to meridian, the Delta and mouth of the great Ventuari tributary is encountered and beyond this the course is in a south-easterly direction and so continues as far as the source. The famous Casiquiare bifurcation is about 150 miles above the mouth of the Ventuari; and Esmeralda, the highest point of attempted permanent civilisation on the Orinoco, is some twenty miles beyond.

Esmeralda was, even in Humboldt's time, a flourishing mission, but has been now for many years little more than a name, the houses being reduced to two or three huts. The name is derived from the quantity of fragments of chloritic and colourless quartz which lie scattered about the grass plains on which the mission was established. All travellers bear witness to the beauty of the position, with the peak of Duida visible beyond the forest to the north-east; but they also agree in considering Esmeralda the worst place for the tiny sandflies (mosquitoes of the Spaniards), which are the great plague of the Upper Orinoco.

Duida appears to be one of the peaks of the vertical-sided tableland type usual in Guayana, belonging to a range of mountains extending into the Piaroa territory, though broken at many points by river valleys, including that of the Ventuari. Though similarity of form cannot always be regarded as indicating identity of composition, the fact that such observations as have been made point to the floor of the whole elevated plateau of Guayana, here as elsewhere, being made of the same granite as that of the Roraima Hills and the Callao goldfields. It seems justifiable to suppose that all these peculiar mountains are of the same probably pre-Cambrian sediments, and it may be that Mount Duida and the range of which it is part will be found to be pierced by the dykes and sills which elsewhere in the Guayanas are often found to be accompanied by gold and other ores.

Beyond Esmeralda several travellers, from the time of Don Francisco de Bobadilla downwards, have reached the Raudal de los Guaharibos, but all have been compelled to turn back from those rapids, on account of the ferocity of the Indians of that name. Only one traveller claimed to have been more fortunate than the rest and to have reached the source of the great river. The Guaharibo Rapids are situated some 120 miles up-stream from Esmeralda.

The Ventuari is the largest Venezuelan tributary of the Upper Orinoco, yet the three hundred miles or so of its course are practically unknown to Europeans. As far as its valley has been explored, alternating forests and savannahs have been found. Across these in colonial times there was once a track uniting Esmeralda directly with the Lower Orinoco by way of the Caura; the route lay up the Padamo and then across the head-waters of the Ventuari to the source of the Erewato, a tributary of the Caura. Along this road there was a chain of forts, but the cruelties of the soldiers at last led the Indians to unite for their examination, and Humboldt tells us that every man in the fifty-league-long chain of forts was slain one night in 1776. The Indians told him that by this road it was ten days from Esmeralda to the headquarters of the Ventuari, and two days thence to the mouth of the Erewato.

Some of the upland savannahs which this road crossed must be excellently situated both for occupation by Europeans and for stock-raising, but the region is naturally very difficult of access at present, lying as it does in the very back of the hinterland of the Guayana. These districts are occupied by the Maquiritare, near relatives of, if not identical with, the Waiomgomo of the Caura. Their territory produces rubber and timber as well as gold. Auriferous quartz is said to have been seen by casual traders up the Ventuari, and the inhabitants collect the precious metal, storing it in jars, with which, by devious waterways and many portages, they travel across to British Guiana to trade for rifles of a quality unobtainable in southern Venezuela.

Separated by a narrow ridge from the Ventuari is the upper valley of the Merevari (Caura), a practically unknown region, scantily peopled by the Waiomgomo, and apparently possessing no particular attractions from a commercial point of view.

On the south side of the main river we have one of the most notable instances of a natural phenomenon peculiar to the elevated inland plain of South America in the celebrated bifurcation of the Casiquiare, some twenty miles below Esmeralda. The watershed between the Orinoco and the Rio Negro is here very ill defined, and near the bifurcation a line of slight elevation on the southern bank of the former river is all that exists to separate the two great drainage systems. At the head of the Casiquiare the elevation is sufficiently reduced to allow some part of the water of the Orinoco to overflow into the southern drainage area, and so affords a through waterway to the whole of the Amazon Valley.

On the eastern side of the *Brazo*, as it is called, there are numerous tributaries, whose upper courses are absolutely unknown, save from the casual reports of wandering Indians. The main stream and its affluents alike flow through great forests, and the immediate neighbourhood of the Casiquiare being level, the valley is damp and abounds in small lakes and swamps.

There is abundant rubber in the forests, but the life of the inhabitants of the small settlements, which are mainly supported by this industry, is a miserable one. They live chiefly on cassava, accompanied by much alcohol in one form or another, from champagne to raw sugar spirit; if other beverages fail, they have even fallen back on eau-de-Cologne, brought from Pará or Ciudad Bolivar and, one would have imagined, too expensive a luxury to be imbibed in quantity.

The Casiquiare discharges its waters into the Guainia, or more correctly, the two streams join to form the Rio Negro, the river being known by that name below the junction. The highest village of importance on the Guainia is Maroa, the seat of government of the Rio Negro district. The Guainia being a clear, deep (*i.e.*, black) stream, with a cloudless sky overhead and no mosquitoes, Maroa enjoys a good climate. Its inhabitants cultivate an excellent quality of manioc and manufacture hammocks.

The forests of the Guainia and Rio Negro are comparatively little known, though some rubber is collected along the banks. The old settlement of San Carlos, on the Rio Negro, is now abandoned, and beyond this there are no Venezuelan villages before the hill known as the Cerro del Cucuhy, which marks the Brazilian frontier, and beyond lies the military station of Cucuhy, occupied by soldiers of the latter republic.

Although, as we have seen, it is possible to travel by water from the Orinoco to the Amazon, the more direct route up the Atabapo and across the "Isthmus" of Pimichin to the Guainia is generally used by the Indians and traders.

Above San Fernando there are no towns on the banks of the Atabapo, though many native villages. To the south-east of the capital is the wide savannah of Santa Barbara, capable of supporting a vast number of cattle. Farther south the banks are forest-covered, and when the head of navigation is reached at Yavita the route across to Pimichin lies between giant trees, which have attracted the attention of many travellers. The watershed here between the two rivers has no great elevation, and it would be possible to excavate a canal and so provide a far shorter waterway between the two great river systems. Whether such a project will ever seem to be justified is another matter.

The great hindrance to progress over the whole of the Amazons territory is at present lack of population, for with less than two persons to the square mile it is impossible to do much towards developing the country. Apart from their natural lack of enthusiasm, the Indians have for over a century been neglected as far as education is concerned, and whether judicious action in this direction on the part of the Government would be possible or profitable one cannot say. The general tendency of the authorities is rather towards colonisation by Europeans, with due regard to the protection of the Indians. However its development may eventually come about, there is no doubt of the great possibilities of the territory, pastoral, agricultural, and mineral resources being alike abundant and untried.

CHAPTER XVI
THE DEVELOPMENT OF VENEZUELA

Commerce—Early history—Pearls and gold—The Guipuzcoana Company—The republic—Years of struggle—Separation from Colombia—Guzman Blanco—British, American, and German trade—Opportunities—Currency—Banking—Banco de Venezuela—Banco Carácas—Banco de Maracaibo—National Debt—Natural resources—Large returns on capital—Coal—Iron—Salt—Asphalt and petroleum—Sulphur—Copper—Gold—The Llanos—Stock-raising—Possibilities of the industry—The Venezuelan Meat Products Syndicate—Agriculture—Coffee—Cocoa—Sugar—Tobacco—Cotton—Rubber—Tonka-beans, balatá, sernambi and copaiba—Fisheries—Pearls—Industries—Chocolate—Cotton-mills—Tanning—Matches, glass, and paper—Cigarettes and beer—Arts and sciences—Academy of History—Universities—Surveys.

The gradual advance of Venezuela into a position of real importance in the commonwealth of nations can hardly be considered to have commenced till the country took approximately its present political boundaries and organisation, since before that time the movement in commercial dealings with the outside world had been fitful and very retrogressive.

The casual coincidence of some of the colonial and republican provinces prior to 1830 is, however, a sufficient excuse for a brief review of the course of such development as took place between the discovery of South America and the final severance of Venezuela from Colombia.

As has been seen in the sketches of the early history of Venezuela, the pearl fisheries of the Caribbean Islands were the lure which first attracted a band of settlers who, however unworthy of the title of pioneers or merchants, were nevertheless the first traffickers who carried the produce of the New World to Europe. The value of the pearls exported in the early years of the sixteenth century appears to have been very great, and equal to, if not in excess of, all the produce and merchandise shipped annually from the colony of Venezuela in the closing years of Spanish rule. After the destruction of the pearl fisheries by the reckless and extravagant exploitation of the *conquistadores*, the value of the exports varied according to the quantity of gold and precious metals extorted from the Indians, and little trading was carried on.

As the easily accessible stores of gold decreased, the Court of Spain sought to acquire gain in a not entirely new fashion from the colonists by selling them to the Compañía Guipuzcoana in 1728, which, at first but a chartered company with special privileges, soon obtained a monopoly, and became by its extortions the cause of the first attempt at revolt on the part of the captaincy-general. At length their rights were abrogated in 1778, and the commerce of the colony was at liberty again to develop in a normal fashion; though the continued arbitrary opening and closing of the ports to foreign nations could not but render any advance very fitful. In 1796 the imports into Venezuela during one of the "open" periods reached a total of over £600,000, and in 1810 the increasing quantity of tropical produce transmitted to the East was nearly one million pounds in value.

Though, under the republic, the commerce of the country has greatly increased, the twenty years following the Declaration of Independence were a period of great industrial depression. For the first ten years or so the war with Spain practically put a stop to ordinary trade with foreign countries; during the joint administration of the three provinces of Venezuela, New Granada, and Ecuador in the Great Colombia of Bolivar, Venezuela suffered in all departments of her life, until at last the union was severed in 1830, and from that date it is possible to compare the progress of Venezuelan commerce with that of other nations; for convenience this has been expressed in a diagram, the solid line corresponding to exports and the dotted line to imports. The zenith of Venezuela's prosperity in the seventy years was reached during the Presidency of Guzman Blanco, the figures for the present day being far below these. The excess and growing excess in value of exports over imports is natural in a country rich, as Venezuela is, in easily won agricultural and mineral resources but poor as yet in manufactures and shipping; and that this is so may be readily seen from the detailed table of exports and imports for 1909-1910 given in Appendix B.

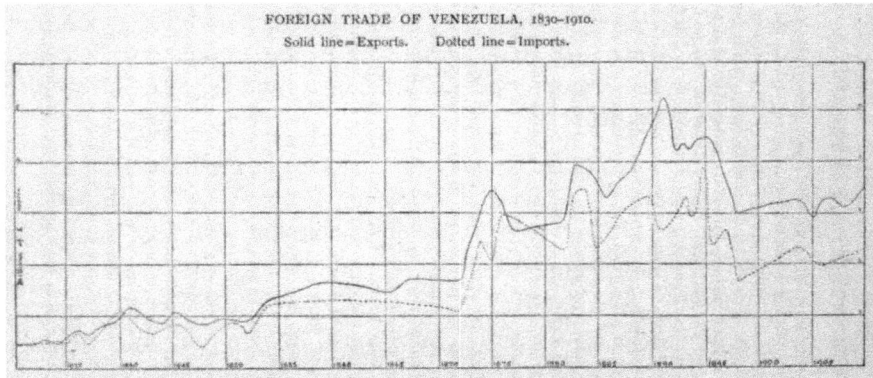

FOREIGN TRADE OF VENEZUELA, 1830-1910.

Solid line = Exports. Dotted line = Imports.

As may be seen from the tables in Appendix B, the largest exporter to Venezuela at the present time is the United States, with Great Britain second and Germany third. It is only within the last two or three years that the United States have advanced to this position of superiority in the trade of the republic, Great Britain having previously held the lead. There is little need to inquire into the cause of this influx of American goods, when in travelling through even remote parts of the country one meets with travellers exhibiting and praising American inventions and manufactures such as are calculated to appeal to the Venezuelan public, and this in spite of the fact that at the present time the American, as such, apart from his personal attractiveness or otherwise, is not *persona grata* in the country. The big stores, with branches in most of the more important towns, are mainly in the hands of Germans, but the goods sold are largely British and American. More than one of them attributed their possession of this trade to the fact that they are willing to live in the country and work there for a far smaller return at present than the British trader; but the day of small things is not to be despised, and in view of the expansion of trade and the amelioration of the standard of living evident at the present time in Venezuela, there is a great opportunity for British merchants to adopt the persevering tactics of the German, and to some extent the pushfulness of the American, not only to increase the sale of their products already shipped in large quantities into Venezuela, but to do the selling themselves.

The chief medium of exchange has been continuously since 1812 the coinage of the republic, which was at first issued after the Declaration of Independence from the old royal mint at Carácas, but for many years all the best known European moneys of the higher denominations were accepted at a fixed rate. In 1848 the franc was for a short time adopted as the unit, followed by the *Venezolano* (1854), and in 1879 the *bolivar*, equivalent to a franc, was first suggested, but only finally standardised in 1891, since which time it has remained the unit.

Banks were first established in the early eighties, but the big commercial houses, both before and since that time, have carried on a good deal of banking business. The recognised banking institutions of the country are three in number, all being permitted to issue notes pending the establishment of a long-mooted National Bank.

The Banco de Venezuela has a nominal capital of B 12,000,000, of which three-quarters is paid up. A charter was first granted by the Government to a group of Venezuelan merchants and capitalists on March 24, 1882, to form a *Banco Commercial*, but in 1903 it became, and has since remained, national as well as commercial. In August, 1890, the bank was reconstructed as the Banco de Venezuela, with a capital of B 8,000,000, the charter to hold good for fifty years; it underwent a second reconstruction in 1899, since which date the nominal capital has been B 12,000,000, divided into 600 shares of B 20,000 each, in the hands of 276 shareholders. The note issue is B 2,000,000, and the reserve fund at the end of 1908 was B 1,200,000. The dividend declared that year was equal to 8 per cent. on the total capital. The bank has its headquarters in Carácas, with fourteen agencies in the towns of the republic.

The Banco Carácas was incorporated on August 23, 1890, the charter holding good for forty years. The nominal capital is B 6,000,000, divided into 600 shares of B 10,000 each, and there are now 137 shareholders. The note issue is B 801,000, the reserve fund at the end of 1908 being B 579,483, while the dividend declared in that year was equivalent to 3·9 per cent. on the capital. The bank is wholly devoted to commercial business, and has its headquarters in Carácas, with various agencies throughout the republic.

The Banco de Maracaibo received a thirty-one-years charter on May 11, 1882, and was incorporated with a capital of B 1,250,000, of which three-quarters has been paid up. The 3,750 shares are held by 161 persons, who received in 1908 a dividend of 9 per cent. on the total capital; at the end of that year the reserve fund was B 125,000, while the note issue was B 1,895,000. The headquarters of the bank are in Maracaibo, and there are various agencies in the western States of the republic.

The National Debt of Venezuela dates in the first place from a few years after the Declaration of Independence, but until 1830 it was, of course, included with that of New Granada and Ecuador in the Great Colombia. At that date the various internal floating debts on the custom-houses were consolidated at 5 per cent. and a further consolidation was authorised in 1840. In 1845 a further arrangement was made under the treaty with Spain for the payment of indemnity to Spanish subjects whose property had been confiscated by the republic. Later loans have been raised for certain public works, &c., bringing the total internal debt in 1909 to over two and a half million pounds.

The external debt has a more eventful history, and dates from 1820, when the first moneys were borrowed by Colombia in London. £547,783 was the amount raised, the interest payable being at 8 per cent. if paid in London and 10 per cent. if paid in Colombia. At the division of Colombia in 1830 the total debt had increased to £9,806,406, of which £3,180,456 was for arrears of interest; the new republic was adjudged responsible in 1834 for £2,794,826, being £1,888,396 of the original debt, with £906,430 arrears. In 1840 an attempt was made to put matters on a regular footing by the issue of bonds for the outstanding capital debt, bearing interest for the first seven years at 2 per cent., with a subsequent increase to 6 per cent. at the rate of ¼ per cent. annually. Deferred bonds were issued for the arrears bearing interest at 1 per cent. for the first year with a ¼ per cent. annual increment up to 5 per cent. The total value of bonds issued was £2,007,159, the interest being paid regularly until 1847, when internal troubles prevented the payment of the October dividend.

After a period of chaos, a further arrangement was made in 1859 by which the earlier ordinary bonds were to be exchanged for others paying 2½ per cent. for the first year, and 3 per cent. subsequently, while similar bonds were to be issued for the arrears on both ordinary and deferred stock. The deferred stock was to be exchanged for 1½ per cent. bonds. Finally the bondholders agreed to accept 3 per cent. stock for the arrears of interest from 1840 to 1847, with a 2 per cent. cash payment in September, 1860.

In 1862 a £1,000,000 loan was arranged through Baring Brothers, in London, the issue to be at 63 per cent., the bonds to bear interest at 6 per cent. with 2 per cent. annual redemption. The security was 55 per cent. of the La Guaira and Puerto Cabello import duties; two years later a further loan on the same terms was issued through the General Finance and Credit Company of London, the issue price being 60 per cent.

In 1880 the bonds and loans since 1859 were converted into a new consolidated debt of £2,750,000 at 3 per cent. By resolution of August 5, 1887, the diplomatic debt (to France and Spain) was added to the National Debt, and these two branches of the external debt were duly recognised in 1889, the diplomatic claims of about £200,000 being paid interest at the rate of 13 per cent. Internal disturbances prevented the payment of interest in 1892 and 1893, but otherwise the amounts were regularly forthcoming.

In 1896 a further loan of £2,000,000 was authorised for the payment of the guaranteed interest to certain railways, and for acquiring and completing other lines. This loan, issued by the Diskonto Gesellschaft in Berlin at 80 per cent., bears interest at 5 per cent., but the requisite sum was not paid by Venezuela either for this or other debts in 1897, and only partial payments were made down to August, 1901, when they ceased altogether.

In 1903 payments were resumed, and between that year and 1907 the amounts awarded to the three favoured nations after the 1903 blockade were paid off, while the sums due to other nations were reduced before 1910 from B 21,000,000 to B 13,000,000. In 1905 also the old English 3 per cent. debt and the 1896 loan were united under the name of the Three Per Cent. Diplomatic Debt. Between 1906 and 1910 over B 33,000,000 of debt were paid off, the total at the beginning of that year being B 207,995,052.72 or £8,111,807. At the close of the year this had been further reduced to B 197,807,477.83, or £7,714,490. Nearly £400,000 was thus paid off in the first year of General Gomez's presidency.

The natural resources of the country have received little attention hitherto, in comparison with the abundance and extent of the opportunities for investment of capital. The desultory attempts at development have in many cases met with extraordinary success, the best known instance being that of the Callao goldmine, while the return obtained for capital has been very high both for Venezuelans and foreigners; the failure of at first successful enterprises or the failure of others from the commencement has in nearly every case been due to lack of foresight, careless management, inadequate or inflated capital.

The republic has been best known to miners as a producer of the rarer metals and minerals, but the more satisfactory, if less showy, resources are not wanting, though some, such as the fine building and ornamental stones, have been absolutely neglected.

In many parts of the Caribbean Hills the Segovia Highlands, the Andes, as well as the Maracaibo and Coro lowlands, deposits of coal are known to exist, and have been worked in a perfunctory manner in various regions. There are *minas de carbon de piedra* west of Maracaibo, where the coal appears to be of very good quality; and similar seams have been extracted near Coro by shallow workings. The most extensive coalmines are those of Naricual, some fifteen miles eastward of Barcelona.

The ores of the other great staple mineral, iron, are vaguely referred to in descriptions of various imperfectly known parts of the country, but the only deposit which has hitherto attracted the interest of capitalists is that of Imataca on the foothills of the range of the same name in the Delta-Amacuro territory, on the banks of the Caño Corosimo. The veins are said to be numerous and extensive, and 700 tons were shipped to Baltimore in 1901, when the ore was examined and described as magnetic with 60 to 70 per cent. of iron. The main deposit is known as Imataca, but neighbouring *minas* bear the names of Tequendama, El Salvador, Nicaragua, La Magdalena, El Encantado, Costa Rica, and Yucatan; a concession for the whole of the known ferriferous area was granted on August 14th of last year (1911) to the Canadian-Venezuelan Ore Company, Limited, of Halifax, N.S.

Salt is, perhaps, the most profitable source of mineral wealth, in view of the Government monopoly, only certain persons being licensed to mine or otherwise obtain it. One of the richest sources is the salina of Araya, discovered by Niño in 1499, where there is an extensive surface deposit of pure sodium chloride; the majority of these salinas are situated on the dry, treeless stretches formed by ancient marine deposits, from which the salt is obtained by digging pits, these being filled with water in such a way as to dissolve out the salt of the surrounding sands and clays, and then evaporated to dryness in the sun. Several thousands of tons are obtained annually in this way near Maracaibo, on the Island of Coche, while some is also produced near Barcelona. The Coche salt is said to be the whitest and finest, but much of the inferior yellow variety is consumed in the Andine States.

THE "PITCH" LAKE, TRINIDAD.

Venezuela has long been known as a source of asphalt, and there are indications of the existence of the parent mineral, petroleum, all over the northern and western States. A few desultory and ill-advised attempts have been made to develop the petroleum resources in such places as Pedernales, in the Delta, and other localities near the coast; but the only satisfactory work has been carried out by the Venezuelan Compañía de Petroleo del Táchira, in the southern part of the State of that name, where for some years the oil was raised in shallow wells, refined, and sold in the neighbourhood for illuminating purposes. The more easily worked and discovered asphalt deposits have been mined both on Pedernales Island and the mainland near the Gulf of Paria, where the Bermudez asphalt "lake" is found near the Guanoco River; the area covered by the black, pitch-like residue of petroleum here is said to be considerably larger than the famous "pitch lake" of Trinidad, but the thickness of the deposit is less. The total amount exported in 1908 amounted to 37,588 metric tons, most of which was from the Bermudez property, Pedernales having only been exploited by a German company for a short time about ten years ago.

The only other non-metallic mineral which has been developed in any way appears to be sulphur, which occurs in considerable quantities near Carúpano, some eighteen kilometres from the port, in the mountains. A

German company was formed in 1903 with a capital of 2,000,000 marks to work the deposit.

Copper ores are believed to exist at many places in the mountains of Venezuela, and the mines of Seboruco, Bailadores, and other places, both in the Andes and the Caribbean Hills, were worked formerly with profit. A rich deposit has recently been opened up near Pao, in the north part of the State of Cojedes, but the chief development of this resource of the country has taken place at Aroa, in the State of Yaracuy. Here extensive plant was set up some twenty years ago by a British company, and large quantities of regulus were shipped from Tucacas, the maximum being 38,341 tons in 1891. This earlier work came to an end, however, owing to the fall in prices, and the mines have only recently been reopened, when on a small capital they have made very large returns under the able management of Mr. Scrutton; the amount of ore exported in 1908 was 3,334 metric tons, and in 1909-10 4,950 metric tons, valued at about £7,000.

Gold has always since the Conquest been one of the principal attractions offered by Venezuela to prospectors and some few capitalists, and it must be acknowledged that the evidence of the various attempts proves that gold in great quantities exists in the Callao region, where the majority of the mines have been located. Lack of experience and carelessness among the managers of the earlier concerns have led to shutting down of mine after mine, when once the more accessible parts of the vein have been exhausted, or it has been lost by faulting. Among the earlier mines the El Callao was perhaps the most famous, but at all times the mining industry in this remote region has been hampered by the cost and difficulty of transport, a drawback only to be removed by the construction by the Government either of proper macadamised roads or of railways, preferably the former to begin with. In spite of the various difficulties, however, the quantity of gold exported from Ciudad Bolivar in 1908-9 was 385·774 kilograms, and in 1909-10, 601·974 kilograms.

No visitor to Venezuela who penetrates far enough into the country to catch a glimpse of the Llanos can fail to be impressed with the possibilities of the country in stock-raising and exporting, and yet this great area of pasturage supports, in proportion to its extent, a mere handful of cattle and horses. The quality of the grass of the Llanos may be inferior to that of the Argentine Pampas, but even such a defect, if existent, may be improved in time, and so far no pedigree stock have ever been introduced, nor has the industry ever been seriously handled.

In 1804, according to Depons, there were 1,470,000 cattle, horses, and mules on the Llanos, and by 1812 the total number had increased to 4,500,000; but during the wars of independence, owing to the depredations by the opposing armies, the number was greatly decreased, and in 1839 was still only a little over 2,000,000. In the meantime, however, the excellent qualities of the Barquisimeto tableland and the Coro and Maracaibo lowlands for breeding goats had been discovered, and the export of goats' horns and hides has been continuously an important item in the trade of Western Venezuela. In 1888 the number of heads of stock on the Llanos had increased to 8,500,000, and at that period many were exported to the other States and islands of America, a few even to the United States. Ten years later revolutions and counter-revolutions had decreased the number to 2,000,000.

The export trade in live stock has never attained very great dimensions, and in 1909-10 the value was £40,374, while the always more important item of hides, horns, and hoofs of cattle and goats was valued at over £320,000. The establishment of the Venezuelan Meat Products Syndicate works for shipping frozen meat from Puerto Cabello should do much to encourage an industry as yet in its infancy and yet of incalculable interest to the country, once properly developed.

As is the case with other resources, of the many agricultural products of Venezuela only a minority have been energetically developed, in some degree on account of lack of population to collect the natural fruits in such prolific regions as Guayana, but also on account of failure to appreciate the natural advantage of the many climates to be found within the northern part of the country, where may be grown, not only the rare fruits of the tropics but the, to many, more pleasant fruits and flowers of the cooler zones.

The three cultivated plants which have multiplied sufficiently to form the basis of considerable industries are coffee, cacao, and sugar-cane. Of these coffee was first introduced from the West Indian Islands towards the end of the eighteenth century, and the plantations now cover much of the cultivated land of the northern hills. The bushes grow anywhere between elevations of 500 and 2,000 metres, but the region immediately below the 1,000 metre line is found to be the best; and at this elevation flourishing plantations are to be found in the central part of the Coastal Cordillera, and in the Andes; the Carabobo and Segovia coffees are not so good, however, as those grown elsewhere. The plants are set from 1,600 to 1,900 to the hectare, each when matured producing ¼ to ½ lb. annually, or 400 to 950 lbs. per hectare, the life of each bush being taken as about fifty years. The value of the coffee exported in the year 1909-10 was nearly £1,500,000.

Cacao is indigenous to Venezuela, and the wild trees abound in the forests of Guayana. Before the advent of Europeans it is believed that no cultivation of cacao was carried on, but the plantations of Venezuela produce some 8,000 tons annually at the present time, of which some is renowned above all other cocoa of the world. The chief cocoa districts are the neighbourhood of Carácas, parts of the Orinoco Delta, and the Maracaibo Lake region. In the financial year 1909-10 the total exports were valued at about £700,000.

Sugar can be grown anywhere in Northern Venezuela, except on the Llanos and in the higher mountains, or where, as near Barquisimeto or Coro, the atmosphere is too dry. In addition to the native or Creole sugar, there are three varieties from the East known as Otahiti, Batavia, and Selangor cane. From the juice of these sugars crude (*papelon*) and refined (*azucar*), with alcohol (*aguardiente*) and rum are manufactured, the greater part of the crop being utilised in distilleries. Most of the sugar comes from the Maracaibo and Carácas districts, but the product is for the most part consumed in the country, as are the million or so bottles of alcohol. The exports for 1909-10 amounted to £20,000.

Tobacco can be grown all through the foothills of the Cordilleras, but the only important centres are the upland valleys south of Cumaná, in the east, and near Capatárida, in the State of Falcón; the latter is said to be the best, and considerable quantities of the leaf are sent to Havana. Cotton also grows wild along the dry northern coast, and has been cultivated to some extent, particularly after the American Civil War; at the close of the last century the exports amounted to 450 tons, but in 1909-10 only 63 tons were shipped, the greater part of the native product being used in the Valencia mills. Of the remaining agricultural produce most is consumed in the country, the principal plants being maize, manioc (of which some is exported), and (in the Andes) wheat.

Of the wild products rubber has been known to occur in Guayana since 1758, and the latter has been collected since 1860 in a desultory manner by individual prospectors; some is also produced in the forests of Zulia, but the largest quantity passes through Ciudad Bolivar, which exported some 440,000 lbs. of caoutchouc in 1909-10, valued at over £116,000. The tonka-beans, balatá-gum (see p. 215), sernambi, and copaiba-balsam of Guayana are also collected and exported, to say nothing of the many valuable timbers, with which little is done as yet, while coconuts have their place among the minor agricultural products of the country.

The fisheries of Venezuela, if these can be considered as existent, are of very slight importance, and even the pearling-grounds have comparatively little value. These are more or less controlled by the Government, and unlimited concessions have been granted to companies from time to time, a system not calculated to secure the greatest possible length of life for this national asset. The value of the stones exported in 1909-10 was about £21,000.

As we have seen, the industries of Venezuela are in their infancy, and have as yet no international importance, and apparently little for the country itself, in spite of the enormous protective duties on all kinds of manufactures.

Chocolate of good quality is made in Carácas, some 45,000 lbs. being turned out by "La India," but the high-priced imported article is more sought after.

Cotton goods are manufactured in Valencia, drills, flannelette, canvas, &c., being the principal varieties, largely made of the local produce. In spite of the great grazing-grounds of Venezuela very little butter is made in the country, and the inhabitants seem here also to prefer the inferior but much more expensive imported (tinned) variety. An important industry throughout Northern Venezuela is that of tanning, dividive and mangrove bark being the principal materials used; the leather is used chiefly for boots and saddles.

Matches are a Government monopoly, and are manufactured in Carácas. The glass industry, heavily protected though it is, does not seem to have acquired any great importance since its inception in 1906, though paper (chiefly of inferior quality) has been manufactured since 1897.

The two most profitable local industries are the cigarette factories and breweries; the former, a heavily protected monopoly, exists in many parts of the republic, though the largest output is from the Federal District. The Cervecería Nacional was established in Carácas in 1894, with a capital of B 600,000, increased in 1901 to B 2,500,000; it has flourished continuously, and bought up the smaller rival breweries of Valencia and Puerto Cabello. There is also a brewery in Maracaibo, and very little beer is imported into Venezuela.

It is, perhaps, early yet to look for development in the arts or sciences in Venezuela, but there have been one or two painters of note; and of a vast output of flowery writing some is worthy of the name of literature. In this connection the Academy and the Academy of History, with the museum and library in Carácas, deserve honourable mention.

There are two Universities, as we have seen, that of Carácas dating from 1725, that of Mérida from 1810; in both the best faculties are those of medicine and law, few of the many "doctors" in the country having any knowledge of other branches.

Although after the separation from Colombia steps were taken to have a survey made of the republic, the first preliminary studies of Codazzi have remained till very recently all that have been done. Since 1907, however, there has been a Commission, under the control of the War Department, which is slowly collecting material for a map of the whole country, but so far only a small area has been completed.

CHAPTER XVII
COMMUNICATIONS AND TRANSPORT

Lack of adequate means—Postal service—A small but growing system—Methods of carriage—Unusual uses of mailbags—Telegraphs—Telephones—Railways—Bolivar Railway—Later lines—Tramways—Abundant water-power—"Roads"—*Carreteras*—Bridle-paths—P.W.D.—Waterways—Less than they seem—Importance—The Orinoco—Ports—Shipping—Steamship lines.

Those who know something of Venezuela away from the few ports and towns generally visited by Europeans will doubtless consider the title of this chapter a misnomer. Indeed, it is the lack of adequate means of communication between the different parts of the republic which hinders more than any single cause its progress and development. Revolutions and internal dissensions have been the immediate trouble, but these, if not caused, are at least fostered, by the absence of better roads than bridle-paths and of more permanent lines of communication than single telegraph wires; though in justice it must be said that in times of peace the last-named service is far ahead of the other branches.

Venezuela is included in the Postal Union, though owing partly to the custom of "farming" the stamps, the cost of transmission of letters in the interior is twopence-halfpenny and from Venezuela to foreign countries fivepence.

The Post Office is considered as a branch of the Ministry of National Development, and employed 358 officials in 1909. The G.P.O. in Carácas is well administered, and from this the quality of the service ranges through the principal offices of each State to the two hundred rural offices scattered up and down the more frequented parts of the republic. More and more money is being spent annually in an endeavour to make the service thoroughly efficient, and in 1908-9 the expenditure under this head was B 848,444, or £33,602. In 1908 the number of interior postal packets carried was about 4,500,000, 2,750,000 letters were received from, or dispatched to, foreign countries, with 18,500 parcels; the number of letters dispatched abroad was rather smaller. The comparison between 4,500,000 and 4,500,000,000, the number of letters handled by our own Post Office some years back, makes the Venezuelan service seem insignificant, but at least it exists and is capable of expansion to an efficient system of communication throughout the country.

In the *Centro* the mails are, of course, carried by train between the big towns, and the deliveries are fairly punctual, while the service to the seaports is sufficiently good; elsewhere, however, the mail-trains of mules wander casually along the "roads," the postbags often forming only an insignificant part of the loads; in more outlying parts still the mails are carried on foot. On one occasion the author with a friend was guided along about thirty miles of obscure track by the "postman" (aged sixteen), who had one U.S.A. mailbag, which during part of the journey was occupied jointly by the letters and tins of sardines and other provisions for the long tramp; the letters did not appear to suffer greatly, but this familiar use of a mailbag of a foreign Government seemed somewhat unorthodox, even though it be less so than the application of the striped remains to sail-patching, many of the small sloops and goletas being wafted on their way by means of fragments of mailbags, generally Uncle Sam's.

But though the postal service outside the principal towns and most populous districts is very primitive, the telegraph service, with its cheap rates, is well managed and efficient.

The first telegraph line in the country was that between La Guaira and Carácas, opened in 1856; in 1909 there were 7,839 kilometres of wires in the country and 179 offices, with a staff of 800 men. In the financial year 1908-9 the cost of the service was B 2,041,385, or £80,847, and 394,792 messages were sent in 1908, at a total charge of B 936,657 (£36,429); more than half of these were official.

In addition to the Government lines there are a few private wires along the railways, and telegraphic communication with the outside world is carried on by means of the French cable, which runs from La Guaira to Curaçao.

Such telephone lines as exist are mainly in the hands of private companies or individuals, and only 10 of the 120 lines existing are owned by the State. The British Telephone Company in Carácas has a very efficient exchange there and trunk lines to the chief towns of the *Centro*, and also a telephone service in Ciudad Bolivar.

Means of transport are in much the same condition as lines of communication—that is to say, there is in existence the nucleus of a complete system; but "the end is not yet," and to-day one must be prepared for anything in travelling over wide areas in Venezuela.

In and around Carácas, and between most of the large towns of the *Centro*, one may travel with as much ease and comfort as in parts of Europe, and better than on a certain line running out of London, but beyond, though there may be in some directions roads on which carts can be used, one is more often reduced to the means of locomotion of sixteenth-century England. Outside the *Centro* there are a few comparatively short lines, which can hardly be regarded as forming part of the railway system of Venezuela, though they may one day become part of it.

There are in all eleven railways in the country, but one has practically ceased to exist, and it is a long time since any train ran on it. The total number of passengers carried in 1908 was 413,000, and nearly 184,000 tons of freight.

Of the eleven lines the oldest, strangely enough, is not in the *Centro*, though, being connected with the main system by steamer, it may be considered as part of it. This is the Bolivar Railway, which commenced in 1873 as a line from Tucacas to the copper-mines of Aroa, and was subsequently extended to Barquisimeto. It has a 24-inch gauge, and its present length is 176·5 kilometres. The La Ceiba line was authorised in 1880, and has a ·91-metre gauge, with a present length of 81·5 kilometres; the same year saw the commencement of the La Guaira-Carácas Line, already described in an earlier chapter. Two years later a 1·07-metre line was commenced from the port of Guanta to Barcelona and the Naricual coalmines. In 1884 the Maiquetia-Macuto street railway was built to afford easy communication with the chief watering-place of Venezuela; it has the same gauge (·91-metre) as the Carácas line and is 8 kilometres in length. The railway from Carenero to Rio Chico was commenced in 1884, and is now 50 kilometres long, but, like the La Ceiba line, this is not part of the central system. The Central Railway, originally planned in 1885 to connect Carácas and Valencia by a circuitous route, never accomplished that end, and merely affords a means of communication between Carácas and the towns of Miranda, and is now 42 kilometres in length, with a gauge of 1·07 metre. The Puerto Cabello and Valencia line was commenced in the same year and is 54 kilometres long, while the Gran Ferrocarril de Venezuela, the German line, was contracted for in 1888, and at one and the same time obviated the extension of the Central, as originally planned, and completed the nucleus railway system of Central Venezuela as it exists to-day. It has a total length of 179 kilometres. The short line connecting Coro and La Vela was built in 1893, and is, like the Táchira line, commenced at the same time, owned in the country; the latter has a length to-day of 114·5 kilometres and is of the standard Venezuelan gauge, 1·07 metre. The Santa Barbara-El Vigia line was the last to be commenced (1896), but it has already fallen into disrepair, and of the 60 kilometres little, if any, remains in usable condition.

In Carácas a system of electric tramways not only provides rapid transit from one part of the city to the other but also runs out southwards to the suburb of El Valle. There are also lines of varying motive power and efficiency in Valencia, Puerto Cabello, Maracaibo, Ciudad Bolivar, Barquisimeto, Carúpano, and Cumaná. In view of the quantity of available water-power in the mountain districts of Venezuela, one imagines that electric traction will one day be very widely used, but, like many of the possibilities of Venezuela, this lies almost entirely in the future.

Descending to the less rapid methods of travelling by road, we find the whole country is in much the same condition as England or Western Europe four hundred years ago, for, with the exception of some ten carreteras of very indifferent quality, the roads of Venezuela are bridle-paths, and occasionally hardly worthy even of that title.

COUNTRY COACH: BARQUISIMETO.

ON THE BOLIVAR RAILWAY.

Such cart-roads as there are have to some extent been engineered, but none are macadamised. The best is that from La Guaira to Carácas, 35·4 kilometres long, but even this is little used by wheel traffic. One of the longest is the high-road from Carácas to Valencia, 168 kilometres, but this is exceeded by that connecting San Felix, on the Orinoco, with Guasipati, which has a length of 219 kilometres, with a 25-kilometre extension to Callao; the whole road is in a fearfully bad state in the rains, however, as to which matter enough has been said in Chapter XIV. From Carácas another main road goes eastward 70 kilometres down the Guaire valley to Santa Lucia, and yet another south-east to Charallave, 47 kilometres away. From Valencia, also, cart-roads radiate to Puerto Cabello (70 kilometres), to Nirgua (90 kilometres), to Güigüe for Villa de Cura (34 kilometres), and to San Carlos (99 kilometres).

There are also cart-roads under construction from Puerto Cabello to San Felipe, between Uracá and San Cristobal, and one or two in other parts of the Andes.

Among the bridle-paths there are a few with cobble-paved surfaces, dating back to early colonial times, but these have fallen into disrepair, and in Guayana they have been disused for so long that their whereabouts is often unknown, save where the Indian trails cross or follow a bit of the old paving here and there. For the rest the way is generally passable, but sometimes up to the animal's belly in mud; here there are bridges over the mountain torrents, there none; the deeper streams may have ferries, but to be held up by an extra heavy fall of rain is no uncommon event. The Government spent nearly £80,000 on the Public Works Department in 1908-9, but since not all even of this small sum is devoted to actual road-making or other improvements, it will be seen that things are being only gradually improved; and it may be long yet before the asphalt and rock of the country are applied to the betterment of the uninspiring yet all-important roadways, at once one of the simplest and one of the most efficient methods of developing the nation's natural resources.

The waterways of Venezuela, numerous and general as they appear on the map, are singularly disappointing on closer investigation. The great Orinoco is a fine natural highway, it is true, as far as Pericos, some 600 miles from the mouth, but here the river is broken by the rapids of Atures and beyond by those of Maipures, and it is impossible for large boats to pass through to the upper river. The Apure, Arauca, and Meta are, of course, useful means of communication with the Colombian border regions and the south-western Llanos, but the numerous tributaries on the north side are generally too variable in depth for permanent traffic, and those on the south, as we have seen, are broken up by rapids for practically their whole length.

On the other hand, if we take the positive value of the river highways, rather than their actual extent as compared with the number of streams indicated on a map, we can see that they are of considerable importance; the rivers of Guayana and of the eastern Llanos may be of little use for large boats, but the Orinoco forms a great central artery, from which roads, and perhaps eventually railways, can diverge to the limits of the basin. Some of the Llano tributaries, too, are navigable for steamers, and thus the State of Apure is now kept in communication with the outside world—all this without speaking of the great advantage accruing to the State of Zulia from its central lake, with its many tributary navigable rivers, along which large boats can travel throughout the greater part of the State, and on to the boundaries of those of the Andes, as well as into the neighbouring republic of Colombia. Along most of these natural and easily utilised lines of communication there are already services of steamers—nothing very advanced, but still a beginning.

There are twelve ports with custom-houses for trade and communication with the outside world, but that number includes the new one of Imataca, on the Caño Corosimo, in the Delta territory, established August 14, 1911. Puerto Cabello ranks first for number of vessels, La Guaira second, and Carúpano third; all, except Caño Colorado, have regular wharves, adequate custom-houses, &c. The total number of vessels received in the year 1909 was 645, with an aggregate tonnage of 937,689, of which two-thirds were steam-propelled. It is interesting to compare the standing of the various countries in tonnage of steamships, as given in the following table:—

Nationality.	Tonnage.	Number of Vessels.
Dutch	212,375	151
United States of America	155,269	85
British	149,565	67
French	149,114	36
German	106,257	53
Italian	71,760	21
Spanish	43,785	13
Norwegian	30,978	42
Venezuelan	10,651	158
Swedish	4,808	7
Russian	2,346	7
Danish	778	3
Colombian	3	2

Thus Holland is far ahead in point of numbers, though by no means first in trade, while France comes above Germany, even though the imports from the latter are much greater. The small number of Spanish vessels speaks eloquently as to the fitness of Spain to retain her South American colonies by force after her decline.

Finally, for communication with the outside world, these are the following chief lines and the ports they run to:—

Nationality.	Line.	Ports.
Dutch	Koninglijke W. I. Mail	Amsterdam to Carúpano, Cumaná, Guanta, La Guaira, Puerto Cabello, and Curaçao
U.S.A.	Red "D"	New York to La Guaira, Puerto Cabello, Curaçao, and Maracaibo
British	R.M.S.P.	Puerto Cabello to Southampton (when so announced)
British	Harrison	Liverpool to La Guaira and Puerto Cabello
British	Leyland	The same
French	Cie. Gén. Transatlantique.	Bordeaux to Carúpano, Pampatar, La Guaira, and Puerto Cabello
German	Hamburg-Amerika.	Hamburg to Cumaná (Puerto Sucre), Pampatar, Guanta, La Guaira, and Puerto Cabello
Italian	La Veloce	Genova to La Guaira and Puerto Cabello
Spanish	Cia. Transatlantica Española	Barcelona to La Guaira and Puerto Cabello
Venezuelan	"Nacional"	Maracaibo, via all ports except Cristobal Colón, and Caño Colorado, to Ciudad Bolivar

The most usual route from England is of course via Trinidad, travelling to Port-of-Spain by the R.M.S.P. and on by Dutch, French, or other line to La Guaira; the Red "D" route, via New York, may be quicker, if other services do not suit, but it is less pleasant, owing to the longer time spent in northern (and stormy) latitudes.

CHAPTER XVIII
THE FUTURE OF VENEZUELA

A great opportunity—The Panama Canal—The Llanos—Petroleum-fields—Liquid fuel—Position of Venezuela—Guayana—Possibilities—Colonisation—Government—The military-political class—The disgrace of labour—Better conditions—Vargas—The "Matos" revolution—General Gomez—Hopes to be realised—Honesty and justice—Development—Roads—Railways—Education—Consular service—Great Britain's trade with Venezuela—A poor third—British capital—The people's responsibility—An opportunity.

What will be the condition of Venezuela twenty or thirty years hence? The question is one to which no exact answer can be given, for it involves the consideration of so many, variable factors. We may, however, safely say that in that period there will be either no advance or a very great one; in the latter case, the country may well rival Argentine in world-importance.

The resources to some of which increased prosperity will be due have already been described in the body of this volume, but we can here pass in review the chief national assets, and glance also at the methods which will have to be adopted to secure the right atmosphere for the full development of the country.

In doing this, we must take into account one external event which may be expected to occur within the next two years, namely, the opening of the Panama Canal, for it will give Venezuela an opportunity such as she has never before had of developing her foreign trade by leaps and bounds. Many of her products are common to other countries equally well situated for taking advantage of the increasing shipping facilities afforded by the "Ditch," but two of her undeveloped assets in respect of which she enjoys exceptional conditions are found in the great natural grazing-grounds and the subterranean stores of petroleum; the latter are as yet untried, but assuming that they fulfil their promise, Venezuela can supply equally well to the Pacific and the Atlantic food and fuel—*i.e.*, not luxuries but necessities.

The area of the Llanos has been estimated as over 100,000 square miles, so that Venezuela has here a space large enough to support a vast herd of cattle. Their markets, it is true, will still lie rather in the populous countries of Europe than in any of those brought nearer by the canal; but increased shipping facilities should encourage the improvement of stock and the development of the industry along lines which will make the country of real international importance, for it must be remembered that Venezuela is a week nearer to Europe than the other great meat-exporting country of the South, Argentina.

The oil resources of Venezuela do not possess any unique qualities either from a strategic or a topographical point of view; in other words, their product is not the nearest to the line of steam-traffic to the Isthmus, nor are the fields so situated in the country that they could be worked with greater ease than, for instance, those of Trinidad or Peru.

We must digress for a moment to notice more fully the importance of a strategic position, from the point of view of commerce, not of war. It is a well-known fact that one of the greatest hindrances to a more general adoption of liquid fuel, apart from the question of permanence of supplies, is the absence of regular oiling-stations, so that steamers burning petroleum are handicapped as to freedom of movement in a way in which coal-burning boats are not.

Now let us glance once more at Venezuela's position, from the point of view of strategic position; the topography of the country and the present means of communication will probably render it more easy to develop these oil-fields than those of the neighbouring republic of Colombia, though the latter lie nearer to the canal-zone; if this be so, Venezuela and Trinidad may be considered together as the largest area of oil-producing country situated in such proximity to the canal as to make it possible for vessels to replenish their stores of fuel conveniently. Whether the oil is taken on board in Trinidad, at one of the Venezuelan ports, or at Colón, the advantageous position of the fields is equally clear for European boats, which would then, on this sea-route, be in a position almost analogous to the oil-burning boats between Japan and San Francisco, where they are in the Californian fuel-oil region.

There seems reason to suppose that Venezuela has extensive areas producing oil of the type requisite, and therefore her future importance depends largely upon the energy with which she discovers or encourages others to discover where and how the mineral can be most profitably won.

Nor must the possibilities of Guayana be ignored in this general summary, for a considerable proportion of some of the larger exports given in Appendix B is shipped through Ciudad Bolivar; these are mainly, of course, forest products and gold, but there are great possibilities of increased output of both these, with the development of more permanent agricultural and pastoral resources in the woods and savannahs of southern Venezuela. The introduction of industrial colonists has, as we have seen, been planned already, and much may come of the wise prosecution of such a scheme.

Under these three heads we have the undeveloped resources of Venezuela, but there remains a long list of products exported, some of which already aggregate a considerable value, while others are capable of great increase. There is no necessity to deal with these various products in detail here, since a glance at the table in Appendix B will show their relative importance. The question remains, What is needed that Venezuela's trade may be free to expand and may be assisted in that expansion by those in authority?

First and foremost, there is the character of the Government itself to be considered. Venezuela, like most of the rest of Latin America, has suffered much at the hands of a military-political class, whose one method of acquiring and retaining power has been that of force; while, once installed in the places of authority, the members of that class have devoted most of their time to acquiring wealth and power for themselves, and little or none to the task for which they have been "elected" (in theory) by the people. To such an extent were the doctrines of this class general that it had been found impossible to persuade good men and true to take control of the national finance, those fitted to do so knowing well that any attempts at reform on their part would at once be thwarted by their self-seeking colleagues in the Ministry, to whom adequate public control of expenditure would be abhorrent.

Nor can the republic be blamed for the existence of this class, whose traditions are merely a slightly exaggerated copy, of those of the early Spanish aristocratic colonists, who deemed it derogatory to work, but thought it no shame to exist upon the forced labour of others; with the break-up of slavery conditions, which occurred before their actual abolition, these men and their descendants, often not of pure Spanish blood, preferred political intrigues and the leadership of revolutions to honest work, and until recent years this caste has held the government in the majority of the Latin-American republics. The belief in the disgrace of labour is not common to any age or any country among men of a certain type, but the class who hold these views have held more power and have been more numerous in South America than in Europe, unless we go back some three or four hundred years to the days when "gentlemen" were supposed to live like the lilies of the field, with an occasional fight at other people's expense to relieve the monotony of existence.

Early in the history of Venezuela's independence an abortive attempt was made, in the election of Doctor Vargas to the presidency, to counteract the evil influence of the military politicians of the revolution, but Mariño and his friends, whose names should surely be reviled by every true patriot in Venezuela, made the succeeding chaos inevitable, and it may be doubted if the spirit which revealed itself in the election of Vargas in 1834 attained such prominence again until the time of the Matos revolution, which was an attempt (in 1902) of the people of Venezuela to do away with the military power by defeating it on its own ground. That revolt failed, but it is noteworthy that the supporters of the present régime were prominent among its leaders.

Whether with the growing dislike for military dictatorships there has come the equally necessary love of justice and straight dealing, and real hatred of political jobbery, time alone will show. High hopes have been fostered by the speeches of General Gomez for the greater stability and responsibility of the Governments of the republic, and it remains for the people of Venezuela to see that these hopes are realised. Just and honest government is the first need of the country; given those conditions, its development should, indeed must, be rapid.

Such a Government should divert the revenue of the country from the private pockets, into which too much of it has hitherto gone, to such beneficent ends as the improvement of ways of communication, the cause of popular education, and the establishment of an efficient consular service abroad.

Real roads, with macadam surface, would cause modern methods of transport to supersede the antique pack-mule method, and railways would follow without direct Government intervention. A system of free popular education is in existence, on paper, but in reality the overwhelming majority of Venezuelans are as yet absolutely illiterate; yet the individuals are far from dull, and increased learning will doubtless, ere long, leave no chance of return for the rule of inefficiency and disorder. The consular service is already being improved, and it is to be hoped that the effect on foreign commerce will soon be felt for good.

From a geographical point of view Great Britain should be more interested in Venezuela than in any other South American republic. Not only is it almost the nearest part of that continent to our shores, but in British Guiana, Trinidad, Tobago, and Barbados, to say nothing of other West Indian islands, we are her next-door neighbours. In spite of these facts the amount of British capital in Venezuela is only some £8,000,000 sterling as compared with £44,000,000 in Uruguay; we are a very poor third in the list of her customers, the next highest, France, buying four times as much as ourselves, and the United States nearly six times. As far as the amount of capital invested is concerned, the comparative stability of the various countries may be urged as a reason, but there seems no reason why we should not foster trade in Venezuela by purchasing more of those of her many products which we need, and since a large proportion of these would be shipped through Trinidad, it might be urged that we should thereby strengthen one of the islands of the Empire.

The future of Venezuela depends primarily on her own people, who will have to rouse themselves to develop in a conscientious and painstaking manner the many resources of their country; but it is certain that in the task which lies before them they will need and obtain the assistance of foreign capital and advice, and in this, if British enterprise is alive to a great opportunity, we, as a nation, should bear no small part.

APPENDICES

APPENDIX A
POPULATION OF STATES AND DISTRICTS UNDER THE CONSTITUTION OF 1909 ACCORDING TO THE CENSUS OF 1891

State.	District.	Capital.	Population.
ANZOÁTEGUI		**Barcelona**	**134,064**
	Aragua	Aragua	36,802
	Bolivar	Barcelona	26,235
	Bruzual	Clarines	12,467
	Cagigal	Onoto	10,811
	Freites	Cantaura	16,665
	Independencia	Soledad	4,092
	Libertad	San Mateo	7,200
	Miranda	Pariaguán	5,222
	Peñalver	Píritu	8,773
	Tadeo Monágas	Mapire	5,797
APURE		**San Fernando**	**22,937**
	Achaguas	Achaguas	4,746
	Muñoz	Bruzual	1,848
	San Fernando	San Fernando	12,186
	Páez	Guasdualito	4,157
ARAGUA		**La Victoria**	**94,994**
	Girardot	Maracay	9,505
	Mariño	Turmero	13,235
	Ricaurte	La Victoria	25,712
	San Casimiro	San Casimiro	9,405
	San Sebastian	San Sebastian	5,292
	Urdaneta	Camatagua	9,533

	Zamora	Villa de Cura	22,312
BOLIVAR		**Ciudad Bolívar**	**55,744**
	Cedeño	Caicara	3,847
	Heres	Ciudad Bolívar	21,582
	Roscio	Guasipati	12,391
	Sucre	Moitaco	7,923
	Píar	Upata	10,001
CARABOBO		**Valencia**	**169,313**
	Bejuma	Bejuma	18,282
	Guacara	Guacara	15,362
	Montalbán	Montalbán	17,469
	Ocumare de la Costa	Ocumare	4,157
	Puerto Cabello	Puerto Cabello	18,489
	Valencia	Valencia	95,554
COJEDES		**San Carlos**	**87,935**
	Anzoátegui	Cojedes	3,697
	Falcón	Tinaquillo	15,964
	Girardot	El Baúl	9,108
	Pao	Pao de San Juan Bautista	20,907
	Ricaurte	Libertad	9,248
	San Carlos	San Carlos	17,963
	Tinaco	Tinaco	11,048
FALCÓN		**Coro**	**139,110**
	Acosta	San Juan	7,910
	Buchivacoa	Capatárida	} 18,898
	Jurado	Urumaco	
	Colina	La Vela	9,655
	Democracia	Pedregal	13,176
	Falcón	Pueblo Nuevo	19,590

	Federación	Churuguara	10,622
	Miranda	Coro	19,686
	Bolivar	San Luis	} 19,438
	Petit	Cabure	
	Silva	Tucacas	3,943
	Zamora	Cumarebo	16,192
GUÁRICO		**Calabozo**	**183,930**
	Bruzual	El Sombrero	21,189
	Infante	Valle de la Pascu	21,564
	Miranda	Calabozo	25,860
	Monágas	Altagracia de Orituco	31,297
	Roscio	Ortiz	27,072
	Zaraza	Zaraza	56,948
LARA		**Barquisimeto**	**189,624**
	Barquisimeto	Barquisimeto	41,321
	Cabudare	Cabudare	16,938
	Crespo	Duaca	12,868
	Quíbor	Quíbor	20,273
	Tocuyo	Tocuyo	41,559
	Torres	Carora	40,140
	Urdaneta	Siquisique	16,525
MÉRIDA		**Mérida**	**88,522**
	Campoelías	Egido	12,457
	Libertador	Mérida	29,437[7]
	Miranda	Timotes	6,601
	Rangel	Mucuchíes	4,783
	Rivas Davila	Bailadores	6,875
	Sucre	Lagunillas	13,166
	Torondoy	Torondoy	1,595

	Tovar	Tovar	13,608
MIRANDA		**Ocumare del Tuy**	**141,446**
	Acevedo	Caucagua	16,776
	Brión	Higuerote	7,963
	Guaicaipuro	Los Teques	25,414
	Lander	Ocumare del Tuy	13,305
	Páez	Rio Chico	18,621
	Paz Castillo	Santa Lucia	13,673
	Plaza	Guarenas	6,817
	Sucre	Petare	17,964
	Urdaneta	Cúa	12,509
	Zamora	Guatire	8,404
MONÁGAS		**Maturín**	**74,503**
	Acosta	San Antonio	8,829
	Cedeño	Caicara	21,852
	Monágas	Maturín	25,874
	Piar	Aragua de Maturín	14,144
	Sotillo	Uracoa	3,804
NUEVA ESPARTA		**La Asunción**	**40,197**
	Arismendi	La Asunción	6,266
	Diaz	San Juan Bautista	8,705
	Gomez	San Ana	9,080
	Maneiro	Pampatar	5,144
	Marcano	Juan Griego	5,309
	Mariño	Porlamar	5,693
PORTUGUESA		**Guanare**	**96,045**
	Acarigua	Acarigua	11,871
	Araure	Araure	12,463
	Esteller	Píritu	8,450
	Guanare	Guanare	30,008

	Guanarito	Guanarito	10,432
	Obispo	Ospino	12,233
	Turén	Villa Bruzual	10,588
SUCRE		**Cumaná**	**92,030**
	Arismendi	Rio Caribe	11,268
	Benítez	El Pilar	12,889
	Bermudez	Carúpano	17,500
	Mariño	Cristobal Colón	8,777
	Mejías	Marigüitar	5,402
	Montes	Cumanacoa	8,133
	Rivero	Cariaco	7,396
	Sucre	Cumaná	20,665
TÁCHIRA		**San Cristobal**	**101,709**
	Ayacucho	San Juan de Colón	8,041
	Bolivar	San Antonio	8,195
	Cárdenas	Táriba	12,882
	Capacho	Independencia	9,091
	Junín	Rubio	12,229
	Jauregui	La Grita	18,804
	Lobatera	Lobatera	5,143
	San Cristobal	San Cristobal	19,504
	Uribante	Pregonero	7,820
TRUJILLO		**Trujillo**	**146,585**
	Betijoque	Betijoque	14,529
	Boconó	Boconó	33,289
	Carache	Carache	33,845
	Escuque	Escuque	12,696
	Trujillo	Trujillo	26,095
	Urdaneta	La Quebrada	12,698
	Valera	Valera	13,433

YARACUY		**San Felipe**	**85,844**
	Bruzual	Chivacoa	8,134
	Nirgua	Nirgua	28,708
	San Felipe	San Felipe	17,959
	Sucre	Guama	} 11,838
	Bolivar	Aroa	
	Urachiche	Urachiche	6,110
	Yaritagua	Yaritagua	13,095
ZAMORA		**Barinas**	**62,696**
	Arismendi	Arismendi	6,929
	Barinas	Barinas	9,157
	Bolivar	Barinitas	7,146
	Obispos	Obispos	10,481
	Pedraza	Ciudad Bolivia	7,579
	Rojas	Libertad	10,430
	Sosa	Nutrias	10,974
ZULIA		**Maracaibo**	**150,776**
	Bolivar	Santa Rita	6,598
	Colón	San Carlos del Zulia	7,161
	Mara	San Rafael	5,538
	Maracaibo	Maracaibo	37,551
	Miranda	Altagracia	7,020
	Páez	Sinamaica	68,707
	Perija	Libertad	5,512
	Sucre	Bobure	5,529[8]
	Urdaneta	Concepción	7,160
DISTRITO FEDERAL		**Carácas**	**113,204**
TERRITORIO AMAZONAS		**San Fernando de Atabapo**	**45,097**
TERRITORIO DELTA-AMACURO		**Tucupita**	**7,222**

APPENDIX B
TRADE OF VENEZUELA, 1909-10

(Compiled from the *Estadística Mercantil y Marítima*, Carácas)

IMPORTS (BY CLASSES).

		£ (at 25·25).
I.	Textiles	821,619
II.	Foodstuffs	444,142
III.	Hardware	341,942
IV.	Machinery	65,091
V.	Other oils (and stearin)	58,612
VI.	Mineral oils	34,198
VII.	Building materials and labour	15,187
VIII.	Cement	12,816
IX.	Coal	11,244
X.	Railway materials	5,791
XI.	Electrical apparatus	1,938
XII.	General merchandise	430,620
	Total	2,243,200

IMPORTS (BY COUNTRIES).[9]

	£ (at 25·25).
United States	730,560
Great Britain	589,700
Germany	422,234
Holland	153,725
France	148,930
Spain	109,173
Italy	58,953
Trinidad	13,821
Belgium	12,110
Austria	1,647

Curaçao	1,183
Other countries	1,164
Total	2,243,200

EXPORTS (BY PRODUCTS).

	£ (at 25·25).
Coffee	1,469,476
Cocoa	689,954
Rubber (caoutchouc, sernambi, and balatá)	557,127
Hides (oxen, goats, and others)	320,571
Gold	65,738
Egret plumes	50,459
Cattle	40,374
Asphalt	36,598
Dye woods and tanning barks	23,101
Pearls	20,941
Sugar	20,080
Timber	16,215
Tonka-beans	7,792
Tobacco	5,737
Hellebore	2,806
Alpargatas (sandals)	2,570
Fish-bladders	2,383
Coco-palm products	2,361
Cotton	2,291
Horns	2,031
Tortoise-shell, mother-of-pearl, &c.	1,642
Fruit	600
Quinine	492
Arrowroot	221
Total	3,363,370

IMPORTS (CLASSES AND COUNTRIES).

		Austria. £	Barbados. £	Belgium. £	Colombia. £	Cuba. £	Curaçao. £	Ecuador. £	France. £	Germany. £
I.	Textiles		120	1,050			92	99	37,635	155,274
II.	Foodstuffs	1,647		270			11		33,912	99,120
III.	Hardware			1,513			2		11,087	67,476
IV.	Machinery			156			614		273	8,880
V.	Other oils (and stearin)			3,667					1,831	2,752
VI.	Mineral oils			3						204
VII.	Building materials and lumber		11						337	1,270
VIII.	Cement			58			19		33	3,843
IX.	Coal						4			1,366
X.	Railway materials									807
XI.	Electrical apparatus								4	115
XII.	General merchandise		5	5,393	99	571	441		63,818	81,127
	Totals	1,647	136	12,110	99	571	1,183	99	148,930	422,234

		Great Britain. £	Holland. £	Italy. £	Porto Rico. £	Portugal. £	Spain. £	Trinidad. £	United States. £
I.	Textiles	417,614	54,397	29,748			47,682	193	77,715
II.	Foodstuffs	17,028	29,606	10,909			34,606	2,673	214,360
III.	Hardware	43,514	7,581[10]	1,831			1,601	1,262	206,075[10]
IV.	Machinery	16,893	1,664	291	139		3,343	54	32,784
V.	Other oils (and stearin)	493	35,558[11]	4,741			5,543	242	3,785
VI.	Mineral oils	37	3					1,062	32,889
VII.	Building materials and lumber	3,983	206	178				456	8,746
VIII.	Cement	1,443	1,352					2,988	3,080
IX.	Coal	8,146	908						820
X.	Railway materials	1,100	528					297	3,061
XI.	Electrical apparatus	51		243				19	1,506
XII.	General merchandise	79,398	21,924	11,012	47	73	16,398	4,575	145,739
	Totals	589,700	153,725	58,953	186	73	109,173	13,821	730,560

EXPORTS (BY PRODUCTS AND PORTS. VALUE IN £ AT 25·25).

	Alpargalas (sandals).	Arrowroot.	Asphalt.	Cattle.	Cocoa.	Coco-palm Products.	Coffee.	Copaiba—Balsam and Oil.	Copper.	Cotton
	£	£	£	£	£	£	£	£	£	£
La Guaira	1,887				334,415		244,836		654	45⁹
Puerto Cabello	582	16		785	96,884	594	441,161		7,019	60⁵
Maracaibo		31	3,056		10,892	24	751,779	7,197		42⁷
Ciudad Bolivar				34,550	374		1,664	2,041		
Carúpano	47			27	151,545		5,556		31	
Pampatar	54						299		61	
La Vela		174		581			2,127		16	1²
Guanta				2,865			950			55⁶
Puerto Sucre							19,610			
Cristobal Colón			270	1,566	91,070	1,743	1,482			
Caño Colorado			33,272		4,774		12	85	11	23²
Totals	2,570	221	36,598	40,374	689,954	2,361	1,469,476	9,323	7,792	2,29

	DYES AND TANNING MATERIALS.		Egrets' Plumes.	Fish Bladders.	Fruit.	Gold.	Hellebore.	HIDES.		
	Barks.	Divisive.						Goats'.	Oxen.	Others, chiefly Deer.
	£	£	£	£	£	£	£	£	£	£
La Guaira			77			674	2,806	2,900	45,355	3,990
Puerto Cabello		1,144	677	19	335	317		26,622	26,035	3,469
Maracaibo	1,884	14,621		2,346				8,063	30,459	296
Ciudad Bolivar	36		49,705			64,747		73	126,245	3,797
Carúpano		27						94	1,053	
Pampatar		487						459	139	
La Vela		4,134						34,681		
Guanta		185						305	883	104
Puerto Sucre		444						684	2,029	45
Cristobal Colón	71	68			265			87	464	
Caño Colorado									2,049	191
Totals	1,991	21,110	50,459	2,383	600	65,738	2,806	73,968	234,711	11,892

	Horns.	Pearls.	Quinine-bark.	RUBBER.			Shells.	Sugar.	Timber.	Tobacco.	Tonka-beans (Sarrapia).
				Caoutchouc.	Semambi.	Balatá.					
	£	£	£	£	£	£	£	£	£	£	£
La Guaira	653	11,889	188			820	133	7,879	79	562	
Puerto Cabello	1,052		279	1,787			11	1,443	392		58
Maracaibo			25	3,230				10,233	15,044		
Ciudad Bolivar	197			116,305	32,089	401,093				1,676	12,429
Carúpano		4,305				239			149		
Pampatar		4,752					1,498		92		
La Vela								525			
Guanta	112								19		
Puerto Sucre						126					
Cristobal Colón						539			440	11	
Caño Colorado	17					899				3,488	
Totals	2,031	20,941	492	121,322	32,089	403,716	1,642	20,080	16,215	5,737	12,487

APPENDIX C
POPULATION, ALTITUDE, MEAN ANNUAL TEMPERATURE AND DEATH-RATE OF PRINCIPAL VENEZUELAN CITIES

(From the *Anuario Estadístico*, 1908, and the data for the military map, 1909)

City.	Population. Census of 1891.	Altitude, in Feet.	Mean Annual Temperature, Degrees Fahrenheit.	Death Rate 1908, per 1,000 Inhabitants.
(*a*) COAST TOWNS.				
Maracaibo	34,740	20	86	36·5
Barcelona	14,089	43	81·5	15·8
Puerto Cabello	13,176	10	81	42·0
Cumaná	11,471	23	80·5	19·7
Carúpano	10,897	26	81	25·9
Coro	10,161	53	81	31·6
La Guaira	8,512	26	84·5	33·1
La Asunción	3,160	356	79	27·3
(*b*) CORDILLERAS AND GUAYANA HIGHLANDS.				
Carácas	72,429	3,036	66·5	34·4
Valencia	54,387	1,577	80	24·5
Barquisimeto	27,069	1,868	78	35·1
San Cristobal	16,797	2,722	70·5	19·6
Villa de Cura	15,792	1,835	75·5	27·6

La Victoria	14,109	1,782	74	29·6
Mérida	13,366	5,415	64·5	29·9
Boconó	13,233	4,336	65	32·9
San Felipe	10,817	808	80	33·9
Trujillo	10,481	2,640	72	26·3
Ocumare del Tuy	7,745	693	79	60·2
Los Teques	6,916	3,864	68	40·6
Guasipati	3,052	?	86	14·3
(c) LLANOS AND ORINOCO VALLEY.				
Ciudad Bolivar	17,535	125	86·5	23·8
Maturín	15,624	244	80·5	11·7
Aragua de Barcelona	15,680[12]	363	82	21·4
San Carlos	10,159[12]	495	83	47·4
Guanare	9,051	636	83·5	9·3
Calabozo	8,159	330	88·5	25·1
San Fernando de Apure	6,695	240	91	26·8
Barinas	5,354	594	82	14·2
Tucupita	823	?	?	?
San Fernando de Atabapo	388	?	?	?

HEIGHTS OF PRINCIPAL MOUNTAINS.

Range.	Peak.	Height, in Feet.
Sierra Nevada of Mérida	La Columna	16,523
	La Concha	16,087
	La Corona	15,609
	El Leon	15,490
	El Toro	15,490
Cordillera of the Andes (outer range)	El Salado	13,949
	Los Conejos	13,761
Cordillera of the Coast	Naiguatá	9,124
	Silla de Carácas (eastern peak)	8,702
Interior Range	Turumiquiri	6,761

APPENDIX D
GOVERNMENT FINANCE, 1908-9

(From the *Anuario Estadístico*, 1908)

REVENUE 1908-9.

	£	£
Taxes on foreign trade:—		
Import duties	1,152,105	
Export duty (live cattle)	3,371	
Sundry port dues	20,204	
Storage and warehousing	655	
Consular fees	2,118	
Other minor imposts	1,310	1,179,763
Internal taxation payable throughout the Federation:—		
Sale of stamps[13]	109,048	
Stamped paper	5,134	
Tax on mining properties	4,895	
Tax on alcohol and tobacco	112,767	
Tax on cigarettes, &c.	85,833	
Tax on matches	10,335	
Trademark and patent dues	160	328,172
Taxes payable in the Federal district and territories:—		
12% duty in territories	220,501	
Public registry of property	3,097	
Direct and local taxes in territories	876	224,474
Public services:—		

Telegraphs and cables	10,566	
Other Government enterprises	2,314	12,880
Revenue from national estate:—		
National lands	632	
Salt-pans	202,744	
Pearl fisheries	494	203,870
Minor sources of revenue:—		
Returns on sundry capital, securities, rights, &c.	15,622	
Other minor sources	31,660	47,282
Total		1,996,441

EXPENDITURE 1908-9.

	£	£
Ministry of the Interior:—		
Legislature	17,593	
Ecclesiastical subsidy	7,264	
Public health	2,577	
Prisons	7,633	
Subsidies to States	224,074	
Charities	13,349	
General	28,146	310,636
Ministry of Foreign Affairs:—		
Consular Service	2,404	
Legations and general	141,279	143,683
Ministry of Finance and Public Credit:—		
Administrative Services	193,475	

Diplomatic claims of 1903	126,404	
Other branches of National Debt	261,667	581,546
Ministry of War and Marine:—		
Army	259,003	
Navy	22,003	
Dockyard	24,699	
Military map of Venezuela	4,566	
General	50,661	360,932
Ministry of Public Instruction:—		
Higher Education	28,465	
Elementary Education	55,561	
General	33,247	117,273
Ministry of National Development:—		
Post Office	33,602	
Telegraphs	80,847	
General	8,634	123,183
Ministry of Public Works		78,928
"Emergencies"		171,693
Total		1,887,874

APPENDIX E
THE NATIONAL DEBT OF VENEZUELA

(Years 1906 to 1910)

INTERNAL DEBT.

Branch.	1906.	1907.	1908.	1909.	1910.
	£	£	£	£	£
Consolidated 3 per cent. stock[14]	1,299,448	2,175,210	2,354,300	2,389,668	2,399,309
Other	1,744,242	551,240	279,885	165,784	119,156
Totals	3,043,690	2,726,050	2,634,185	2,555,452	2,518,465

FOREIGN DEBT.

Branch.	1906.	1907.	1908.	1909.	1910.
	£	£	£	£	£
National 3 per cent. bonds by diplomatic agreements	483,169	466,919	453,295	433,309	417,414
Provisional (Spanish) certificates	62	62	62	62	62
Diplomatic 3 per cent. debt	4,993,627	4,868,978	4,735,958	4,604,572	4,418,987[15]
Claims awarded by Hague Tribunal, 1903	883,799	777,514	647,344	518,409	359,562
Totals	6,360,657	6,113,473	5,836,659	5,556,352	5,196,025

FOOTNOTES

[1] This lake has recently been drained by an English syndicate, who have already found some evidence which tends to show that the story is substantially correct.

[2] "Another fourth part was discovered ... by Amerigo Vespucci: wherefore I do not see why it should not be justly permissible to name it after Amerigo the discoverer ... Amerigē, the land of Americus, or America."

[3] "MOST MAGNIFICENT SIR,—Among other papers of your worship's found in this city, there was a letter addressed to me, with more offers and preambles than there are stars in the sky."

[4] "Our Lord protect the most magnificent person of your worship,

"Your servant,

"LOPE DE AGUIRRE."

[5] As usual, the second part of the original title was the name, or supposed name, of the local Indians.

[6] The word Guacharo connotes crying or lamenting in Spanish.

[7] Includes the municipality of Independencia. *See* **Zulia**.

[8] Does not include the municipality of Independencia. *See* **Mérida**.

[9] Omitting *coal* and *coined gold*, the totals for the four leading countries are as follows: U.S.A., £585,953; Great Britain, £581,559; Germany, £420,868; Holland, £152,501.

[10] Includes coined gold, £317 from Holland; £143,700 from U.S.A.

[11] Principally stearin.

[12] Very scattered.

[13] Includes postage stamps, for which allowance should be made under "Public Services."

[14] Created in 1906 and increased by conversion of other branches in 1907.

[15] Great Britain, Italy, and Germany were paid in full before 1908; Belgium, France, Mexico, United States, Spain, Holland, Sweden, and Norway are still creditors.

A BIBLIOGRAPHY OF WORKS RELATING TO VENEZUELA

I. GENERAL

1. **Appun, C. F.** Unter den Tropen. Bd. i. *Jena*, 1871.

2. **Bénard, C.** Le Vénézuéla. Pp. 106, map. *Bordeaux*, 1897.

3. **Bolet-Peraza, N.** The Republic of Venezuela. 8vo. *Boston*, 1892 (reprinted from *New England Mag.*).

4. **Bolivar, G. de.** Venezuela. *Journ. Manchester Geogr. Soc.*, vol. xxv, pp. 18-31 [1909].

5. **Brown, G. M. L.** Three old Ports on the Spanish Main. *Nat. Geogr. Mag.*, vol. xvii, pp. 622-38 [1906].

6. **Bruycker, P. de.** Le Vénézuéla. *Bull. Soc. Géogr. Anvers*, t. x, pp. 303-31 [1885].

7. **Bürger, O.** Reisen eines Naturforschers in tröpischen Südamerika. Pp. vi, 395, 8vo. *Leipzig*, 1900.

8. **Caseneuve, P. de** and **François**. Les États-Unis de Vénézuéla. Map. *Paris*, 1888.

9. **Chaffanjon, J.** Vénézuéla et Colombie. *Bull. Soc. Géogr. Comm. Paris*, t. xiii, pp. 431-42 [1890-1].

10. **Chaper**, ——. La Côte Nord du Vénézuéla. *Arch. Miss. Sci. Litt. Paris*, sér. 3, t. xiv, pp. 337-43 [1888].

11. **Creveaux, J.** Voyages dans l'Amérique du Sud. *Paris*, 1883.

12. **Curtis, W. E.** Venezuela: her Government, People, and Boundary. *Nat. Geogr. Mag.*, vol. vii, pp. 42-58, map [1896].

13. ——. Venezuela: a Land where it's always Summer. Pp. 315, map, 8vo. *New York* and *London*, 1896.

14. **Dance, C. D.** Four Years in Venezuela. *London*, 1876.

15. **Dauxion-Lavaysse, J. F.** A Statistical, Commercial, and Political Description of Venezuela, Trinidad, Margarita, and Tobago. *London*, 1820.

16. **Dawson, T. C.** The South American Republics. 2 vols. *London*, 1904.

Den Kati, H. *See* **Ten Kate, H.**

17. **Depons, F.** Voyage dans l'Amérique méridionale. 3 vols., 8vo. *Paris*, 1806.

18. ——. Travels in South America during 1801-4, containing a Description of the Carácas. Map, 8vo. *London*, 1807.

19. **Duane, W.** A Visit to Colombia in the Years 1822 and 1823. *Philadelphia*, 1826.

20. **Eastwick, E. B.** Venezuela: or, Sketches of Life in a South American Republic. Map by R. Rojas. *London*, 1868.

21. **Erbach, E. Graf zu.** Wandertage eines deutschen Touristen im Strom- und Küstengebiet des Orinoko. 8vo. *Leipzig*, 1892.

22. **Engel, F.** Mittheilungen über Venezuela. *Globus*, bd. xiv, pp. 44-119, 145-84 [1868].

23. **Ernst, A.** Der erste Census in Venezuela. *Globus*, bd. xxvi, pp. 75-7 [1874].

24. **Fitzgerald, D.** Du Vénézuéla. *Bull. Soc. Géogr. Comm. Bordeaux*, t. i, pp. 262-9, 285-93, 313-5, 352-4 [1878].

25. **Gazzurelli, A.** Il Venezuela. *Rome*, 1901.

26. ——. Venezuela, Ordinamento, Produzioni e Scambi. Pp. 62. *Rome*, 1904.

27. **Gerstächer, F.** Neue Reisen durch die Vereinigten Staaten, Mexico, Ecuador, West Indien und Venezuela. *Jena*, 1868-9.

Goiticoa, N. V. *See* **Veloz-Goiticoa, N.**

28. **Halle, F.** Colombia. 8vo. *London*, 1824.

29. **Hawkshaw, J.** Reminiscences of South America from two and a half years' Residence in Venezuela. 8vo. *London*, 1838.

30. **Hondius, J.** Brevio et admiranda Descriptio Regni Guianæ. ?1599.

31. **Jonas, P.** Nachrichten über Venezuela. *Petermann's Mitt.*, bd. xxiv, pp. 11-14 [1878]; bd. xxv, pp. 212-16 [1879].

32. **Landaeta Rosales, M.** Gran recopilacion geografica, estadística e historica de Venezuela. 2 vols., fo. *Carácas*, 1889.

33. **Lisboa, M. M.** Relaçao de uma Viagem a Venezuela, Nova Granada e Equador. 8vo. *Brussels*, 1866.

34. **Mozans, H. J.** Up the Orinoco and down the Magdalena. *New York* and *London*, 1910.

35. **Olinda, A.** Venezuela in der Gegenwart. *Deutsch. Rundschau Geogr.*, bd. xxiv, pp. 337-48, 398-407 [1902].

36. **Risquez, D. F. A.** Venezuela. *Rev. Geogr. Col. y Mercantil*, t. vi, pp. 275-98 [1909].

37. **Rojas, F. V.** Guia Commercial de la Republica de Venezuela. *Port-of-Spain*, 1901, &c.

38. **Roncayolo, M.** Au Vénézuéla. *Paris*, 1894.

Rosales, M. L. *See* **Landaeta Rosales, M.**

39. **Scruggs, W. L.** The Colombian and Venezuelan Republics. 8vo. *Boston*, 1905.

40. **Sievers, W.** Venezuela. *Mitt. Geogr. Ges. Hamburg*, 1885-6, pp. 134-48.

41. —. Census von Venezuela. *Ibid.*, pp. 316-26.

42. —. Zur Kenntniss Venezuelas. *Globus*, bd. lii, pp. 134-7, 149-52 [1887].

43. —. Zweite Reise in Venezuela in den Jahren 1892-3. Map, 1: 1,000,000. *Mitt. Geogr. Ges. Hamburg*, bd. xii, pp. 328 [1896].

44. **Spence, J. M.** The Land of Bolivar. 2 vols., 8vo. *London*, 1878.

45. **Tallenay, J. de.** Souvenirs de Vénézuéla. 12 mo. *Paris*, 1884.

46. **Tejera, M.** Venezuela pintoresca e ilustrada. 8vo. *Paris*, 1875.

47. —. Venezuela en la exposicion de Paris en 1878. 8vo. *Paris*, 1878.

48. **Ten Kate, H.** Travels in Guiana and Venezuela. *Rev. Col. Internat. Amsterdam*, t. ii, pp. 527-40 [1886].

49. **Veloz-Goiticoa, N.** Les États-Unis de Vénézuéla. *Bull. Soc. Géogr. Comm. Bordeaux*, t. xiv, pp. 33-9 [1891].

50. —. Venezuela. Pp. 608, map, 8vo. *Washington*, 1904.

51. **Villavicencio, R.** La Republica de Vénézuéla bajo el punto de vista de la Geografia y Topografia médicas y de la Demografia. Pp. 137, 8vo. *Carácas*, 1880.

52. **Vincent, L.** Notice sur les États-Unis de Vénézuéla. *Bull. Soc. Géogr. Comm. Bordeaux*, t. xiii, pp. 57-69, 89-109 [1890].

53. **Wappäus, J. E.** Die Republiken von Süd Amerika. *Göttingen*, 1843.

54. **Anon.** Letters written from Colombia during a Journey from Carácas to Bogotá. Pp. 208, map. *London*, 1824.

55. —. Tropical Information: a Treatise on the History, Climate, Soil, Productions, &c. of Venezuela. 12mo. *London*, 1846.

56. —. Appun's Wanderungen durch Venezuela. *Ausland*, vol. xliv, pp. 817-21 [1871].

57. —. Notice politique, statistique, commerciale, &c., sur les États-Unis du Vénézuéla. Map, 12mo. *Paris*, 1889.

58. —. Die Vereinigten Staaten von Venezuela. *Deutsch. Rundschau*, bd. xi, pp. 459-63, map [1889].

59. —. Venezuela: Laws regulating Immigration and Public Lands. *Washington*, 1895.

60. —. Venezuela: Short Sketch of its History, Geography and Industries. *Scottish Geogr. Mag.*, vol. xii, pp. 184-95 [1896].

61. —. Official History of the Discussion between Venezuela and Great Britain on their Guiana Boundaries. *Atlanta, Ga.*, 1896.

62. —. Notes on Venezuela. *Scottish Geogr. Mag.*, vol. xix, pp. 97, 98, map [1903].

63. Official Publications, 1. Annual Reports of the Ministers of State to the National Congress.

64. —. 2. Messages of the President of the Republic to the National Congress.

65. —. 3. Codigos de Venezuela.

66. —. 4. Recopilacion de leyes y decretos de Venezuela.

67. —. 5. Venezuela: Ministerio de Relaciones. World's Colombian Exposition at Chicago. The United States of Venezuela in 1903. Pp. 149, map, 8vo. *New York*, 1903.

68. **Anon.** 6. Ministerio de Fomento. Direccion general de Estadística. Estadística mercantil de Venezuela y Anuario Estadístico.

69. —. 7. Reports of the Council of the Corporation of Foreign Bondholders (annual). *London*.

70. —. 8. British Foreign Office Consular Reports, Annual Series (Venezuela, Carácas, &c.).

II. GEOGRAPHICAL.

71. **Aguerrevere, F., &c.** Trabajos del Cuerpo de Ingenieros encargado del levantamiento del Plano Militar de Venezuela. 4to. *Carácas*, 1908.

72. **Berthelot, S.** Sur les travaux géographiques et statistiques exécutés dans toute l'étendue du territoire du Vénézuéla par M. le colonel Codazzi. *Bull. Soc. Géogr. Paris*, sér. 2, t. xiv, pp. 161-78 [1840].

73. **Bianconi, F.** Carte des États-Unis de Vénézuéla. 1: 3,400,000. *Rev. Franç.*, t. viii, pp. 413-19 [1888].

74. **Boussingault**, —. Rapport sur les travaux géographiques et statistiques exécutés dans la république de Vénézuéla, d'aprés les ordres du Congres par M. le colonel Codazzi. *Compt. Rend.*, t. xii, pp. 462-79 [1841].

75. **Codazzi, A.** Atlas fisico y politico de la Republica de Venezuela. Pp. 8, 33 maps, &c. *Carácas*, 1840.

76. —. Rapport sur les travaux géographiques, &c., dans le Vénézuéla. 4to. *Paris*, 1841.

77. —. Résumen de la Geografia de Vénézuéla. Pp. 648. *Paris*, 1841.

78. **Ernst, A.** Demarkation der Venezuelanisch-brasilianischen Grenzlinie. *Zeitschr. Ges. Erdk., Berlin*, bd. xxi, pp. 167-72 [1886].

79. **Hondius, H.** Venezuela cum parte Australi Novæ Andalusiæ. 1630.

80. **Humboldt, F. H. A. v.** Geognostische Skizze von Süd-america. *Ann. Phys.*, t. xvi, pp. 394-449 [1804].

81. **Huot, V.** Nouveaux travaux topographiques au Vénézuéla. *Bull. Soc. Géogr. Paris*, t. xvii, pp. 458-60 [1908].

82. **Jahn, A.** Contribuciones a la geografia fisica de Venezuela. I. Observaciones al Plano Militar de la Republica. *Carácas*, 1907.

83. —. Contribuciones a la Hidrogafia del Orinoco y Rio Negro. Map, 1: 1,000,000. *Carácas*, 1907.

84. **Level, A. A.** Nomenclator de Venezuela, contentivo de su censo en orden alfabetico. T. 2, 8vo. *Carácas*, 1883.

85. **Oltmann**, —. Don José de Ituriaga's astronomische Beobachtungen am Nieder-Orinoco.... 1754 bis 1758. *Abh. K. Akad. Wiss. Berlin*, bd. ii, pp. 115-27 [1830].

Rosa, R. *See* **Eastwick, E. B.** (No. 21).

86. **Sievers, W.** Bemerkungen zur Karte der Venezolanisch-Brasilianischen Grenze. *Zeitschr. Ges. Erdk. Berlin*, bd. xxii, pp. 1-5, map, 1: 2,000,000 [1887].

87. —. Die Grenzen Venezuelas, *Globus*, bd. lxix, pp. 53-5. map [1896].

88. —. Eine neue Karte von Venezuela. *Petermann's Mitt.*, bd. liv, pp. 69, 70, map, 1: 1,500,000 [1908].

89. **Tejera, M.** Mapa Fisico y Politico de Venezuela. 4 sheets, *Paris*, 1876.

90. **Anon.** Residuum Continentis (Viz. Caribana & Nova Andalusia) cum adjacentibus insulis. 1598.

91. —. Carta plana de la Provincia de Carácas o Venezuela. 1787.

92. —. Memoria de la Direccion general de estadística al Presidente de los Estados Unidos de Venezuela en 1873. 3 vols. *Carácas*, 1873.

93. —. Texte et carte commerciale des États-Unis de Vénézuéla avec notice descriptive. *Paris*, 1888.

94. —. Orinoco-Essequibo Regions.... map, 2, Senate Doc. U.S. (Boundary Commission), 1897.

See also Nos. 79, 119, 120, 366, 367.

III. GEOLOGICAL.

95. **Ahrensburg, H.** Erdbeben in Carácas. *Mitt. Géogr. Ges. Jena*, bd. xix, pp. 56-8 [1901].

96. **Attwood, G.** A Contribution to South American Geology. *Quart. Journ. Geol. Soc.*, vol. xxxv, pp. 582-590, map [1879].

97. **Bendrat, T. A.** Geologic and Petrographic Notes on the Regions about Caicara, Venezuela. *Amer. Journ. Sci.*, ser. 4, vol. xxxi, pp. 443-52 [1911].

98. **Bonssingault,—.** Les Sources Thermales de la Chaîne du littoral du Vénézuéla, *Compt. Rend.*, t. xci, pp. 836-41 [1880].

99. **Buch, L. v.** Von Aptychus, und über die Anden von Venezuela. *Zeitschr. deutsch. geol. Ges.*, bd. ii, pp. 339-44, pl. x [1850].

100. **Cortese, E.** Escursioni geologiche al Venezuela. *Boll. Soc. Geol. Ital.*, vol. xx, pp. 447-69 [1901].

101. **Drevermann, Fr.** Ueber Untersilur in Venezuela. *N. Jahrb.*, 1904, vol. i, pp. 91-3, pl. [1904].

102. **Foster, C. Le Neve.** On the Caratal Goldfield. *Quart. Journ. Geol. Soc.*, vol. xxv, pp. 336-43 [1869].

103. **Gerhardt, K.** Beitrag zur Kenntniss der Kreideformation in Venezuela und Peru. *N. Jahrb.*, Beilage-Band xi, pp. 65-117 [1897].

104. **Humboldt, F. H. A. v.** Esquisse d'un Tableau Géologique de l'Amérique méridionale. *Journ. Phys.*, t. liii, pp. 30-59 [1801].

105. ——. Account of the Earthquake which destroyed the Town of Carácas on the 26th March, 1812. *Edinb. Phil. Journ.*, vol. i, pp. 272-80 [1819].

106. **Karsten, H.** [Letter from Puerto Cabello on the Geology of Western Venezuela.] *Ber. Acad. Wiss. Berlin*, 1849, pp. 197-200.

107. ——. [On Neocomian Rocks near Trujillo.] *Ibid.*, pp. 370-6.

108. ——. [Tertiary and Cretaceous in Cumaná and Barcelona.] *Zeitschr. deutsch. geol. Ges.*, bd. ii, pp. 86-8 [1850].

109. ——. Beitrag zur Kenntniss der Gesteine des nördlichen Venezuela. *Ibid.*, pp. 345-61.

110. ——. Ueber die geognostische Verhältnisse des nördlichen Venezuela. *Archiv. Min. Geogn.*, bd. xxiv, pp. 440-79 [1851].

111. ——. Geognostische Bemerkungen über die Umgebungen von Maracaibo und über die Nordküste von Neu Granada. *Ibid.*, bd. xxv, pp. 567-73 [1853].

112. **Karsten, H.** Reise-notizen über die Provinz Cumaná in Venezuela. *Westermann's Monatshefte*, 1859.

113. ——. Die geognostische Beschaffenheit der Gebirge der Provinz Carácas. *Zeitschr. deutsch. geol. Ges.*, bd. xiv, pp. 282-7 [1862].

114. ——. Geologie de l'ancienne Colombie Bolivarienne. Pp. 62, map, 4to. *Berlin*, 1886.

115. **Lorié, J.** Fossile Mollusken von Curaçao, Aruba und der Küste von Venezuela. *Samml. geol. Reichs-Mus. Leyden*, sér. 2, bd. i, pp. 111-49, [1887].

116. **Salomon, W.** Ueber angebliches Untersilur in Venezuela. *Monatsb. deutsch. geol. Ges.*, 1909, pp. 193. [Shows that specimens described by Drevermann (No. 101) were bought in U.S.A. and not from Venezuela.]

117. **Sievers, W.** Das Erdbeben vom 26 März, 1812, an den Nordküste Südamerikas. *Mitt. Geogr. Ges. Hamburg*, pp. 265-71.

118. ——. Reiseberichte aus Venezuela. *Ibid.*, pp. 272-87; 1885-6, pp. 1-133.

119. ——. Venezuela. Pp. viii, 359. *Hamburg*, 1888.

120. ——. Karten zur physikalischen Geographie von Venezuela. *Petermann's Mitt.*, bd. xlii, pp. 149-55, 197-201, 3 maps, 1: 3,000,000 [1896].

121. —. Das Erdbeben in Venezuela von 26 Okt., 1900. *Jahrb. Veroffnet. Geogr. Ver. Bonn*, 1905, pp. 35-50.

122. **Stevens, R. P.** [Geology and Mineralogy of Venezuela.] *Proc. Ac. Nat. Sci. Philadelphia*, 1868, pp. 303, 304.

123. **Tate, R.** Notes on the Geology of Guyana, in Venezuela. *Quart. Journ. Geol. Soc.*, vol. xxv, pp. 343-50 [1869].

See also Nos. 314, 319, 320, 342.

IV. BOTANICAL AND ZOOLOGICAL.

124. **Appun, K. F.** Beiträge zur Insecten-Fauna von Venezuela und Britisch Guyana. *Ausland*, bd. xlv, pp. 41-7, 67-70 [1872].

125. **Bellermann, P.** Landschaft- und Vegetations-Bilder aus den Tropen Südamerika's nach der Natur Gezeichnet. *Berlin*, 1894. [Text by **Karsten**.]

126. **Berlepsch, H. v.** and **E. Hartert**. On the Birds of the Orinoco Region. *Novitates Zoologicae*, vol. ix, 1902.

Bonpland, A. *See* **Humboldt, F. H. A. v.**

127. **Braun, A.** Uebersicht der Characeen aus Colombien und Guyana. *Monatsb. k. preuss. Akad. Wiss.*, 1858, pp. 354-67.

128. **Dozy, F.** Prodromus floræ bryologicæ Surinamensis. Accedit pugillus specierum novarum floræ bryologicæ Venezuelanæ. Pp. 54. *Düsseldorf*, 1854.

129. **Ernst, A.** On the Medicinal Plants of Carácas, Venezuela, and their Venezuelan Names. *Journ. Botany*, vol. iii, pp. 143-50, 277-84, 306-22 [1865].

130. —. Plants growing in the Streets of Carácas. *Ibid.*, pp. 322, 323 [1865].

131. —. Formas caracteristicas de la flora Venezolana. Las palmas. *El Porvenir*, vol. i, no. 6; vol. ii, no. 7; vol. iii, no. 8 [1866].

132. —. List of Venezuelan Woods, with their Venezuelan Names and Specific Gravity. *Journ. Botany*, vol. iv, pp. 359, 360 [1866].

133. —. On the Plants cultivated or naturalised in the Valley of Carácas, and their Vernacular Names. *Ibid.*, vol. v, pp. 264-75, 287-90 [1867].

134. —. On the Plants common to the Southern United States and Venezuela. *Ibid.*, pp. 290-6 [1867].

135. —. Los Helechos de la Flora Caracasana. *Vargasia*, 1868-9, pp. 100-103.

136. —. Plantas interesantes de la Flora Caracasana. *Ibid.*, pp. 178-94.

137. —. Verzeichniss der auf den venezuelanischen Inselgruppe Los Roques im Sept., 1871, beobachteten Pflanzen. *Botan. Zeit.*, bd. xxx, pp. 539-41 [1872].

138. —. Sertulum Naiguatense.... *Journ. Botany*, vol. x, pp. 261-4 [1872].

139. —. Observationes aliquot in plantas nonnullas rariores vel novas floræ Caracasanæ. *Flora*, vol. lvii, pp. 209-15 [1874].

140. —. Descriptive Catalogue of the Venezuelan Department at the Philadelphia International Exhibition, 1876. Pp. 55. *Philadelphia*, 1879.

141. **Ernst, A.** Estudios sobre la flora y fauna de Venezuela. Pp. 330. *Carácas*, 1877.

142. —. Florula Chelonesiaca. *Journ. Botany*, vol. xiv, pp. 176-9 [1876].

143. —. Vargas considerado como botanico. *Carácas*, 1877.

144. —. Enumeracion de las plantas mas notables que fueron observadas en la excursion a Naiguatá. *Repertoria Caraqueño*, 1879, pp. 141-6.

145. —. On some Interesting Cases of Migration of Marine Fishes on the Coast of Venezuela at Carúpano. *Nature*, vol. xxxiii, pp. 321, 322 [1886].

146. —. Eine botanische Excursion auf der Insel Margarita. *Nederl. Kruidk. arch. Nijmegen*, bd. iv [1886].

147. —. La vegetacion de los Páramos de los Andes Venezolanes. *Bol. Ministr. Obras. Publicas, Carácas*, 1892, pp. 159-63.

148. —. Sertulum Aturense.... *Rev. Cient. Univ. Central Venezuela*, t. i, pp. 219-23 [1900].

149. —. Bibliographia. *Jena*, 1900.

Gaillard, A. *See* **Patouillard, N.**

150. **Goebel, K.** Die Vegetation der venezolanischen Páramos. *Pflanzenbiol. Schild.*, 1889-93, pt. 2, no. 1. and *Marburg*, 1891.

151. **Goering, A.** Zur Thiergeographie Venezuelas. *Mitt. Ver. Erdk. Leipzig*, 1876, pp. 14-24.

Hartert, E. *See* **Berlepsch, H. v.**

152. **Humboldt, F. H. A. v.** and **A. Bonpland**. Plantæ æquinoctiales. 2 vols. *Paris*, 1808.

153. — and **C. S. Kunth**. Nova genera et species plantarum. 7 vols. *Paris*, 1815-25. [Vol. 7 has lists of Venezuelan plants.]

154. **Jahn, A.** Las palmas de la flora venezolana. Pp. 126, 8vo. *Carácas*, 1908.

155. **Johnston, J. R.** Flora of the Islands of Margarita and Coche, Venezuela. *Proc. Boston Soc. Nat. Hist.*, vol. xxxiv, pp. 163-212, map [1909].

156. **Karsten, H.** Auswahl neuer und blühender Gewächse Venezuelas. 4to. *Berlin*, 1848.

157. —. Floræ Colombiæ terrarumque adjacentium specimina selecta.... *Berlin*, 1858-69.

Kunth, G. S. *See* **Humboldt, F. H. A. v.**

158. **Loefling, P.** Reise nach den spanischen Ländern in Europa und America in den Jahren 1751 bis 1756. Pp. 406. *Berlin* and *Stralsund*, 1766.

159. **Loriol, P. de.** Note sur quelques espéces nouvelles appartenant à la classe des Echinoderms. *Mém. Soc. Phys. Hist. Genève*, t. xxiv, pp. 659-73 [1876].

160. **Maury, P.** Enumération des plantes du Haut-Orénoque récoltées par Mm. J. Chaffanjon et A. Gaillard. *Journ. Botanique*, t. iii, pp. 129, 157, 196, 209, 260, 166 [1889].

161. **Patouillard, N.** and **A. Gaillard.** Champignons du Vénézuéla et principalement de la région du Haut-Orénoque, récoltées en 1887 par M. A. Gaillard. *Bull. Soc. Mycol. France*, t. iii, pp. 7-46, 92-129 [1887].

162. **Ritter, C.** Ein Blick auf die Vegetation der Cordilleren in Venezuela (über 12-13° N. Br.) aus handschriftlichen Mittheilungen der Herrn. Berg. *Monatsb. Ges. Erdk. Berlin*, sér. 2, bd. viii, pp. 152-6 [1851].

See also Nos. 51, 315, 317, 401.

V. HISTORICAL.

163. **Acosta, Joaquin.** Compendio historico del descubrimiento y colonizacion de la Nueva Granada en el siglo decimo sexto. 8vo. *Paris*, 1848.

164. **Alcala, A. P. de.** Consectario de la ciudad de Cumaná. 1790.

165. **Altoguirre y Duvale, A. de.** Relaciones geograficas de la Gobernacion de Venezuela (1767-8) con prologo y notas. *Madrid*, 1908.

166. **Anglerius, Petrus Martyr.** De rebus oceanicis et novo orbe decades tres. *Basiliæ*, 1516 etc. *Coloniæ*, 1574. [Many editions and translations.]

167. **Austin, J. B.** Venezuela's Territorial Claims. *Bull. Geogr. Club Philadelphia*, vol. ii, pp. 1-19 [1896].

168. **Baker, M.** The Anglo-Venezuelan Boundary Dispute. *Nat. Geogr. Mag.*, vol. xi, pp. 129-44, map [1900].

169. **Baralt, R. M.** and **R. Diaz.** Résumen de la Historia de Venezuela. Tt. ii. Pp. 398, 370. *Paris*, 1841.

170. **Benzoni, G.** La historia del mondo nuevo. 8vo. *Venice*, 1565.

171. **Berthelot, S.** Analyse du premier volume de l'Histoire du Vénézuéla. *Bull. Soc. Géogr. Paris*, sér. 2, t. xv, pp. 319-29 [1841].

172. **Blanco, E.** Venezuela heroica; cuadros historicos. 8vo. *Carácas*, 1881.

173. **Briceño, Manuel.** Los Ilustres. Paginas para la Historia de Venezuela. Pp. 239, 8vo. *Bogotá*, 1884.

174. **Barney, J.** A Chronological History of the Discoveries in the South Sea or Pacific Ocean. 5 vols. 4to. *London*, 1803-17.

175. **Casas, B. de** las. Brevissima relacion de la destruycion de las Indias.... 4to. *Seville*, 1552.

176. **Cassani, J.** Historia de la Provincia de la Compañía de Jesus del Nuevo Reyno de Granada. Fol. *Madrid*, 1741.

177. **Castellanos, J. de.** Elegias de Varones ilustres de Indias. *Madrid*, 1589.

178. **Caulin, A.** Historia coro-graphica, natural y evangelica de la Nueva Andalusia. Provincias de Cumaná, Guayana y Vertiente del Rio Orinoco. Pp. 482, map. *Madrid*, 1779, and 8vo. *Carácas*, 1841.

179. **Colón, Cristobal.** Relaciones y cartas de.... In *Biblioteca Classica*, t. clxiv. *Madrid*, 1892.

180. **Daly, C. P.** Is the Monroe Doctrine involved in the Controversy between Venezuela and Great Britain? *New York*, 1896.

181. **Davie, R.** The Victorious Voyage of Captaine Amyas Preston, now Knight, and Captaine George Sommers to the West India, begun in March, 1595. In *Hakluyt's Principal Navigations* ... Hakluyt Society edition, 1904, vol. x, pp. 213-26.

182. **Diaz, J. D.** Recuerdos sobre la rebelion de Carácas. 4to. *Madrid*, 1829.

Diaz, R. *See* **Baralt, R. M.**

183. **Ducoudray-Holstein, H. L. V.** Historia de Bolivar ... 2 t., 8vo. *Paris*, 1831.

184. **Dudley, R.** [Voyage to Trinidad and the Coast of Paria.] *Hakluyt's Principal Navigations*, 1600, vol. iii, pp. 574-8.

185. **Esteller, A.** Catecismo de historia de Venezuela, desde su descubrimiento hasta la muerte del Libertador. 8vo. *Carácas*, 1886, &c.

186. **Fernandez de Oviedo y Valdes, G.** La historia general de los Indias. Fo. *Seville*, 1535.

187. **Figueiras, G.** Une première occupation allemande au Vénézuéla (xvie siècle). *Questions Diplom. et Col.*, t. xv, pp. 240-4 [1903].

188. **Flinter, G. D.** The History of the Revolution of Carácas ... with a Description of the Llaneros or people of the Plains of South America. 8vo. *London*, 1819.

Fortoul, J. *See* **Gil Fortoul, J.**

189. **Gaffarel, P.** Étude sur les rapports de l'Amérique et de l'ancien continent avant Christophe Colomb. 8vo. *Paris*, 1869.

190. **Gil Fortoul, J.** Historia Constitucional de Venezuela. Tom i. Pp. 570. *Berlin*, 1907.

191. **Gilij, F. S.** Saggio di Storia Americana. 4 Tt. 8vo. *Rome*, 1780-4.

Gomara, F. L. de. *See* **Lopez de Gomara, F.**

192. **Guinan, F. G.** Historia del Gobierno del Doctor J. P. Rojas Paul ... 1888 à 1890. Pp. 560. 8vo. *Valencia*, 1891.

193. **Gumilla, J.** El Orinoco illustrado y defendido. 4to. *Madrid*, 1745.

194. **Hassert, K.** Die Welserzüge in Venezuela. *Beiträge Kolonial-politik*, bd. iii, pp. 297-317 [1902].

195. **Heilprin, A.** Notes on the Schomburgk Line and the Guayana Boundary. *Bull. Géogr. Club Philadelphia*, vol. ii, pp. 20-30, map [1896].

196. **Herrera Tordesillas, A. de.** Descripcion de los Indias Occidentales. 8 Dec. Fo. *Madrid*, 1601-15.

197. **Hippisley, G.** A Narrative of the Expedition to the Rivers Orinoco and Apure. Pp. 653. *London*, 1819.

198. **Humbert, J.** La première occupation allemande du Vénézuéla au xvie siècle, période dite des Welser (1528-56). *Journ. Soc. Americanistes, Paris*, t. i, no. 3 [1904]. *See* Vincent, L.

199. **Hylacomylus, M.** Cosmographiæ Introductio ... Insuper quatuor Americi Vespucci navigationes. 4to. *St. Dié, Lorraine*, 1507.

200. **Keymis, L.** A Relation of the second Voyage to Guiana, performed and written in the Year 1596. 4to. *London*, 1596.

201. **Klöden, K. v.** Die Welser in Augsburg als Besitzer von Venezuela und die von ihnen veranlassten Expeditionen der Deutscher dahin. *Zeitschr. Allgem. Erdk. Berlin*, bd. v, pp. 433-55 [1855].

202. **Laet, J. de.** Nieuvve Wereldt ofte Beschrijvinghe van West-Indien.... Pp. 510, maps, fo. *Leyden*, 1625. Other editions in Latin. Fo. *Leyden*, 1633, &c.

203. **Lameda, L.** and **M. Landaeta Rosales.** Historia militar y politica del general Joaquin Crespo. 2 vols. Pp. xcii, 528; xlii, 528. 4to. *Carácas*, 1897.

204. **Landaeta Rosales, M.** Gobiernos de Venezuela desde 1810 hasta 1905. Pp. 115, 8vo. *Carácas*, 1905.

205. **Lopez de Gomara, F.** La Istoria de las Indias, y Conquista de Mexico. 2 parts. Fo. *Zaragoza*, 1552.

206. **MacNutt, F. A.** Bartholomew de las Casas: his Life, his Apostolate, and his Writings.... 8vo. *New York* and *London*, 1909.

207. **Mendoza, L. Torres de.** Coleccion de Documentos ineditos ... del archivo de Indias. 8vo. *Madrid*, 1864.

208. **Olavarria, D. A.** Estudios historico-politicos, 1810 à 1889. Pp. 289, 8vo. *Valencia*, 1894.

209. **Oviedo y Baños, J. de.** Historia de la conquista, y poblacion de la provincia de Venezuela. Pt. I. Pp. 380, fo. *Madrid*, 1723.

Oviedo y Valdes, G. F. de. *See* Fernando de Oviedo y Valdes, G.

Pacheco, J. F. *See* Mendoza, L. T. de.

210. **Páez, J. A.** Autobiografia. 2 vols., 8vo. *New York*, 1867-9.

211. **Pepper, E.** Apuntes para la historia contemporanea de Venezuela, 1892-4. Pp. 93, 8vo. *Curaçao*, 1895.

Petrus Martyr d'Anghiera. *See* Anglerius, P. M.

212. **Raleigh, W.** The Discoverie of the large, rich and bewtiful Empyre of Guiana, with a relation of the great and Golden Citie of Manoa (which the Spaniards call El Dorado). Pp. 112, 4to. *London*, 1596.

213. **Rivero, J.** Historia de las Misiones de las Llanos de Casanare y los rios Orinoco y Meta, escrita en el año de 1736. 8vo. *Bogotá*, 1883.

214. **Robinson, J. H.** Journal of an Expedition 1,400 miles up the Orinoco and 300 up the Arauca. Pp. 397. *London*, 1822. [An absurd title, the total length of the Orinoco being about 850 miles, and the portion below the mouth of the Arauca only 360.—L.V.D.]

215. **Rodway, J.** The West Indies and the Spanish Main (Story of the Nations Series). *London*, 1896.

216. **Rojas, A.** Estudios indigenas. Contribuciones a la historia antiqua de Venezuela. 8vo. *Carácas*, 1888.

217. **—.** Primeras paginas de un libro de leyendas historicas de Venezuela. 8vo. *Carácas*. 1888.

218. **—.** Historia Patria. Leyendas historicas de Venezuela. 8vo. *Carácas*, 1890.

219. **—.** Do. Estudios historicos. Origenes Venezolanos. 8vo. *Carácas*, 1891.

220. **Scruggs, W. L.** British Aggressions in Venezuela. *Atlanta, Ga.* Map. 1895.

221. **Simon, Pedro.** Primera Parte de las Noticias historiales de las Conquistas de tierra firme en las Indias Occidentales. Pp. 671, fo. *Cuenca*, 1627.

222. **Steinen, K. v. den.** Ausgrabungen am Valenciasee. *Globus*, bd. lxxxvi, pp. 101-8 [1904].

223. **Strickland, J.** Documents and Maps on the Boundary Question between Venezuela and British Guayana from the Capuchin Archives in Rome. *London*, 1896.

224. **Tavera-Acosta, B.** Anales de Guayana, vol. i. *Ciudad Bolivar*, 1905.

225. **Tejera, F.** Manual de Historia de Venezuela. Ed. iii. Pp. 291. *Carácas*, 1895.

226. **Tejera, M.** Compendio de la Historia de Venezuela. 12mo. *Paris*, 1875.

227. **Tello Mendoza, R.** Viaje del General Cipriano Castro ... al Centro, sur y Oriente de Venezuela en Abril y Mayo de 1905. Pp. 427, 4to. *Carácas*, 1905.

228. —. Complemento. [General Cipriano Castro.] Pp. 326, 8vo. *Carácas*, 1905.

229. **Tello Mendoza, R.** Documentos del General Cipriano Castro. 5 vols. *Carácas*, 1906.

230. **Ulloa, A. de.** Noticias Americanas. 4to. *Madrid*, 1772.

231. **Vespucci, A.** *See* Hylacomylus, M.

232. **Vincent, L.** and **J. Humbert.** Le Vénézuéla; période des Welser (1528-46). *Bull. Soc. Géogr. Comm. Bordeaux*, t. xx, pp. 444-57 [1897]: t. xxi, pp. 7-12 [1898].

Waldsee Mueller, M. *See* Hylacomylus, M.

233. **Weinhold, M.** Ueber Nicolaus Federmann's Reise in Venezuela, 1524-31. 3 *Jahresb. Ver. Erdk. Dresden*, 1867, Appendix, pp. 91-112, maps.

234. **Yanes, F. J.** Historia de Venezuela. 1840.

235. **Anon.** *Cartas edificantes de la Compañía de Jesus*, t. xvi., p. 92 [1757].

236. —. Documentos para los anales de Venezuela desde el movimiento separatista de la Union Colombiana hasta nuestros días. *Carácas*, 1889.

237. —. The United States of Venezuela in 1893. (World's Columbian Exposition at Chicago.) Pp. 149, map, 8vo. *New York*, 1893.

238. —. Brief submitted by Venezuela to the Commission appointed to investigate and report upon the true Divisional Line between the Republic of Venezuela and British Guiana. Pp. 28. *Washington*.

239. —. U. S. Commission on Boundary between Venezuela and British Guiana. Documents, &c. 8 vols. *Washington*, 1897.

See also Nos. 293, 324, 325, 338, 343.

VI. ETHNOLOGICAL

240. **Appun, K. F.** Die Goajira-Indianer. *Ausland*, 1868, pp. 1220-22.

241. **Breton, R.** Dictionnaire Caraibe-Français. Tt. 2., 4to. *Auxerre*, 1665-6.

242. —. Grammaire Caraibe. 8vo. *Ibid.*, 1667.

243. **Brinton, D. G.** The Dwarf Tribe of the Upper Amazon. *Washington*, 1898.

244. **Calcaño, J.** El Castellano en Venezuela. Estudio Crítica. 8vo. *Carácas*, 1897.

245. **Costambert, E.** Coup d'Œil sur les productions et sur les peuplades géophages et les autres populations des bords de l'Orénoque. *Bull. Soc. Géogr. Paris*, sér. 5. t. i, pp. 205-20 [1861].

246. **D'Orbigny, A.** L'homme Américain (de l'Amérique méridionale). Tt. 2. *Paris*, 1839.

247. **Du Pouget, J. F. A.** L'Amérique préhistorique. 8vo. *Paris*, 1883.

248. **Engel, F.** Pfahlbauten in Venezuela. *Ausland*, 1865, pp. 254-8.

249. —. Die Goajiros. *Ibid.*, pp. 798-802, 834-9.

250. —. Volksbilder aus Venezuela. *Ibid.*, 1867, pp. 11-14.

251. **Ernst, A.** Anthropological Remarks on the Population of Venezuela. *Mem. Anthrop. Soc.*, vol. iii, pp. 274-87 [1870].

252. —. Ueber die Reste der Ureinwohner in den Gebirgen von Mérida. *Zeitschr. Ethnol.*, vol. xvii, p. 190 [1885].

253. **Garcia, G.** Origen de los Indios de el Nuevo Mundo, e Indias occidentales. Pp. 525. *Valencia*, 1607.

254. **Goering, A.** A Visit to the Guajiro Indians of Maracaibo. *Illustr. Travels H. W. Bates*, vol. ii, pp. 19-21 [1869].

255. —. Venezuelanische Alterthümer. *Mitt. Ver. Erdkunde Leipzig*, 1874, pp. 21-3.

256. —. Bei den Chaymas-Indianern von Caripe. *Mitt. Ver. Erdk. Halle*, 1879, pp. 40-48.

257. **Hervas y Panduro, L.** Catalogo de las lenguas de las naciones conocidas.... 6 vols. 4to. *Madrid*, 1800-1805.

258. **Level, A. A.** Informe sobre el estado actual de los Distritos de reducción de indigenas Alto Orinoco, Central y Bajo Orinoco. *Carácas*, 1850.

259. **Lopez Borreguero, R.** Los Indios Caribes. 2 vols. 16mo. *Madrid*, 1875.

260. **Lugo, B. de.** Gramatica en la lengua general del Nuevo Reyno, llamado Mosca. 8vo. *Madrid*, 1619.

261. **Marcano, G.** Ethnographie précolombienne de Vénézuéla. [Valleys of Aragua and Carácas and Atures district.] *Mém. Soc. Athrop. Paris*, sér. 2, t. iv, pp. 1-86, 99-218 [1889-93].

262. **Marcano, G.** Ethnographie précolombienne du Vénézuéla. *Bull. Soc. Anthrop. Paris*, sér 4, t. i, pp. 857-65, 883-95 [1890].

263. —. Ethnographie précolombienne du Vénézuéla. *Ibid.*, t. ii, pp. 238-54 [1891].

264. **Morisot**, —. Notes ethnographiques recueillies dans le bassin de l'Orénoque. *Bull. Soc. Anthrop. Lyon*, t. viii, pp. 115-20 [1890].

Nadaillac, Marquis de. *See* **Du Pouget, J. F. A.**

265. **Orsi di Broglia di Mombella, G.** Sculture di Indigene del Alto Orinoco. *Bull. Soc. Geogr. Ital.*, ser. 3, t. iii, pp. 474-9 [1890].

266. **Plassard, L.** Les Guaraunos. *Bull. Soc. Géogr. Paris*, sér. 5, t. xv, pp. 568-92 [1868].

267. **S— M. D. L.** Dictionnaire Galibi.... Précédé d'un essai de grammaire. 8vo. *Paris*, 1763.

268. **Tauste, F. de.** Arte y Bocabulario de la Lengua de los Indios Chaymas, Cumanagotos, Coros, Parias.... 4to. *Madrid*, 1680.

269. **Tavera Acosta, B.** En el Sur (dialectos indigenas de Venezuela). *Ciudad Bolivar*, 1907.

270. **Anon.** Dr. Crevaux' Besuch bei den Guaraunos im. Orinoko Delta. *Globus*, bd. xliii, pp. 1-8 [1883].

See also No. 313, 376.

VII. CARÁCAS AND THE "CENTRO."

271. **Andral**, —. Trade of Carácas District for the Year 1899. *Foreign Office Cons. Rep.*, Ann. Ser., No. 2466 [1900].

272. **Appun, C. F.** and **L. Martin**. Beobachtungen auf ihrer Reise nach Venezuela im December, 1848, und Januar, 1849. *Monatsb. Ges. Erdk. Berlin*, ser. 2, bd. vi, pp. 123-30 [1849].

273. **Blume**, —. Die Verhältnisse von Venezuela und die dortige deutsche Colonie Tovar nach neueren handschriftlichen Mitteilungen und eigner Erfahrung. *Monatsb. Ges. Erdk. Berlin*, ser. 2, bd. x, pp. 111-27 [1853].

274. **Curtis, W. E. C.** The Capitals of Spanish America. 8vo. *New York*, 1888.

275. **Engel, F.** Die Küste von Carácas. *Zeitschr. Ges. Erdk. Berlin*, bd. iv, pp. 404-29 [1869].

276. —. Carácas, die Hauptstadt von Venezuela. *Globus*, bd. xv, pp. 210-12, 234-6 [1869].

277. **Ernst, A.** Das Thal von Carácas in Venezuela. *Globus*, bd. xx, pp. 25-9, 43-6, 56-9 [1871].

278. —. Die Witterungsverhältnisse der Thäler von Carácas. *Zeitschr. Ges. Erdk. Berlin*, bd. vii, pp. 248-58, map [1872].

279. **Fendler, A.** [Meteorology of Colonia Tovar.] *Smithson Rep.*, 1857, pp. 178-282 [1858].

280. **Fitzgerald, H. D.** Valencia (Vénézuéla). *Bull Soc. Géogr. Comm. Bordeaux*, t. ii, pp. 417-24 [1879].

281. **Galli, A.** Del Discoprimiento di un Nuovo Baco da Seta nelle vicinanze di Carácas. *Boll. Consol. Firenze*, t. v, pt. 2, pp. 343-8 [1868-9].

282. **Goering, A.** [Puerto Cabello to Valencia.] *Globus*, bd. xiv, pp. 281-3 [1868].

283. **Gronen, D.** Puerto Cabello. *Deutsche Rundschau*, bd. ix, pp. 123-6 [1887].

284. **Herzog, A.** Eine Besteigung der Silla de Carácas. *Globus*, bd. lvi, pp. 277-81 [1889].

285. **Hesse-Wartegg, E. v.** Beobachtungen über den See von Tacarigua im nördlichen Venezuela. *Petermann's Mitt.*, bd. xxxiv, pp. 321-31, map, 1: 420,000 [1888].

286. **Kiesselbach, W.** Von Bremen nach Carácas und der deutschen Niederlassung Tovar in Venezuela. *Globus*, bd. ix, pp. 276-9 [1866].

Martin, L. *See* **Appun, C. F.**

287. **Ritter, C.** Ein Tag in San Estevan. Geschildert von Herrn Carl Appun. *Monatsb. Ges. Erdk. Berlin*, ser. 2, bd. vi, pp. 131-42 [1849].

288. **Rivera, A.** An Illustrated Guide to Carácas. *Philadelphia*, 1897.

289. **Spence, J. M.** Primera Ascension al Pico de Naiguatá. 8vo. *Carácas*, 1872.

See also Nos. 5, 13, 20, 21, 98, 105, 113, 119, 133, 222, 381, 382, 383, 387.

VIII. ZULIA.

290. **Delechaux, —.** Renseignements sur le port et sur la barre de Maracaibo. *Ann. Hydrogr. Paris*, t. xiii, pp. 126-7 [1857].

291. **Eggers, H.** Die Asphalt-Quellen am See von Maracaibo. *Deutsche Geogr. Blätter*, bd. xix, pp. 183-94 [1896].

292. **Engel, F.** Maracaibo. *Zeitschr. Ges. Erdk. Berlin*, bd. v, pp. 418-52 [1870].

293. **Humbert, J.** Un Gibraltar ignoré. *Bull. Soc. Géogr. Comm. Bordeaux*, sér. 2, t. xxiv, pp. 109-12 [1901].

294. **Plümacher, O.** Maracaibo. *Ausland*, bd. lxi, pp. 781-5, 812-14, 836-9 [1888].

295. **Pocaterra, J. D.** Derrotero del Golfo de Venezuela ó saco de Maracaibo. *New York*, 1864.

See also Nos. 6, 111, 119, 248, 254, 393, 395.

IX. THE ANDES.

296. **Engel, F.** Eine Ersteigung der Sierra Nevada de Mérida in Venezuela. *Globus*, bd. xv, pp. 278-81, 298-301, 330-32 [1869].

297. —. Auf der Sierra Nevada de Mérida. *Samml. gem. verstand. Wiss. Vorträge*, n.f., bd. iii, no. 58. *Hamburg*, 1888.

298. **Goering, A.** Sierra Nevada von Mérida. *Mitt. Ver. Erdkunde Leipzig*, 1875, pp. 101-5.

299. —. Vom tröpischen Tieflande zum ewigen Schnee. *Leipzig*, n.d. [1895?].

300. **Guerrero, E. C.** El Táchira fisico, politico é ilustrado. Pp. 306. 8vo. *Carácas*, 1905.

301. —. El Táchira. *Bol. R. Soc. Geogr. Madrid*, t. xlviii, pp. 133-6 [1906].

302. **Sievers, W.** [Communication relative to his journey to the Cordillera of Mérida.] *Mitt. Geogr. Ges. Hamburg*, 1884, pp. 339-45.

303. —. Ueber Schneeverhältnisse in der Cordillere Venezuela's. *Jahresb. Geogr. Ges. München*, 1885, pp. 54-7.

304. —. Bemerkungen zur Original Routenkarte der Venezolanische Cordillere. *Mitt. Geogr. Ges. Hamburg*, 1885-6, pp. 309-16, map, 1: 1,000,000.

305. **Sievers, W.** Landschaftlicher Charakter der Anden Venezuelas. *Globus*, bd. li. pp. 8-11, 26-9, 41-4 [1887].

306. —. Die Cordillere von Mérida nebst bemerkungen über das Karibische Gebirge. *Geogr. Abhand.*, bd. iii. Pp. 238, map [1888].

See also Nos. 99, 107, 119, 147, 150, 162, 252.

X. FALCÓN, &c.

307. **Sievers, W.** Richard Ludwig's Reisen auf Paraguana (Venezuela). *Globus*, bd. lxxiii, pp. 303-9 [1898].

308. —. Die Inseln von der Nordküste von Venezuela. *Ibid.*, bd. lxxiv, pp. 163-5, 291-4, 302-7 [1898].

309. ——. Richard Ludwig's Reisen in Coro. *Ibid.*, bd. lxxv, 177-10 [1899].

See also Nos. 43, 106, 119, 137, 403, 404.

XI. THE "ORIENTE."

310. **Ahrenburg, H.** Die Perlenfischerei auf der Insel Margarita. *Mem. Geogr. Ges. Jena*, bd. xxv, pp. 37-9 [1907].

311. **Beebe, Mary B.** and **C. W.** Our Search for a Wilderness. *London*, 1910.

312. **Erbach-Erbach, E. Graf zu.** Im Delta des Orinoko. *Jahresb.* ix *u.* x *Württemberg Ver. Handelsgeographie*, pp. 50-66 [1892].

313. **Ernst, A.** Bemerkungen über das Delta des Orinoco und die Guaraunen. *Globus*, bd. xvii, pp. 316-18 [1870].

314. **Fostin, E.** Une plaine de bitume au Vénézuéla. *Compt. Rend. Soc. Geogr. Paris*, 1895, pp. 221-4.

315. **Goering, A.** Ausflug nach den neuen Guacharo-höhlen in der Venezolanischen Provinz Cumaná. *Globus*, bd. xiii, pp. 161-7 [1868].

316. **Hirzel, H.** Erdöl und Asphalt auf der Inseln Pedernales, Pesquero und del Plata in Venezuela. *Chem. Rev. Fett. Harz. Ind.*, bd. x, pp. 275-7 [1903].

317. **Humboldt, P. H. A. v.** Account of the Great Cavern of the Guacharo. *Edinb. Phil. Journ.*, vol. iii, pp. 83-92 [1820].

318. **Level, A. A.** Esbozos de Venezuela. I. Margarita. *Carácas*, 1881.

319. **Sievers, W.** Ein Schlammvulkan, Hervidero, in der Llanos von Maturín. *Deutsche Rundschau Geogr.*, bd. xx, pp. 394-8 [1898].

320. **Wall, G. P.** On the Geology of a Part of Venezuela and Trinidad. *Quart. Journ. Geol. Soc.*, vol. xvi, pp. 460-70 [1860].

321. **Anon.** Recollections of Cumaná. *Orient. Herald*, vol. xv, pp. 495-501 [1827].

322. ——. Wanderungen an der Küste Venezuela's. *Ausland*, 1865, pp. 745-51.

See also Nos. 5, 21, 108, 146, 155, 164, 178, 256, 270, 386, 397.

XII. THE LLANOS.

323. **Bingham, H.** The Journal of an Expedition across Venezuela and Colombia. 8vo. *New Haven* and *London*, 1909.

324. **Carvajal, J. de.** Relacion del descubrimiento del Rio Apure hasta su ingreso en el Orinoco.... MSS. Printed *Leon*, 1892.

325. **Cortes de Madariaga, J.** Diario y observaciones ... en su regreso de Santafé a Carácas. 8vo. *Carácas*, 1832.

326. **Gagliardi, —.** Le condizioni delle colonie italiane nel Venezuela e la miniera di Naricual. *Bol. Soc. Geogr. Ital.*, sér. 4, t. vii, pp. 1251-3 [1906].

327. **Humboldt, F. H. A. v.** Ansichten der Natur.... 16mo. *Stuttgart* and *Tübingen*, 1826.

328. **Páez, R.** Travels and Adventures in South and Central America. Life on the Llanos. 8vo. *New York*, 1868.

329. **Anon.** Die Landschaft am Apurestrom in Venezuela. *Globus*, bd. v, pp. 244-7 [1864].

See also Nos. 34, 108, 188, 197, 213, 214.

XIII. BOLIVAR CITY AND STATE.

330. **André, E.** The Caura Affluent of the Orinoco. *Geogr. Journ.*, vol. xx, pp. 283-306 [1902].

331. —. The Caura. 4to & fo., map. *Trinidad*, 1902.

332. **André, E.** A Naturalist in the Guianas. Pp. 310, map. *London*, 1904.

333. **Bendrat, T. A.** Karte der Umgebung von Caicara in Venezuela. *Petermann's Mitt.* 1910, pl. xlvi.

334. —. Ciudad Bolivar. *Journ. Geogr.*, bd. viii, pp. 218-22 [1910].

Blair, Dr. *See* No. 354.

335. **Campbell, W. H.** By the Cuyooni to the Orinoco in 1857. *"Timehri,"* *Demerara*, vol. ii, pp. 133-58 [1883]. *See* No. 354, *infra*.

336. **Du Marais, —.** Renseignements sur l'Orénoque. *Ann. Hydrogr. Paris*, t. xiii, p. 127 [1857].

337. **Eckermann, —.** Orinoco Fahrten. *Ann. Hydrographie*, bd. xxxi, pp. 166-72 [1903].

338. **Elliot, C.** Proposed Exploration of the River Orinoco, &c. *Proc. R. G. S.*, vol. i, pp. 251-5 [1856-7].

339. **Ernst, A.** Die Goldregion des venezuelanischen Guayana. *Globus*, bd. xvi, pp. 124-6, 137, 138 [1869].

340. **Fernandez-Duro, C.** Rios de Venezuela y de Colombia. Relaciones ineditas (Antonio de la Torre, &c.). *Bol. Soc. Geogr. Madrid*, t. xxviii, pp. 76-174 [1890]; t. xxix, pp. 161-219 [1890].

341. **Foster, C. Le Neve.** A Journey up the Orinoco to the Caratal Goldfield—Raleigh's "El Dorado." *Illustr. Trav. H. W. Bates,* vol. i, pp. 257-63, 297-302, 335-8, 376-8, map [1869].

342. **Galli, G.** Sulle Miniere Aurifere delia Guayana. *Bol. Consol. Firenze,* t. vi, pt. 2, pp. 24-35 [1870].

343. **Gumilla, P. J.** Histoire naturelle, civile et géographique de l'Orénoque. 3 vols., 12mo. *Avignon,* 1758.

Holmes, —. *See* No. 354.

344. **Lemos, — de.** Trade of Ciudad Bolivar for the Year 1899. *For. Off. Cons. Rep.,* Ann. Ser., No. 2388 [1900] and others.

345. **Morisse, L.** Excursion dans l'Eldorado (El Callao). 4 maps. *Paris,* 1904.

346. **Paquet, N.** L'Or en Guyane Vénézuélien. 8vo. *Paris,* 1904.

347. **Passarge, S.** Reise im venezolanischer Guiana. *Mitth. Geogr. Ges. Hamburg,* bd. xix, pp. 253-5 [1903].

348. **—.** Reise im Gebiet des Orinoko. *Mitt. Ver. Erdk. Leipzig,* 1903, pp. 33-6.

349. **Passarge, S.** Bericht über eine Reise in venezolanischer Guyana. *Zeitschr. Ges. Erdk. Berlin,* 1903, pp. 5-43, map, 1: 300,000. [Astronomical work by W. M. S. Selwyn.]

350. **Paterson, S.** In the Wilds of Venezuela. *Scottish Geogr. Mag.,* vol. xiv, pp. 591-9 [1898].

351. **—.** In the Valley of the Orinoco. *Geogr. Journ.,* vol. xiii, pp. 39-50, map [1899].

Selwyn, W. S. *See* **Passarge, S.**

352. **Wears, W. G.** Prospects of Gold Mining in Venezuela. Plan. 8vo. *London,* 1888 [2 editions].

353. **Anon.** Journal of a Trip from San Thomé de Angostura, in Spanish Guayana, to the Capuchin Missions of the Caroni. *Quart. Journ. Sci.,* vol. viii, pp. 260-87; vol. ix, pp. 1-32 [1820].

354. **—.** Die Expedition der Herren Dr. Blair, Holmer und Campbell nach den Goldwäschen von Caratal in Venezuela, im Spätsommer 1857. *Zeitschr. Ges. Erdk. Berlin,* n.f., bd. iv, pp. 365-78. Map [1858].

See also Nos. 21, 34, 85, 97, 102, 123, 193, 245.

XIV. THE TERRITORIO AMAZONAS.

355. **Chaffanjon, J.** Le Bassin de l'Orénoque. *Gazette Géogr. Paris*, t. ii, pp. 201-4 [1885].

356. ——. Das Becken des Orinoco. *Ausland*, bd. lix, pp. 323-7 [1886].

357. ——. L'Orénoque et ses Sources. *Bull. Soc. Géogr. Comm. Bordeaux*, t. x, pp. 682-8 [1887].

358. ——. Exploration du bassin de l'Orénoque. *Compt. Rend. Soc. Géogr. Paris*, 1887, pp. 97-100.

359. ——. Mon dernier Voyage au Vénézuéla. *Bull. Soc. Géogr. Comm. Paris*, t. x, pp. 9-20 [1887-8].

360. ——. Un Voyage au Vénézuéla. *Bull. Soc. Géogr. & Mus. Comm. St. Nazaire*, t. iv, pp. 13-25 [1888].

361. ——. Le Bassin de l'Orénoque. *Rev. Géogr. Internat. Paris*, t. xiii, pp. 64, 133-5 [1888].

362. ——. Voyage à travers les Llanos du Caura, et aux sources de l'Orénoque. *Jour. du Monde*, t. lvi, pp. 305-84. Sketch map [1888].

363. ——. Voyage au sources de l'Orénoque. *Bull. Union Géogr. Nord. France*, t. ix, pp. 97-147 [1888].

364. ——. L'Orénoque et le Caura. 2 maps. *Paris*, 1889.

365. **Hübner, G.** Reise in das Quellgebiet des Orinoco. *Deutsche Rundschau Géogr.*, bd. xx, pp. 14-20, 55-65 [1897].

366. **Humboldt, F. H. A. v.** Note sur la communication qui existe entre l'Orénoque et la rivière des Amazonas. *Journ. École Poly.*, t. iv, pp. 65-8. Map [1810].

367. ——. Ueber die Verbindung zwischen dem Orinoco und Amazonen fluss. *Zach's Monatl. Correspondenz*, bd. xxvi, pp. 230-35 [1812].

368. **Michelena y Rojas, F.** Exploracion Official por la primera vez desde el Norte de la America del sur siempre par Rios.... Map. 8vo. *Brussels*, 1867.

369. **Montolieu, F.** L'Ynirida. *Bull Soc. Géogr. Paris*, sér. 6, t. xix, pp. 289-301 [1880].

370. **Morisse, L.** Le Caoutchouc du Haut-Orénoque. *Arch. Miss, Sci. Litt. Paris*, sér. 4, t. i, pp. 177-200 [1891].

371. **Rusby, H. H.** Concerning Exploration upon the Orinoco. *Alum. Journ. Coll. Pharm. N.Y.*, vol. iii, pp. 185-91 [1896].

372. **Schomburgk, R. H.** Journey from Fort San Joaquim, on the Rio Branco, to Roraima, and thence by the Rivers Parima and Merevari to Esmeralda on the Orinoco in 1838-9. *Journ. R. Geogr. Soc.*, vol. x, pp. 191-247 [1841].

373. —. Journey from Esmeralda on the Orinoco to San Carlos and Moura on the Rio Negro.... *Ibid.*, pp. 248-67 [1841].

374. **Stradelli, E.** [Expedition up the Orinoco.] *Boll. Soc. Géogr. Ital.*, ser. 2, t. xii, pp. 354-6, 500 [1887].

375. —. Nell' alto Orinoco. *Ibid.*, ser. 3, t. i, pp. 715-44, 832-54. Map [1888].

376. **Tavera-Acosta, B.** Rio Negro. Pp. 149. 8vo. *Ciudad Bolivar*, 1906.

377. **Anon.** Robert Schomburgk und seine Reise in Guyana, am Orinoco, &c. *Globus*, bd. xiv, pp. 151-4, 186-9 [1868].

378. —. J. Chaffanjon's Reisen im Gebiete des Orinoko und Caura. *Globus*, bd. lvi, pp. 70-74, 88, 99, 195, 212, 231 [1889].

See also Nos. 148, 160, 161, 245, 265, 327.

XV. RESOURCES, COMMERCIAL DEVELOPMENT, COMMUNICATIONS, &c.

379. **Berthelot, S.** Notice sur les nouveaux établissements agricoles fondés au Vénézuéla. *Bull. Soc. Géogr. Paris*, sér. 2, t. xviii, pp. 37-55 [1842].

380. **Briceño, M. de.** La gran cuestion fiscal de Venezuela.... Reforma del sistema aduanero. 8vo. *Carácas*, 1864.

381. **Carruthers. J.** The Trincheras Steep Incline on the Puerto Cabello and Valencia Railway, Venezuela. *Proc. Inst. Civ. Eng.*, vol. xcvi, pp. 120-30 [1888-9].

382. **Church, G. E.** The Venezuela Central Railway and its Sources of Traffic. 8vo. *London*, 1888.

Diaz, M. V. *See* **Rojas, A.**

383. **Engel, F.** Die Fahrstrasse von La Guayra nach Carácas. *Globus*, bd. xiv, pp. 334-7 [1868].

384. **Ernst, A.** A Descriptive Catalogue of the Venezuelan Department at the Philadelphia International Exhibition. 12mo. *Philadelphia*, 1876.

385. —. La Exposicion Nacional de Venezuela en 1883. Fo. *Carácas*, 1884.

386. **Fiebeger, G. J.** Report on Bermudez Asphalt. *Rep. Operat. Eng. Dept. D.C.*, 1894, pp. 143-6.

387. **Heinke, E. H. A.** "La Guaira and Carácas Railway." *Proc. Inst. Civ. Eng.*, vol. cx, pp. 299-303 [1892].

388. **Hortensio, G. and M.** Literatura venezolana. 2 vols. *Carácas*, 1883.

Houston, J. L. *See* **Punchard, W. C.**

Humbert, J. *See* **Vincent, L.**

389. **Magliano, R.** L'Industrie delle Miniere e del Caffe nel Venezuela. *Bol. Ministr. Afari Esteri*, 1891, vol. ii, pp. 357-60 [1891].

390. **Navarro, E.** Venezuela. Ferrocarriles, comercio y navegacion. *Rev. Géogr. Col. y Mercantil*, t. iv, pp. 182-219 [1907].

391. **Oppel, A.** Die wirtschaftliche Verhältnisse von Venezuela. *Globus*, bd. lvii, pp. 171-4 [1890].

392. **Palacio, R. M.** El Progreso de Venezuela. 8vo. *Carácas*, 1877.

393. **Plümacher, E. H.** Petroleum Deposits in Venezuela. *Rep. Comm. Rel. U.S.*, 1880, pp. 11-16.

394. —. Petroleum Development in Venezuela. *Rep. Cons. U.S.*, vol. xxi, pp. 556, 557 [1887].

395. **Plümacher, E. H.** Asphalt and Petroleum Deposits in Venezuela. *Ibid.*, vol. xxvi, pp. 487-91 [1888].

396. **Punchard, W. C.** and **J. L. Houston**. La Guaira Harbour Works. *Proc. Inst. Civ. Eng.*, vol. cxv, pp. 332-42 [1893-4].

397. **Quievreux, H.** La pêche des perles au Vénézuéla. *Rev. Maritime*, t. cxlvi, pp. 444-8 [1900].

398. **Richardson, C.** On the Nature and origin of Asphalt. *Journ. Soc. Chem. Ind.*, vol. xvii, pp. 13-32 [1898].

399. —. The Modern Asphalt Pavement. *New York*, 1905 and 1908.

400. **Rizzetto, R.** Un episodio della Emigrazione Italiana nel Venezuela. *Boll. Soc. Géogr. Ital.*, t. ii, pp. 141-56 [1886].

401. **Rojas, A.** and **M. V. Diaz**. Apuntes para el repertorio de plantas utiles de Venezuela. 8vo. *Carácas*, 1866.

402. **Ruiz, P. M.** Anuario Estadístico de Venezuela, 1908. Pp. lxxx, 495. *Carácas*, 1910.

403. **Schottky, A.** Die Kupfererze der Districtes von Aroa, Venezuela. Pp. 36. *Breslau*, 1877.

404. ——. Ueber die Kupfererze des Minen-Districtes von Aroa in Venezuela. *55 Jahresber. Schles. Ges. Kultur*, pp. 45, 46 [1878].

405. **Sievers, W.** Die wirtschaftliche Bedeutung Venezuela's und die deutschen Interessen daselbst. *Die Natur*, bd. li, pp. 61-4 [1902].

406. **Vincent, L.** and **J. Humbert.** L'instruction publique au Vénézuéla. *Bull. Soc. Géogr. Comm. Bordeaux*, t. xx, pp. 241-6, 381-9, 422-30 [1897].

407. **Anon.** The London Venezuelan Guyana Mutual Emigration Society. Prospectus, with Code of Laws, etc., in the Settlement and Colony of Pattisonville. 12mo. *London*, 1869.

408. ——. Petroleum in Venezuela. *London Iron Trades Exchange*, vol. xxviii, p. 397 [1880].

409. ——. Les Sources du Pétrole de Vénézuéla. *Ann. Industr.*, t. xix, p. 393 [1887].

410. ——. The Asphalt Deposits of Venezuela. *Eng. Min. Journ.*, vol. lxxi, p. 303 [1901].

411. ——. Der Bermudez Asphalt-streit. *Asphalt Teerind. Zeit.*, bd. v, pp. 287, 288 [1905].

See also Nos. 68, 69, 70, 132, 281, 291, 314, 316, 326, 342, 345, 346, 352, 370.

Milton Keynes UK
Ingram Content Group UK Ltd.
UKHW042144281024
450365UK00010B/599

9 789362 922069